D1174549

COLOURED, TYPE AND SONG CANARIES

A Complete Guide

G.B.R. WALKER

Photographs and Drawings by
DENNIS AVON

BLANDFORD PRESS
POOLE · NEW YORK · SYDNEY

Following the publication of Coloured Canaries *some ten years ago, I have been fortunate in being invited to visit several countries to judge at numerous exhibitions. On these visits I have made innumerable good friends whose encouragement has enabled me to complete this edition. To them this book is dedicated – with thanks.*

GBRW

First published in the UK 1987 by Blandford Press
Link House, West Street, Poole, Dorset BH15 1LL

Copyright © 1987 G.B.R. Walker and Dennis Avon

Distributed in the United States by
Sterling Publishing Co, Inc,
2 Park Avenue, New York, NY 10016

Distributed in Australia by
Capricorn Link (Australia) Pty Ltd
PO Box 665, Lane Cove, NSW 2066

British Library Cataloguing in Publication Data

Walker, G.B.R.
    Coloured, type, and song canaries : a
    complete guide.
    1. Canaries
    I. Title   II. Avon, Dennis
    636.6'862   SF463

ISBN 0 7137 1620 7

Typeset by Best-set Typesetter Limited Hong Kong
Printed in Great Britain by Butler and Tanner Frome and London

CONTENTS

ACKNOWLEDGEMENTS

Such has been the amount of assistance given to both of us that it is difficult to know where or how to start offering our grateful acknowledgement of the help given.

Initially, it is perhaps correct to thank most sincerely the five specialist authors, Jill Pearson, Alan Ellison, Chris Goodall, Edwin Henshall and Gerry Wolfendale, for their contributions. Next, thanks must go to Joel Le Banner and Mario Ascheri for their in-depth and expert comments on the birds illustrated in the colour plates. Our special thanks also go to Louis Tielens for agreeing to write the foreword.

Bob Yates has once again undertaken the onerous task of checking the entire text and to him we are greatly indebted, as we are to John Scott, a highly-respected breeder and judge of type canaries, for commenting upon and correcting the text on the 'English' breeds; to Joel Le Banner for completing a similar task on the 'continental' breeds of type canary and to Jim Lyon for his help with the song-canary section.

Information has been given on the origin and peculiarities of specific national breeds by Roger Le Duff and Claude Edouard (France), Fritz Herrmann (Switzerland), Elise and Paul Putz (West Germany), Hiroshi Matuskawa (Japan), Edward D'Arcy (Eire), Clarice and Walter James, Robert Wild and Els Gerritson (USA), Oscar Presmantes Mateu and Honorio Gimeno Pelegri (Spain) and Del Prete Michele (Italy) and of various breeds by Harry Williamson, John Scott, Walter Lumsden, G.H. Perks, Gordon Plumb, Fred and Ken Rix, A. Durrell, A. Piper, P. Scott, P. Warne and N. Barrett.

Jan van Mol (Netherlands) has been particularly helpful in arranging and assisting at photographic sessions and varying amounts and types of assistance have been given by Walter

Vermeullen (Belgium), George van Lochem (Netherlands), Bernard Dufresne, Michel Vimeux, Pierre Groux and Jacques Faivre (France), Don Perez, Bob and Pattye Roberts and Ramon Lamelas (USA) and Mike Seery (Eire).

To the translation team of June Cable, Christianne Fischer, Kaye Poutney and Charles de Bono grateful thanks, with particular thanks to Michelle Barber and Kaye Poutney for typing the manuscript.

To attempt to list everyone who has been so helpful in allowing us to photograph their birds would result in an additional volume being published. To you all our most grateful and sincere thanks.

Thanks also to Bob Roberts Jnr of Bob Roberts Photography, Austin, Texas, USA, and to Paul Putz of West Germany for so kindly loaning us colour slides of the breeds we found impossible to locate on our travels.

Lastly, it would indeed be remiss not to thank our wives and families for their encouragement and tolerance, without either this book would not have become a reality.

FOREWORD

When Geoff Walker's first book, *Coloured Canaries*, appeared, everyone agreed that this work was the best English language edition written on the subject since A.K. Gill's *New Coloured Canaries* published many years ago. It was therefore with great enthusiasm that I heard from Geoff that he was writing a new book encompassing not only coloured canaries but also canaries judged on shape or song.

The author is known throughout the avicultural world for his skill in describing the various mutations of coloured canaries with his research on the other breeds enabling him to write authoritatively on these.

On 14 February 1952, the Confederation Internationale d'Amateurs et Eleveurs de Canaries (CIC) was founded in Utrecht (Netherlands). The most important aim of this organisation was to bring together all canary breeders worldwide into one association and to organise each year a World Championship Show.

In 1956, the CIC joined with the Association Ornithologique Mondiale (AOI – another international body representing breeders of cage birds other than canaries) and the Confederation Ornithologique Mondiale (COM) was founded in Paris.

The COM gained in size and is proudly preparing to present its 36th World Show in the northern hemisphere (this will be held in Paris in France in January/February 1988).

Since the COM was founded, there have been a number of new mutations appearing in coloured-canary circles which makes an almost impossible task for novices trying to identify each variety. Added to this have been the innovations in the COM classifications, where classes have been added for a combination of song plus colour and new type varieties. Geoff Walker's new comprehensive book is thus even more welcoming giving not only the novice but the more

11

experimental breeder as well a clear and scientific work on the subject.

As one of the international judges from the well-known judges' panel of the OMJ of COM (Ordre Mondial des Juges of the COM), Geoff has been selected on more than one occasion to judge at our World Championship Shows and, in recent years, has judged throughout Europe and the USA, where his knowledge on the subject of coloured canaries has been fully appreciated.

I am sure that this new work by Geoff Walker, enhanced as it is by the superb photography of Dennis Avon, will prove to be a *must* for all canary fanciers throughout the world.

Louis J. Tielens
General Secretary of the COM

AUTHOR'S PREFACE

It is most noticeable, whilst travelling to different countries and discussing aviculture in general and canary culture in particular, that there is a general unawareness of the large number of canary breeds in existence. It is also apparent that, whilst many excellent books exist on specific breeds or groups of breeds, there is none that covers the whole spectrum. With this in mind the idea of producing this book was conceived.

It is accepted that specialisation is now essential if anyone is to gain success at exhibitions and, therefore, no one can truly be sufficiently knowledgeable to write authoritatively on every species of the canary. The author is a coloured-canary specialist but has built up friendships over the years with many experts in all sections of aviculture. With their considerable help, and with the help of the many other people who have so freely supplied information, it is hoped that, whilst perhaps every question that could be posed is not answered in this edition, there is sufficient information for any intending breeder to make a reasoned decision on the direction which he intends to follow. There is little substitution for practical experience and, having been given the basic guidelines within which a breeder can work, it is then up to the individual to build up his own knowledge.

The four breeds of type canary that attract most support internationally are the Border, Norwich, Yorkshire and Gloster and, for this reason, specialist authors were approached for these chapters. Alan Ellison, Chris Goodall, Edwin Henshall and Gerry Wolfendale are all acknowledged experts in these specialist fields and their contributions have greatly enhanced this edition.

Little real research has been carried out on either the nutritional needs of canaries or the prevention and control of disease. Such information that has been published has, unfortunately, been

13

written for and directed towards qualified veterinary practitioners and, therefore, is too technical to be of use to the average canary fancier. It is particularly gratifying therefore, to have found Jill Pearson, who not only possesses the information so craved by the Fancy but is able to communicate this information in a manner that everyone can understand and learn from.

It is always pleasurable to work with a true professional and to earn this accolade it is necessary that technical expertise should be coupled with extreme patience and attention to detail. Dennis Avon possesses all of these qualities in abundance and it is confidently thought that the colour plates, black-and-white photographs and drawings will be appreciated by everyone. In many instances, hours have been spent travelling extensively throughout the UK and mainland Europe, visiting noted breeders' birdrooms and major exhibitions in an attempt to present first class plates of top quality examples. Many hundreds of photographs have been taken in order to present those included herein and Dennis Avon is still not convinced that his work is completely acceptable. This is the mark of a true professional.

The writing of this book has been a huge educational exercise for the author. Regardless of the amount of knowledge any of us think that we possess, it is not until such a venture is embarked upon that we realise how little we do know. At times, the sheer frustration of lack of information has almost caused the cessation of the project. Only by the help and encouragement of the many friends in the Fancy has it reached fruition. It can only be hoped that everyone reading it will benefit in some way. If so, then the exercise will have been truly worthwhile.

· PART ONE ·
KEEPING CANARIES

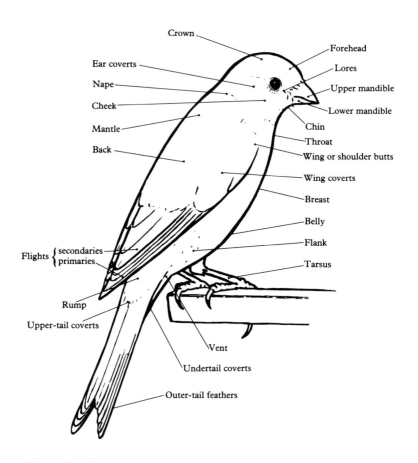

Crown

Forehead

Lores

Ear coverts

Nape

Upper mandible

Cheek

Lower mandible

Mantle

Chin

Throat

Back

Wing or shoulder butts

Wing coverts

Breast

Belly

Flank

Flights { secondaries
primaries

Tarsus

Rump

Upper-tail coverts

Vent

Undertail coverts

Outer-tail feathers

Topography of the canary.

· CHAPTER 1 ·
MANAGEMENT AND BREEDING TECHNIQUES

Put together any ten experienced canary breeders and you will in all probability arrive at ten different methods of managing and breeding canaries. This, whilst perhaps somewhat confusing to the beginner, should be good news in that it confirms the adaptability of the canary and the fact that, if a few simple rules are followed, anyone can achieve success with this fascinating hobby.

The notes are guidelines which the breeder can adopt and adapt to suit himself in the areas of housing, acquisition of stock, general management, breeding, show preparation, etc. The systems described are roughly relevant to all species of canary. Some modifications need to be made for specific varieties and where these apply they are covered in the chapter covering that species.

BIRDROOMS

Canaries for many years have been housed in the most unlikely types of premises and in a great variety of cages. It is, however, recommended that either a separate room or a specific building is used to house your birds. In many instances, circumstances dictate the size, siting and building materials and, apart from perhaps adapting them to include desirable characteristics, little can be done. The only negative areas which certainly preclude the use of any building as a birdroom are lack of light (although this can be supplemented by artifical means), uncontrollable dampness, absence of ventilation and, conversely, uncontrollable draughts. Also, any building where extremes of heat cannot be avoided during the breeding season is unsuitable.

Assuming, however, that the would-be breeder has few, if any, major constraints on the erection of a birdroom, what should he seek and what should he avoid? Birdrooms can be made from almost any material. In the UK, the most popular are of a wooden construction, although brick, rendered concrete or breezeblocks, prefabricated concrete etc., are all used with success. Although less common in the UK than in mainland Europe and North America for example, a spare room within a breeder's residence is also used to advantage. If a wooden building is to be constructed, assuming that a floor is to be fitted, firstly ensure that the underside is coated with a wood preservative. Secondly, when erecting the building, ensure that it is raised above the ground to a height suitable still for access. This is to enable vermin to be detected and to prevent their entry.

Although the size of a breeding room is not necessarily relevant to good breeding results, it is advisable to erect the largest room possible, subject to monetary restrictions, available space and, if applicable, local authority restrictions. It is often found that, as enthusiasm grows, the breeder may wish to increase his stud size and, therefore, the number of offspring and it is far better to have an underpopulated birdroom than an overpopulated one. It is also difficult in many instances to expand a birdroom once it is erected and in use. When deciding on the site for a birdroom, thought should be given to ensuring that all sides are accessible for repairs etc., and that the site is not particularly exposed to extremes of weather conditions. Thought should also be given at this time as to whether it is intended to have a sink unit with running water installed in the birdroom. This obviously makes sense if feasible and is a valuable asset to the breeder. If it is intended to incorporate this feature, the laying of connecting water pipes should be completed prior to the erection of the building, as also should either soakaways or pipes for the disposal of waste matter.

Light in general, and daylight in particular, is necessary to most living creatures. Canaries are no exception and as much space as possible should be given to windows and/or roof lights. Before deciding on the position of windows and a door, however, a plan should be made of the proposed layout of cages, indoor flights, storage areas etc., so as to maximise the use of the available floor and wall areas. Once this is done, it is again emphasised that as much space as possible should be devoted to windows. It is the author's opinion that light is of major importance in ensuring the good health and condition of stock for most of the year. Opinions differ on the direction in which windows should face and obviously this varies from place to place, depending upon the direction of prevailing winds etc. Once all of these points have been resolved and the building erected, the exterior, particularly if wooden, should be coated with wood preservative or hard-wearing exterior paint. Ventilation of a building is also necessary and this can be achieved by various means. If the birdroom is of wooden construction, small pieces of panelling can be cut out and steel ventilation panels put in their place. One should be close to the floor and another sited on the opposite wall close to the roof. With brick or concrete-block buildings, ventilation bricks can be built in while the building is being erected.

Once the building is erected, thought should then be given to the installation of any electrical wiring that may be required, together with the number and location of electrical sockets. As with windows, it is recommended that a generous number of sockets are fitted as it is surprising just how many can be needed at the same time in modern birdrooms. Canaries do not, in normal circumstances, need either artificial light or heat but sometimes such aids can be used to advantage, as will be explained later. Through unavoidable circumstances, some birdrooms will have an inadequate natural light source and, in some instances, no natural light whatsoever. When this is the case, advice should be sought from a qualified electrical contractor on the lighting requirements necessary to imitate natural light. Natural light varies in brightness according to the season and, if a breeder seeks success, he must try to match the natural conditions, particularly in the spring when breeding takes place. Once this advice has been received, the breeder will know how many lighting sockets will be required and can plan the installation to ensure even coverage of the birdroom. Where heat and light is to be employed, tubular heaters and fluorescent tubes are recommended, natural daylight tubes being particularly effective, especially in a birdroom where coloured canaries are housed. This is because normal tubes distort the colour and make it impossible to assess accurately the quality of the resident stock.

It is an unfortunate fact of modern life that crime is on the increase and, all too frequently, one hears of birdrooms being entered and the contents stolen. It is well worthwhile, therefore, to install some form of burglar alarm when erecting a new birdroom. There are several types on sale and advice should be sought from the local crime prevention officer on the most practical for use in the particular building. If these appliances are to be used, they should also be installed during the erection process.

19

The author in his breeding room.

The author has noted the use of air conditioners on his visits to birdrooms in countries with a warmer climate than the UK. Although a most accommodating bird, the canary is unlikely to breed in extremely hot conditions and fanciers should consider the installation of such equipment where necessary and ensure that this is completed prior to the introduction of stock.

Once electrical installations have been completed the building should be lined so as to give a flat surface wherever possible. This has the advantage of making cleaning easier as well as presenting a more attractive finish. Where the building is of wooden construction the frame is normally made of 2 × 2 inch (50 × 50 millimetre) material. When the building is constructed from brick etc., it is recommended that a frame of 2 × 2 inch (50 × 50 millimetre) material is constructed inside onto which the lining can be affixed. This includes the roof. Plywood and hardboard are the materials most used for lining. The use of insulation materials is advised by some breeders and condemned by others. The writer is firmly of the opinion that insulation should be used as he has found it invaluable for maintaining a more even temperature during the extremes of summer and winter. There are a number of insulation materials available and fibreglass roof-insulation sheets are probably the most practical to install. Obviously, if such materials are to be used, they should be installed prior to the building being lined.

Having erected a birdroom, two further tasks remain to be completed prior to the introduction of cages and birds. Firstly, it is recommended that the interior be painted throughout with light-coloured paint to assist in light reflection and, secondly, that a wire-netting safety door be fitted. This can be a wooden frame covered with wire netting, fitted on the inside of the door and opening in the opposite direction. Alternatively it can take the form of a wire-netting-covered structure covering the door on the outside. Wire-netting covers should also be affixed to any windows which open, and these should be sited on the opposite side to the direction in which the windows open. The obvious value of such arrangements is that the door and/or windows can be left open on hot days with no danger of the birds escaping.

The use of these structures will also normally prevent predators gaining entry. Within the UK one tends to think of predators such as cats, rats, mice and stoats or weasels and thought should be given to ensure that these structures are not only strong enough to withstand attack, but also that the wire mesh used is small enough to prevent

21

the smaller animals from passing through. More exotic problems can face fanciers in other countries. Snakes entering a friend's birdroom and eating birds whole is a case in mind and, whilst the author is totally unqualified to give advice on the exclusion of these and, presumably, other unwelcome visitors, preventive measures need to be thought out when the birdroom is erected. Local fanciers are probably the best persons from whom to seek advice. Mosquitoes are also considered a significant pest in countries where they are prolific. In such areas, the use of wire netting as a window/door covering is obviously unsuitable. A fine-gauge mesh is normally available, however, and its use as a substitute is recommended.

Finally, thought should be given to a suitable floor covering. The main criterion to be employed here is that it should be easy to keep clean. The author has seen ceramic and rubber tiles, together with vinyl floor covering, all used successfully. The use of a covering rather than a bare wood or concrete floor is essential because a non-covered floor inevitably contains various cracks and flaws in which dirt accumulates, allowing disease to proliferate.

CAGES AND ACCESSORIES

Once the building has been erected, thought must be given to the number and type of cages and/or indoor flights to be installed. Cages are manufactured in a number of shapes and sizes and from different materials. Alternatively, anyone with only minimal ability as a do-it-yourself person can build his own cages. The author, falling very firmly into this category, is loath to give precise advice on cage building but will, instead, attempt to give guidelines around which more accomplished carpenters can work. Cages can come in three forms: free standing individual or blocks of cages, or cages actually built into the birdroom. Single cages can be literally that or can take the form known as a double or treble-breeder, they can also be made in a form which extends along the length of the birdroom wall. Once purchased or made, they can then be placed on shelves, or affixed either permanently or in a way facilitating their easy removal for cleaning purposes. A double-breeder is a cage which allows a partition to be inserted, thus effectively converting the unit to two cages; a treble-breeder allows two partitions to be inserted and the highly recommended form of a continuous run allows several partitions. These partitions are removable and are referred to as

A double breeding cage.

'slides'. The advantage of the continuous run is that it allows cages of variable size to be used, which is beneficial during specific times of the year.

The actual size of a cage which is to be used for breeding is not too important. Canaries have been bred in cages 12 × 12 inches (300 millimetres) × 12 inches (300 millimetres) high but, in the author's opinion, each compartment ideally needs to be about 18 × 15 inches (380 × 340 millimetres) × 12 inches (300 millimetres) high. In the UK, it is usual to use box-type wooden cages with a wire front; in other countries similar cages made with plastic are used, as are galvanised steel wire cages. Providing that the birdroom is free from damp and draughts, any type of cage will suffice. Although wire fronts made from netting can be used, specially-manufactured cage fronts are more generally employed. These need to be surrounded by a wooden frame into which they fit. Cage fronts can be purchased with a single central door or with a second door normally placed in the centre section and either to the right or to the left of the central door. Later, when breeding is discussed (p. 31), details will be given of the various types of nest pan which can be used. These should be carefully studied so that the nest pan can be chosen before the cage fronts are purchased. The reasons will be obvious later. When making cages, and when designing the fronts, space should be

23

allowed for a removable tray, which will form the floor. The use of these trays is highly recommended to facilitate easy cleaning. The front of the tray in the author's opinion should be about 1½ inches (40 millimetres) deep. The reason for this is discussed on p. 28.

When cages are being built into a birdroom, similar rules apply but one advantage is that back panels need not be fixed to the cages as the wall of the birdoom fulfils their function. When this system is adopted it is comparatively easy to extend the cage around corners so that valuable space is not wasted. More options are also open when this type of caging is used, one being the ability to construct them so as to give entry to interior and exterior flights. All bottom cages need to be sited on a platform not less than 4 inches (100 millimetres) from the ground, the height of the top cage being unimportant. Should cages be sited this low, it is obviously necessary to block the fronts down to the ground as it will be difficult to clean under the cage block.

Once constructed, the cages should be painted with a lead-free paint. White is the most popular colour used for the interior of cages, mainly because it reflects light, while the fronts and surrounds are often painted black. Some breeders, however, prefer to use paint of the same colour as is used in the show cages of the canary variety kept. The type of paint used is unimportant, both gloss and emulsion having advantages. If gloss paint is used, it is more easily washed and is less liable to stain. With modern-day vinyl-emulsion paints, a solution of insect-repelling products can be mixed in.

Although it is possible to use inside or outside flights for breeding purposes, this practice is not recommended to breeders seeking to produce exhibition-quality birds. This apart, inside and outside flights are most useful for housing the stock at other times of the year. The term 'flight' is used to describe either a large wire-covered enclosure sited inside a birdroom or one attached to the exterior which allows birds access to the interior. An aviary is a similar exterior enclosure, which is normally free standing. If inside flights are being constructed, a simple frame covered with wire netting will suffice and, ideally, should reach from floor to ceiling to enable the birds to have beneficial upward flight. They can be joined to cages and access gained through small doors or they can be free standing. To gain entry to the flight, a door, preferably as small as possible, should be made with its height extending from the floor to no more than half of the height of the flight. This normally prevents birds from flying out over the shoulder of the breeder when he enters. The inside of the door should also be provided with a small hook-like catch so that it can be firmly closed once the breeder is inside. Exterior flights or aviaries should be constructed with strong weather-insulated timbers over which ⅜ inch (10 millimetre) wire netting is fixed. Where there is a possibility of interference from cats, birds of prey or other predators, a second layer of wire netting should be placed on the inside of the timber. In countries where mosquitoes abound the use of a fine mesh is required. If the aviary is not to stand on a concrete base, a trench should be dug around the bottom member, which should be erected on a brick base, and fine mesh netting extended at least 39 inches (1,000 millimetres) below ground extending outwards at a right angle for 12 inches (300 millimetres) at the bottom. The trench is then refilled. This obviously is to protect the birds by preventing the entry of predators, such as rats, which will burrow and tunnel into a flight. If the flight is not connected to the birdroom, one end should be enclosed to afford the birds draught-free quarters that are protected from the elements. In all instances a wire safety door should be fitted.

Once cages have been purchased or manufactured, there are a number of accessories that are needed. All commercially-manu-factured cage fronts have head holes through which a bird can feed. There are normally two per front. Over these can be hung seed hoppers and/or drinking water or grit-holding receptacles; two-hooked 'D'-shaped drinkers are generally used. Alternatively, water can be offered in a fountain-type drinker and two-hooked drinkers containing grit and/or seed can be hung on the inside of the cage front. At certain times a 'softfood' mixture and/or small quantities of a special conditioning seed mixture may need to be offered and these are normally given in either small plastic finger drawers or round egg drawers that are held in place by the door fitting into a groove on their handle. Ideally two of everything should be purchased for each cage. Perches should be of wooden or plastic construction and can be either round, oval or square (with the edges planed down). Natural twigs can also be used. The only real stipulations are that they are firmly fixed and are neither too small nor too large for the bird to stand on comfortably. A diameter of ⅜ inch (10 millimetres) is approximately the right size; some breeders, however, will use one of ⅜ inch (10 millimetres) and one of ½ inch (13 millimetres) in each cage. Two perches are normally fitted per cage unit but these can be reduced to one per unit when slides are withdrawn to extend the cage size. The siting of perches is normally one third of the

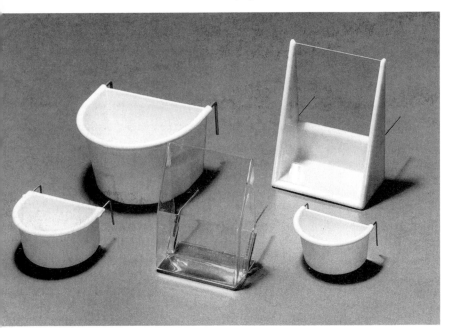

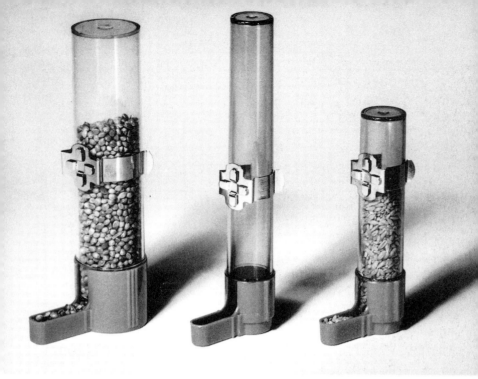

(*opposite top*) Two-hook 'D' pots and seed hoppers.

(*opposite bottom*) Various containers (clockwise from top left): top-hat glass drinkers (two), salad or nesting material holder, two-hook drinker, egg drawers (two).

(*top*) Three types of seed or water flow-feed containers.

(*right*) Floor-standing seed or water gravity-feed containers.

Perches: wooden (left), plastic (right)

distance from the bottom to the top of the cage and sufficiently far inside the cage to allow the bird to stand naturally without its tail touching the cage end. One other useful accessory is a net for catching birds which have escaped from their cages or for catching birds in a large flight or aviary. The preferred net is one that has lightweight cotton netting suspended on a thin wire frame. Linen or cotton sheeting nets suspended on a thicker padded frame are also available but are generally unsuitable for canaries.

The type of cage-floor coverings used varies from breeder to breeder, with paper, sand, sawdust and wood shavings being the substances most used. The choice of floor covering must, to a certain degree, be dictated by the time available to the breeder for cleaning cages. If paper is used, the cages must be cleaned daily but, with the other three options, less frequent attention is necessary. The dis-advantage of using sand is that, when dampened by faeces or water from a bath, the sand will stick to the birds' feet, causing soreness. Sawdust tends to be easily displaced by the wind caused by the birds' wing movements and, when displaced, will cover seed in hoppers or in free-standing pots. Wood shavings, if used to a depth of 1–1½ inches (25–40 millimetres), are in the opinion of the author the most satisfactory. Admittedly, they also will be displaced by the birds' wing movements but not to such a degree as sawdust. Also, being deeper than a sawdust covering, the cages need cleaning less regularly and illnesses that may result in diarrhoea are less likely to be passed on. All types do, however, have their advantages and disadvantages and, by employing a trial-and-error system, the beginner will quickly determine the one which most suits his or her requirements.

STOCK ACQUISITION

Many beginners are drawn to the Fancy having seen a particular canary in a pet shop. They immediately acquire stock of this variety and then often find other varieties that are more pleasing to their eye. In succeeding chapters some indication of the various breeds being kept today is given and it is recommended that, prior to purchasing the stock, the newcomer should initially determine whether song, shape or colour is the major quality sought. He can then, within these three areas, select the breed that pleases him most. Rather than accept written descriptions backed up by photographs, the newcomer is then recommended to visit a number of exhibitions to confirm his original preference. Once this is established beyond doubt, a check should be made on the breeders who achieve consistent success on the showbench, followed by an approach to those exhibitors to see whether they have stock for disposal or can recommend another breeder. Once the choice has been made, the beginner should present himself to the vendor as a newcomer and should ask and be prepared to accept advice on the selection of his initial stock. It is fortunate that, within the canary fraternity, most experienced breeders are genuine and rarely will a newcomer find himself deceived.

Many of the birds offered for sale will not resemble in every aspect the published standard for the breed involved. It is a fact that very few birds possess all of the characteristics sought and a compromise is needed, with perhaps one of a pair chosen possessing some of the required qualities and its partner the others. In most instances, if the vendor has kept precise records, he will have good reason to suggest certain pairings as he will be confident that they will produce birds of an acceptable show standard.

Whilst the newcomer must, by virtue of his lack of knowledge and experience, accept the recommendation of the vendor on stock selection, he can make one or two observations to safeguard himself against faulty advice. The most important is that the stock purchased is fully fit. This can be determined by observation. The bird should be alert and lively when in the flight or cage, not sitting around listlessly. Any bird that does not hold its feathers tight to the body should also be discarded. Fluffed-out feathers indicate that a bird is not fully fit. In most instances a pair should consist of one intensive (yellow) and one non-intensive (buff) bird. There are exceptions to this and, if the breeder offers stock which does not conform to the general rule, he should be expected to explain why. The feathers should appear silky and not in any way coarse and, finally, the prospective purchaser should be allowed to handle the stock offered for sale. At this time, the bird's head should be held close to the ear to determine whether there are any sounds of wheezing. Canaries are susceptible to asthmatic conditions and, while these are not generally fatal, birds showing any such symptoms are to be avoided. Where possible a last-minute check should be made to determine whether there are any signs of heavy scaling on the bird's legs and toes. This is an indication that the bird is quite old and, unless satisfactory reasons have been given for such a bird to be offered for sale, it should be refused. Occasionally, a breeder will offer a bird of 4 or 5 years of age for sale. If it is a male and all the criteria mentioned above are met then the beginner would be well advised to purchase the bird. Inevitably, if a bird is retained by an experienced breeder for more than 2 years it has proved itself to be capable of producing top-quality youngsters. Were this not the case, the bird would have been disposed of earlier.

When purchasing stock, thoughts inevitably turn towards the cost. Some vendors have a flat rate for all birds offered, others will value their birds separately according to their quality. The newcomer has two options when purchasing stock. If working to a budget, the maximum price he can afford to pay should be mentioned to the vendor at the start of their discussions. If the price to be paid is not a prime consideration, then the best-quality birds should always be chosen. It is recommended that a minimum of two pairs of birds should form the initial stock of any intending fancier and these should be bought from the same breeder. Individual birds may be of a higher quality if bought singly from different breeders but no guarantee can be given that their genetical make-up will combine to give the desired result in the progeny. It is far more advantageous, in the long term, to make an initial purchase of say two or three good-quality pairs than five or six pairs of mediocre quality. Controversy also exists on whether it is better for a newcomer wanting to breed a more difficult type to start by purchasing birds of one of the more easily-bred types and then graduate to his chosen variety after he has gained some experience of breeding systems. The author is opposed to this system believing that, however unrewarding the first breeding season might be, the real enthusiast, although disheartened by his possible lack of success, will not be so discouraged that he will leave the Fancy. Also, no guarantees can be given that the so-called easier breed will perform in the expected manner and it is far better to be disheartened by a breed which the fancier really wants to keep than by a substituted variety.

A breeder should not purchase too many birds for his first breeding season. This season is the busiest time of the year for the fancier and the volume of work involved will vary considerably from pair to pair but obviously, the larger the number of pairs used, the greater will be the work entailed. The newcomer, not fully realising the amount of work necessary until he has evolved his own systems, would be well advised to start with a moderately-sized stud.

Finally on the subject of stock procurement, it is recommended that all stock is acquired 3 or 4 months before breeding commences to allow time for the birds to adapt to the new environment and the management techniques used. This applies particularly to females.

BREEDING

The breeding season, for most fanciers, is the most important and exciting part of the year. Canaries, like all other creatures, cannot be expected to perform all tasks successfully and, whilst some make excellent parents, others do not. For this reason the breeding season can be one long series of disasters or, and this is to be hoped, a period of constant delight where most, if not every expectation, is fulfilled.

Preparations

For too many people thoughts turn to preparation for the breeding season 2 or 3 weeks before the birds are expected to commence their breeding cycle. This is a folly that can only lead to disappointment. Preparation for the breeding season should start at the end of the preceding one or, in the case of the newcomer, as soon as his stock has been purchased. At this time, the birds should be placed in the largest cages available or, preferably, in indoor or outdoor flights.

The greater the flight area the better, as vigorous exercise is most important. If there is any possibility of dampness affecting the birdroom, artificial heaters, controlled by a thermostat set at 45–50°F (7–10°C) should be installed. Canaries are not normally adversely affected by the cold weather but they will often become sick if subjected to damp or draughts. The use of a heater will keep damp at bay. Until recently, the use of tubular heaters was recommended in preference to any other form. Fan heaters, even when thermostatically controlled, can cause problems if sited incorrectly and the use of any other form of heating, particularly where a naked flame is employed, is to be avoided at all costs.

The diet at this time should be restricted to a basic selection of seed, known as seed mixture; the author offers 80% plain canary seed, 10% black rape and 10% pinhead oatmeal or groats. Experience has shown that, given a diet of mixed seeds in a single container, birds will search out their particular favourite and scatter the balance on the floor. To overcome this problem, the different seeds should be offered in the proportions mentioned but in separate seed pots. Each pot should be cleared before the seed is replenished. The seed mixture is supplemented by a modest supply of titbits, such as apple, carrot, cucumber, orange, leaves from plants of the brassica family, lettuce and various wild plants. It is emphasised that the amounts offered should be of modest quantities – as a guide no more than will be eaten by the birds in the cage in 1 hour – and that only one of the selection mentioned should be offered daily. Also under no circumstances should any of the products be offered wet. A constant supply of mineral grit should also be made available as the birds, having no teeth, need the grit as an aid to digestion. Some breeders advocate offering a piece of cuttlefish bone as a source of calcium. The author is opposed to this practice as he believes that sufficient calcium can be obtained from a well-balanced diet and the use of cuttlefish bone can lead to the consumption of a surfeit of calcium, causing egg binding later in the year.

He does, however, ensure that, throughout the year, an iodine and mineral block is sited in every cage, believing this to be a necessary source of vitamins and minerals.

Baths, either suspended on the front of the cage over the door opening or free standing on the floor of the cage or flight, should be offered daily if possible throughout the year. If using the suspended

(*opposite*) A selection of seeds and other ancillary food. (×2)

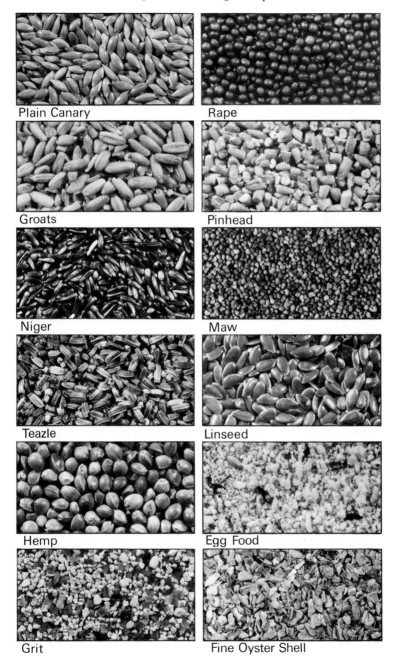

Plain Canary	Rape
Groats	Pinhead
Niger	Maw
Teazle	Linseed
Hemp	Egg Food
Grit	Fine Oyster Shell

external bath, care must be taken to check that the door does not drop down during use, thus trapping the bathing bird. Baths should always be given in the morning and removed at lunchtime to ensure that the feathers of the birds are fully dried out before roosting. This is desirable rather than essential, so if this practice of early removal is not feasible, the beginner should not be too concerned, although he should not use it as an excuse to avoid providing baths at regular intervals.

If, at any time, a bird shows any signs of inactivity accompanied by distress, as evidenced by sitting around with feathers fluffed out, it should at once be caged separately and its seed diet restricted to plain canary and maw seed in equal proportions. Should the condition not improve within 48 hours, the bird should further be transferred to a specially thermostatically controlled heated cage, the thermostat being set at 86°F (30°C). Such cages can be purchased from a manufacturer but it is relatively easy for a breeder to make his own temporary hospital cage using electric light bulbs as a source of heat. When in the hospital cage, the bird should be offered only dry bread which has been soaked in milk and sweetened with a little glucose. If necessary, advice should be sought from a veterinary practitioner.

Approximately 8 weeks prior to the intended commencement of the breeding season, males and females should be separated. It is recommended that the males are caged individually and the females allowed to remain in either flights or large cages.

If the environment is an artificial one, the amount of artificial light should be adjusted to correspond with the hours of natural daylight found in an average room at the relevant time of the year. It must be remembered that dwellings, unless of glass construction, get lighter later in the morning than a garden does and also start to darken earlier in the evening.

When a false environment is created intentionally in order to force the stock into breeding condition earlier than would be natural, heat should be employed and the thermostat set at 50–54°F (10–12°C). Lighting should also be adjusted so that the daylight hours are gradually extended by half an hour every second week so that, by the time the pairing-up process is completed, the birds are enjoying 13½–14 hours of sunlight daily. Opinions differ on whether the additional light should be given before dawn or after dusk. In practice, whatever the time chosen, it must be adhered to and should suit the lifestyle of the breeder. Should dawn be preferred, it is obviously better for the breeder to have an automatic time switch installed in the breeding room to eliminate the need for early rising. The light can then be switched off either manually or by an automatic time switch. It is important that the light is not switched off until the sun has risen sufficiently to afford maximum natural light in the birdroom.

If the system of putting on the light in the afternoon is preferred, this must be done at least 2 hours before dusk and it must then be gradually dimmed to darkness. In this way, the birds will roost naturally instead of being frightened by sudden darkness, which may result in panic flight and injury. Also the females will have warning that dusk is approaching and so will ensure that the youngsters have sufficient food in their crops to last them through the night. Appliances can now be purchased that will gradually dim a fluorescent tube. Alternatively, there is the basic time-switch/dimmer that simultaneously switches off the fluorescent tube and switches on a normal light bulb which itself gradually dims.

Although the practice is somewhat controversial, the author is a firm believer in giving all of his stock a course of a broad-spectrum antibiotic when the males and females are separated, and he repeats this process 4 weeks later. The course lasts for 5 days and, whenever the antibiotic is being given, a multi-vitamin preparation is also offered. To ensure that all stock receives both, the antibiotic and the vitamin preparations are given in the water. At the same time, a modified rearing food is offered in small quantities, initially once a week and later daily for 2 weeks prior to pairing up.

It must be added that the use of antibiotics in this way is frowned upon by the veterinary profession and problems might be faced in acquiring the necessary antibiotics. The author has adopted this practice because, being a practical breeder rather than a qualified veterinarian, he is of the opinion that minor illnesses in birds, which are normally undetectable, can, if untreated, be a cause of infertility and/or dead in shell (failure of a fertilised egg to reach maturity and the chick to hatch out). Also, a significant increase in the number of chicks per pair reared each season has been noted since its introduction.

There are many types of rearing food available. Most commercially-produced products are readily accepted by the birds and prove to be quite suitable for rearing young. Some need additives, some do not, but instructions for use are clearly printed on the label. It is strongly recommended that these instructions are followed. Many breeders, in an attempt to economise, are wont to mix foods or to add bulky fillers to reduce their financial outlay. This is false economy because all commercially-prepared foods are made to a recipe which ensures a properly-balanced diet and any changes to them can lead to imbalances and subsequent lack of success in the breeding room. One point to look for when purchasing rearing foods is the guaranteed date of validity of the vitamin content. This is normally clearly printed on the packet. Products that are past their 'sell-by date' should not be purchased. Some breeders prefer to mix their own rearing foods and recipes vary greatly both in composition and in the way they are administered. Until a breeder has gained experience, he would probably be better advised to choose a com- mercially-made product. Whatever product is selected, it should not be changed until the breeding season is complete. This advice also applies to the seed mixture. Another task that needs to be completed about 4 weeks prior to pairing up is examining the claws of all birds to be used for breeding and trimming them if they are excessively long. This is a simple exercise which takes only a few seconds, causes the bird no pain and, if done properly, lessens the risk of eggs being accidentally punctured during the incubation period. To trim the claws, the bird should be firmly held in the palm of one hand allowing some freedom of movement of the thumb and first finger which are required to firmly hold each claw. Examination will reveal a vein running down the centre of the claw and any claw more than about 1/20 inch (2 mm) from the end of the vein should be cut off using either sharp scissors or nail cutters. In the event of the vein being accidentally severed, the bird's foot should be thoroughly washed in cold water, dried and an antiseptic lotion or powder applied. Fortunately, such occurrences never seem to cause the bird any lasting distress and, apart from the blood staining the perches, necessitating re-cleaning, little else need be done.

Finally, it is desirable to spray each bird thoroughly with an anti-mite preparation. This process should be repeated at least twice more during the succeeding 3 weeks. This ensures the extermination not only of any mites present during the initial treatment but also of generations that may emerge later.

Pairing

For a beginner, the question of stock selection and pairing has been dealt with at the time of purchase. For breeders in their second

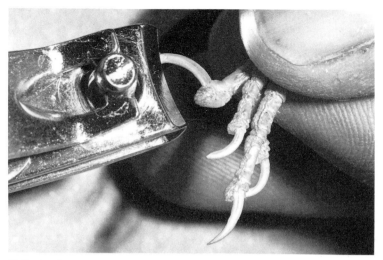

Nail trimming.

season, however, it may be a combination of either duplicating the first season's pairings, if the results obtained were satisfactory, introducing new stock into the existing stud, or commencing a line-breeding or inbreeding experiment. In every instance, it is assumed that advice will be sought from the more experienced breeders and, therefore, the many possible combinations are not dealt with here. The theories of line- and inbreeding are fully described in the section (p. 147) on Yorkshire canaries. Therefore the only explanation needed here is of the systems to be used to breed from the stock in our possession.

Before moving birds into breeding cages, the cages should be thoroughly scrubbed with hot water containing a strong disinfectant and a solution of a malathion-based product specially manufactured as a preventive against infestation by red mite. When dry, the cages should be divided into single units by the use of slides. If a male is to be mated with more than one female, an empty compartment should be left beside each compartment housing a female. The slides separating them, if wooden, should have a number of holes of about ¾ inch (20 millimetres) diameter drilled into them about 2 inches (50 millimetres) from the bottom. Alternatively, a wire slide similar in construction to a cage front can be used. This enables the partners to see each other and allows the male to feed the female but prevents other contact. If the birds are fully fit and in prime

37

breeding condition there are usually no problems in introducing the partners. Occasionally, however, the breeding condition of one of the partners will be further advanced than the other and fighting will take place.

If the birds are fit, after a period of 5 or 6 days the male can normally be seen feeding the female through the holes in the slide and it is then generally safe to withdraw the slide. If more than one female is to be mated with a male, he should be introduced to each of them in rotation. Females are best kept separately or fighting many ensue. If the male is in peak breeding condition, he will be observed drawing in his feathers tightly to his body and singing lustily. The female will be observed calling to her mate and carrying around any loose pieces of paper, wood shavings, etc. and, when the male is singing, squatting on the perch with her tail raised. This is a good indication that each member of the pair has accepted the other and copulation will take place.

If two or more females are to be paired with one male, some breeders will withdraw the male immediately after copulation has been observed and then introduce him to the next female 4 or 5 hours later. Others prefer to leave the male with the first female for half a day and then move him onto the next. Where this is not practical, the male may be transferred from one female to another on a daily basis. If this method is employed, and more than two females are to be paired with the one male, the two females which appear to be nearest to peak breeding condition should be used first. Subsequent females should be isolated in their cages until one of the first two has completed laying her clutch. At this point the process of introduction already described should commence with the third female, and so on. The life of the original pairs should continue in this manner for a further week and then nest pans can be introduced.

Nesting and Nest Pans

Nest pans come in a variety of forms and can be manufactured or purchased. The more usual ones are commercially produced from plastic, wicker and earthenware. Some breeders, however, prefer to make their own from wood with a wire-netting bottom. Should this be the case they should be approximately 3½ inches (90 millimetres) square and 2 inches (50 millimetres) deep. The back should be higher and usually has a hole drilled into it so it can be fixed to a screw placed on the back of the cage. If wood, wicker or earthenware

Clockwise from top left: three types of nesting receptacle – plastic, wicker and wooden – and nesting felt.

nest pans are used, these should be thoroughly soaked in an insect-repellent solution and then dried a week or two before use. Nest pans can be fitted almost anywhere in a cage providing that they are easily accessible and are fixed so that they will not fall. Traditionally, nest pans are hung centrally on the back of a cage but some people prefer to adapt them to hang on the front of the cage. Experiments carried out by the author suggest that, given an option, a bird will normally choose to nest in a site nearest the light source and he therefore recommends that cage fronts with two doors are fitted and the nest pans are placed in specially-manufactured attachments that hang on the outside of the cage in a similar fashion to a bath. These have been found particularly useful because, firstly, the nest pan is not taking up space in the cage and, secondly, inspection of the nest and its contents can be made so much more easily without unduly disturbing the parent(s). On the rare occasions when a female refuses to use the nest pan, wherever it is sited, and starts to build a nest on the floor, she should be discouraged by removing the partly built nest and placing an obstacle in the same position. Should she persist, a nest pan should be sited in the chosen area and the partly built nest should be placed within it. At this point, any other nest pan should be withdrawn.

Canaries are the most accommodating of creatures in that they will usually build their nests from any material supplied for the purpose. It is customary to offer dried moss, soft dried grasses and small pieces of soft string. Because materials collected from the countryside may be contaminated with chemical pesticides, more people, particularly in mainland Europe, are now using manmade or natural fabric offcuts. The author uses specially-packed cotton offcuts. These are cut to a length of ½ inch (10 millimetres) and then whisked in an electric coffee grinder/food processor. The end result is a soft light mixture that is readily used by the canary. Occasionally a female will construct her nest badly or will use wood shavings etc. rather than the offered materials. Should this occur, the fancier should prepare a nest himself; a small electric light bulb can be used to compress the orthodox materials into a suitable shape. Once the female has laid her second egg, the nest should be exchanged and it is almost unknown for a female not to accept the substitute. Some fanciers put a prescribed amount of the preferred nesting material into the nest pan, allowing the female to shape the nest herself; others offer the nesting material in special wire containers placed on the cage front. Neither method can be considered superior to the other.

Plastic and earthenware nest pans have a shiny smooth surface so

Outside-fitting nest-pan holder with earthenware nest-pan and foam insert.

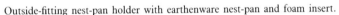

a lining is required so that the female, when building her nest, can attach the chosen nesting material firmly. Traditionally, felt or baize is used; some people purchase specially-manufactured 'nest felts' others use cut-up pieces of felt or baize. A thin-gauge sponge sheet has been introduced recently and has been used successfully by the author. Most commercially-produced nest pans have small holes drilled into the bottom and the linings, therefore, can be sewn into the nest pan. Alternatively, they can be stuck in using glue or rendered carbolic soap. A minimum of two nest pans per pair will be required. Because of problems experienced in the past or a desire to take no chances, the author liberally dusts the nest lining with a malathion-based insect repellent, to deter mite, before placing the nest pan in the cage.

At no time should a nest pan be sited in direct sunlight. If this is unavoidable, steps should be taken to counteract the problem either by fixing a cover into the cage front, to create a shaded position, or by painting the windows with diluted emulsion paint.

Eggs and Egg-Laying

A female canary will lay four eggs in a normal clutch. As each one is

A clutch of eggs in a nest made from soft hay and moss.

Egg-storage drawer.

laid, it should be removed and replaced with a plastic or china substitute. It should then be stored in a site which is not subject to extremes of temperature and clearly labelled so that it is known from which pair it originated. The eggs are returned to the female on the day she lays, or should lay, her fourth egg. The normal incubation period for canary eggs is 14 days although, if the weather is warm, it is not unusual for them to hatch a day earlier and if cold a day later. The eggs are removed and replaced in this way so that they should all hatch on the same day. This is essential because, within 4 days of hatching, the size of a baby canary increases dramatically and a larger chick, because of its size and strength would receive more food from its mother than its smaller nest mates. This frequently results in the smaller birds literally being starved to death. Once the eggs have been replaced a record should be made of the expected hatching date.

When a female is not fully fit she will be unable to pass her egg. This condition is known as 'egg binding'. In the morning, an egg-bound female will be found huddled in the corner of the cage or on the nest, in an obviously distressed state, and no egg will have been laid when one could reasonably be expected. On examination the lower area of the body will appear greatly extended. The remedy is to the coat the area of the vent with a warm solution of olive oil and to place the female in a hospital cage with the thermostat set at about 86°F (30°C). Normally, the egg will be passed within an hour of this treatment being applied. Sometimes the female will go on to complete her clutch with no further problem; sometimes no more eggs appear. If this happens, withdraw the nest pan and if possible, return the bird to a flight. Failing that, leave her alone in her cage and then start the breeding cycle procedure 2 or 3 weeks later.

Once the clutch has been returned and the female starts her incubation (this is termed 'setting the clutch' or 'sitting the hen'), the male is normally withdrawn totally and either used elsewhere or housed separately. If, however, the female refuses to sit, he should be reintroduced for a day or two until she becomes very broody, when he should again be withdrawn. Prior to replacing the eggs it is advisable to dust the nest liberally again with a malathion-based insect-repellent powder. It is recommended that, if possible, more than one female is 'sat' on the same day. If it is discovered that only the odd egg is fertile or, later, that two nests contain only one or two chicks or that there are a number of chicks growing at different rates in two or more nests, the eggs or chicks can be interchanged to allow

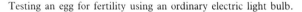

Testing an egg for fertility using an ordinary electric light bulb.

43

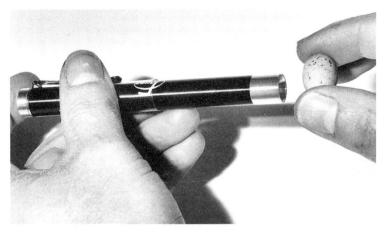

The same operation using a recently-developed battery-operated high-power light source.

either viable numbers or evenly-sized chicks to be reared together.

At all times, careful records should be kept of the dates on which females start to incubate and when the eggs are due to hatch. An easy way to do this is to use a desk diary, preferably one with 1 day per page. The author finds this system easy and convenient, as well as allowing him to jot down useful reminders of other tasks that need to be completed on specific days. Also, space is available for notes which can be later transferred to the breeding register.

After 7 days the nest can be removed and the eggs tested for fertility. This is done by holding the egg up to a bright light. In an infertile egg, the yolk will be clearly visible rising to the top; a fertile egg will appear dark throughout. If the eggs are fertile, the nest should be quickly returned; if infertile, the nest should be totally withdrawn. Those eggs found to be infertile are called 'clear'. Once a nest has been 'broken up' (this being the term used for the withdrawal of a nest), the female will usually show signs of wanting to build another nest about a week to 10 days later, whereupon the breeding process already explained should be recommenced. In the event of only one or two eggs being found fertile, many fanciers prefer to foster out these eggs to other females who are due to hatch on the same day. Should this system be used, it is recommended, wherever possible, to place the eggs in nests belonging to a different colour or type of canary. Alternatively, a breeder may find that one female is incubating four or five fertile eggs whilst another female is incubating only one or two and, in such instances, often two nests of three are made up. Occasionally eggs that are found to be fertile fail to hatch because the chick has either failed to reach maturity or is unable to force its way from the egg. This is known as 'dead in shell'. There are innumerable reasons for this occurrence. Lack of humidity is often the cause and, to overcome this, it is helpful to place a container of water over the room heaters so that moisture is released into the atmosphere; other more sophisticated methods are also available, such as electric humidifiers.

Chicks

Assuming, however, that all is well and the chicks hatch on schedule, a constant supply of rearing food should be offered. Should additives be required, this will be noted on the instructions printed on the packet and these should be followed from the start. Soaked seeds and a variety of greenfoods, such as chopped lettuce and spinach in addition to, or in place of, seeded weed heads (chickweed and dandelion being the British favourites) can also be introduced. The results achieved by the author over several years show that such additions, whilst probably not harmful, are not essential and the choice is left to the individual fancier. Should greenfoods be used, only small quantities should be offered at any one time and

A recently-hatched chick.

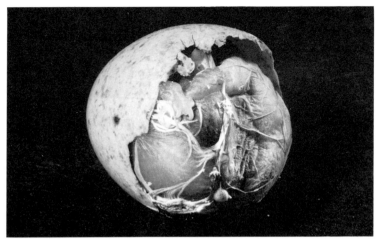

A 'dead-in-shell' chick.

any stale surpluses should be removed quickly. When soaked seeds are used, care must also be taken to ensure that they are thoroughly cleaned by washing in running water before being offered. Some breeders prefer to prepare their own soaked seeds from a commercially-available soaked-seed mixture which generally consists of rape, teazle, niger, hemp and Japanese millet. This should be soaked in water for 24 or 48 hours and then thoroughly washed and left to germinate in a warm dark place for a further 24 hours before being offered to the birds. The author prefers to prepare his own but uses only rape seed – which should be of the black variety (the red is treated to prevent germination) – which is mixed with his rearing food rather than being offered separately. At this stage, he also follows the practice, widely used in mainland Europe but rarely used in the UK, of offering a weak solution of a broad-spectrum antibiotic mixed with a multi-vitamin mixture in the drinking water for the 5 days following the emergence of the chicks from the shell. The first week of a young canary's life is the most critical as it is born blind and without feathers and, although growth is rapid, it is very small and vulnerable. At this time, any minor ailment passed on from the feeding parents can prove to be a major problem with a delicate chick and the suggested precautions help to prevent more serious problems occurring. It should be mentioned here that antibiotics should never be offered without adding a multi-vitamin preparation and never for more than 5 days at a time, as they will destroy vitamins within the bird.

When the first egg shells are noticed on the floor of the cage, thus announcing the arrival of the first chicks, the nests should be checked to ensure, firstly, that part of a broken shell has not slipped over the end of another and, secondly, that a chick which was starting to emerge has not, for some reason, failed to completely crack open the shell. The remedies for both mishaps are quite simple. In the first instance, the whole egg should be put into a shallow dish of water, whereupon the loose shell will easily separate from the whole egg, and, in the second instance, the shell should be gently eased open from the area already cracked.

The necessity for recording all the relevant occasions in a breeding season has been briefly mentioned. The accumulation of knowledge linked with stock improvement is based mainly on personal observation of the stock in ones own birdroom. Memory cannot be relied upon to recall these observations and it cannot be emphasised too strongly that accurate and complete records are absolutely essential. Observations should start at pairing up and continue throughout nesting, incubation and, particularly, from the day a chick hatches until it has completed its moult. Particular attention should be given to anything that could be of relevance in the future. This can include the number of eggs per clutch, the construction of the nest, the female's nervousness when incubating, her capability as a mother and, in the case of a male, his assistance or hindrance in rearing a brood. When the chick hatches, observations should be made on the colour of the skin, legs, feet and beak, nest feather as it forms and also the lipochrome colour and the deposition of melanistic pigment. Similar observations should later be made of the adult plumage.

For the first 6 or 7 days, the female will keep her nest clean by eating the droppings passed by the chicks. These droppings are contained in a faecal sac and, if the chick is healthy, the sac will remain intact. Should the chick have some form of internal disorder, the sac will burst when being passed, making it impossible for the female to keep the nest clean. The droppings are thus deposited round the nest and are eventually transferred onto the plumage of the mother so that she appears to be sweating – a term used to describe this condition. Should this occur, all rearing foods, particularly soaked seeds and greenfoods, should be withdrawn and substituted with a mixture of stale wholemeal bread and boiled milk

Chicks 7 days after hatching.

which has been cooled to an acceptable temperature. To make the mixture more appetising, a small quantity of glucose and maw seed can be added. There are many reasons for the cause of such upsets, the most common one being a rearing mixture that is too rich for the chicks to digest properly – a problem that occurs more often when home-made mixtures are used in preference to commercially produced ones. Alternatively, they are caused by the excessive intake of greenfoods and/or soaked seeds. It is for this reason that the author uses commercially-produced rearing foods and offers no greenfoods/soaked seeds other than those previously described. The use of bread and milk will usually correct problems caused by an over-rich or unbalanced diet. Once the faecal sacs return to normal the usual diet can be slowly reintroduced.

When the chicks are about 1 week old, the female will stop cleaning the nest and it is at this time that the youngsters should be fitted with a closed metallic ring stamped with an identifying number and the year of issue. Such rings come in various sizes and advice should be sought from an experienced breeder of the variety kept on the correct size to be purchased. Alternatively, most ring manufacturers are conversant with the regulations concerning ring sizes for the different varieties and will proffer the correct information. In most countries, it is compulsory to close-ring birds should the breeder intend placing them in an exhibition. In the UK

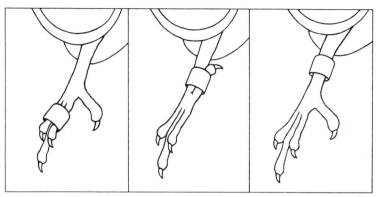

Fitting a closed ring.

this is not so but the practice is recommended as it affords a permanent means of identification. The bird's genetic history can thus be traced, providing that details are properly recorded at the time when the ring was fitted. This is particularly important with coloured canaries in which a bird may be carrying two or more factors.

The method of fixing rings is shown in the illustration above and is similar to the technique used for clipping a bird's claw. The bird should be held firmly in one hand, with the chosen leg held by the thumb and first and second fingers. The ring should initially be placed over the front three toes with the back toe pulled back along the leg. The ring should then be pushed as far up the leg as is necessary to clear the back claw and then released. Although the age of 6 to 8 days is suggested as being the ideal time to fit closed rings, it could be either too late or too soon. Canaries do not always increase in size uniformly; some remain comparatively small and, when the ring is fitted, it will slip off. Others grow very fast and, at the suggested age, the thick part of the foot is too large for the ring to pass over easily. If this is the case, the foot should be lubricated with oil, grease or water and then a firm but gentle attempt made to pass the ring over the thick part of the foot. If it is obvious that it will be possible to fix the ring only by applying great pressure, the attempt should be abandoned. In the event of the chick being too small, attempts to fix the ring should be made daily until the ring remains in place. Only by experience will the breeder be able to judge at what time his birds need to be ringed

If rings are fitted before the female has finished cleaning the nest

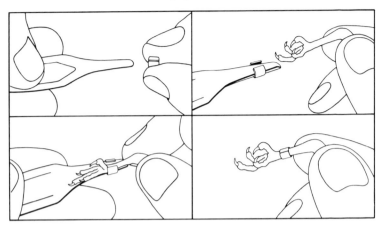

Fitting a celluloid split ring.

she may succeed in ejecting the offending ring from the nest, as she will see it only as a foreign body. Often the chick will be attached. It is better always to ring chicks late in the evening when the light is starting to fade but, regardless of when it is done, checks should be made up to roosting time and first thing the following morning to ensure that no chick has been ejected.

Should a chick be found on the floor at this or any other time, even if it appears cold and dead, it may not in fact be beyond revival. The chick should be cupped in the hand and warmed by breathing onto it. Often the bird will start to revive and, once fully warmed and moving, it can then be replaced in the nest.

Occasionally problems occur whereby removal of a closed ring is required to ensure that no distress to the bird occurs. This normally happens only in the event of accidental damage to a bird's leg. Should removal be required it is obviously a delicate matter. Most closed rings are made from aluminium and are easily cut by either a sharp strong pair of nail scissors or specially-manufactured tools.

Should a breeder decide not to fit closed rings, split plastic ones can be affixed instead. These rings can be acquired in a variety of colours and can either be plain or printed with successive numbers. A special grooved tool is supplied over which the ring is pushed. The ring then opens, allowing the tool to be placed over the bird's leg and gradually withdrawn whilst the ring is held in place. Once totally withdrawn, the ring can then be pinched together. If removal of the ring is required for any reason the reverse procedure is applied.

50

Once the nest, empty of its occupants, has been removed it is advisable to dust it once more with a malathion-based insect repellent. Although it might seem that the author is obsessed with insect repellent, it is a fact that red mite and northern mite can invade the cleanest and most hygienic of birdrooms without warning. The use of repellents, as described, will normally prevent red mite infestation although no preventive seems to work with northern mite. These pests, although not fatal to healthy adult birds will seriously weaken a chick, particularly one that is not fully feathered, firstly by their action as an irritant and, secondly, because they live on blood sucked from their hosts. If there is an infestation, it will soon be detected because hordes of the parasites will crawl over the breeder's hands when he is in contact with the nest. To combat these pests, a quantity of the malathion-based powder should be sprinkled into the breeder's hands and unfeathered chicks should then be gently rolled in the powder, taking care that the underside of the wings is exposed to the treatment. Feathered birds should be dusted using a puffer appliance, again ensuring that the bird is completely covered by the power. A similar exercise should take place with the parents. A nest, if badly infested, should be removed and burned and the nest pan placed in a solution of insect repellent. A duplicate nest then needs to be constructed, dusted with powder and returned, with the chicks, to the cage. The cage should also be cleaned and sprayed with repellent, particular attention being paid to the ends of perches. Strangely, such drastic measures will rarely disturb rearing females to the extent of making them desert their young. Because these parasites strike indiscriminately and without warning checks should be made on their presence at least twice daily.

When the chicks are 14 or 15 days old they will be almost fully feathered and the mother will probably stop brooding them. At this time, the nest pan should be placed on the floor in the corner of the cage and a new one fitted in its place. To prevent the cage from being excessively soiled, a right-angled metal or wooden surround for the nest pan can be fitted into the corner of the cage before putting down the nest. Nesting material should be offered, as with the first nest, and the female, after a day or two, will usually start to build a second nest while at the same time continuing to rear her brood. The male should then be re-introduced and can either be left with the family or removed immediately after copulation has taken place depending on how many females are being serviced.

By the time the female has nearly completed her second nest, her

Chicks 14 days after hatching

A chick which has been badly feather-plucked showing the replacement feathers appearing.

first brood of youngsters will have become adventurous enough to start leaving the nest and to feed themselves. At this time, should the female pluck the feathers from them to line her second nest, or should the young become a nuisance by deserting their first nest and claiming the new one, they should be separated by replacing the slides which were used when the male was first introduced to the female. The chicks should, of course, be put on the opposite side of the partition from the new nest. When this is done, it will be seen that their mother will then feed them through the holes in the slide.

Initially, a small amount of rearing food should be offered to the youngsters in a dish and, if not eaten, it should be replaced with a fresh supply at least twice a day. It is normal for the youngsters to be seen feeding themselves prior to the female's second clutch being set but, if they are not, there is no need to worry. The female, whilst incubating her second clutch, will continue to feed them as required until they are self-sufficient. Whilst it is advisable to separate the youngsters from their mother as soon as possible, 21 days from hatching being the prescribed date, care should be taken to ensure that the chicks are self-sufficient before finally weaning them. As it is not normally practical for many breeders to inspect the birdroom throughout the day, it is useful to separate the youngsters from their mother totally on the morning of their 21st day, leaving them in a cage with a shallow dish containing rearing food. In the evening, this should be removed for half an hour and replaced with a fresh supply. Those chicks that are feeding themselves will usually start to eat within 5 or 10 minutes and can then be removed to weaning cages. Those that are obviously distressed, or who have not been seen to feed themselves, can be returned to their mother for the night; the process should be repeated each day until all chicks are observed to be feeding themselves.

Opinions differ on how often the cages should be cleaned between the time when the female starts to build her nest and when the youngsters are weaned. The author ensures that the cage is totally cleaned out on the morning the clutch is set but only superficial cleaning is carried out until the chicks are ringed, whereupon the cage is again totally cleaned out. This process is repeated when the nest is placed on the floor, with another total clean-out when the second clutch is set. No females have shown undue distress or have been observed to desert their nests when this system has been implemented.

Precautions

While the female is incubating, regular checks should be made to ensure that she has not deserted her nest, something which happens occasionally. If the eggs have not been properly covered during the first day, they should be removed and replaced with dummy eggs. Occasionally a female will not go totally broody until a fifth or sixth egg has been laid. Should this happen, the eggs should be set once the full clutch has been laid. Should desertion take place after this period, the eggs should be marked with a felt-tip pen – care being taken to see that the shell is not accidentally cracked – and the eggs placed in other nests as a temporary measure. Where the eggs are placed must obviously be recorded. Dummy eggs should then be placed in the nest and a watch kept to see whether the female returns to her incubation duties. Often she does and, if so, once the breeder is sure of the female's intentions, the eggs can be returned. In the event of her total disinterest, the eggs must be placed with other females whose clutches are due to hatch either at the same time or on the day after. Again, care should be taken to ensure that they are placed, wherever possible, in nests where the expected progeny will be of a different colour or variety. The original female should have her nest pan removed and a fresh one should be given to her 4 or 5 days later, whereupon the pairing procedure should be repeated.

Occasionally, a breeder may wish to produce two clutches of youngsters from one female using different males. Where this is required, the male used on the first pairing should be withdrawn immediately the clutch is set and the second male introduced when she starts to build her second nest. By the time of the second nest, both members of a pair are normally fully fit and no problems occur. Sometimes, however, the birds will fight and, in this instance, they should be separated (this is known as breaking up the pair) with the male being reintroduced each successive 24 hours until he is accepted by the female. This process should also be used with the first-round pairings should fighting occur.

THE MOULT

When the youngsters are initially placed into weaning cages, their diet for the first week should consist of rearing food. During this week the increasing strength and stamina of the young birds will be noticeable. For the second week following weaning, seed is

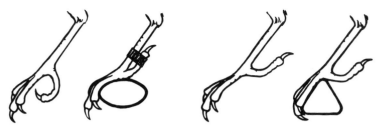

Abnormal claws: undershot (left), slipped (right).

introduced to the diet for the first time. The author offers a dish of plain canary seed and a dish of black rape mixed with pinhead oatmeal, i.e. the mixture normally offered to all of his stud throughout the year; rearing food should also continue to be offered. Youngsters on weaning food will drink copious quantities of water and care should be taken to ensure that supplies are always available. At the beginning of the sixth week of life, they can be transferred to a moulting area. This can be a flight or a large flight cage and opinions vary considerably on the diet to be offered at this time. The majority of breeders continue with the diet offered in the previous week and persist with it until the moult is complete. The author stops giving rearing food daily at this stage, offering it only once a week as a treat. Greenfoods, sweet apples, oranges etc. can be offered daily but are not essential.

When youngsters are first weaned, their cages should be fitted with perches of varying heights; some breeders also ensure that the perches are of varying thickness.

Sometimes on weaning, it will be noticed that a youngster does not grip the perch properly and the back toe projects forward with the three front toes. This is known as 'undershot claw'. In other cases the back toe will lay back along the leg, a condition called 'slip claw'. The treatment required for these problems is shown in the illustration above.

If the claw is undershot, it should be pulled back and taped to the leg with adhesive tape. If the bird has a slipped claw, very thin or triangular-section perches should be installed to force the bird to grip with all claws in order to maintain its balance. These treatments should continue until the problem has been corrected.

As the birds approach 7 weeks of age, it will be seen that the tail and wing feathers are fully grown. This is a sign that they will soon commence their first moult.

During this moult they will replace their body feathers but not their long wing and tail feathers. A bird at this time is referred to as being 'unflighted' and will remain so until 12 months later at its second moult, when all of its feathers will be replaced. It is then 'flighted'. If all or part of the stud are of a variety that needs colour feeding it is now that it should commence. Obviously, if a mixed stud is kept, the varieties which do not require colour feeding need to be segregated and housed either in separate flights or in the higher cages of a block.

Manufactured colour food can usually be offered in the drinking water or mixed into rearing food, but this depends on whether the product is oil- or water-based.

In the UK the most commonly-used substance is a product sold under the brand name Carophyll Red*. It is a water-soluble product and can therefore be offered in either way. Traditional methods of colour feeding non-red-ground canaries, e.g. Yorkshires and Norwich, involved mixing prepared cayenne with rearing food. This custom, although still preferred by a few, has largely been discontinued and the vast majority of breeders now use Carophyll Red®.

If rearing foods are not regularly offered to youngsters during the the moult, which is the author's practice, the colouring agent must be added to the drinking water. Apart from the mess caused by birds bathing in the drinking water and splashing the red liquid throughout the cages, this method has caused no problems. The product is purchased in powder form and small quantities are mixed with hot water which is then allowed to cool before being given to the birds. It is difficult to be precise about the actual quantities used but, as a guideline, a level coffeespoonful per pint of water (about 2 milligrams per litre) is sufficient. As an indication of whether the solution is of the correct strength, its colour should resemble tomato soup and droppings passed by the birds should be red in colour. Should the breeder prefer to offer colour food mixed into his rearing food he can either moisten the rearing food with a solution of colouring agent of the strength described above or he can mix the agent into his rearing food in a dry state, the approximate quantities being about ¹/₁₀ ounce (3–4 grams) per 3¼ pounds (1.5 kilograms) of rearing food. Whatever method is employed, the colouring agent should be offered

* Roche Products Ltd

Two types of hang-on bird bath.

every day until the bird has completed its moult and then offered once a week until the show season is completed. This ensures that any feathers accidentally lost after the moult will, on growing again, attain the same colour as those lost, which is essential if the bird is to be exhibited. In the UK, classes are normally provided for both unflighted and flighted birds. In most other countries, however, only unflighted birds can be exhibited. In these countries it is not unusual to find that a colouring agent is offered in the rearing mixture given to the rearing females. This allows for the wing and tail feathers to appear in a coloured state giving the bird a more balanced appearance after completion of its first moult. Birds similarly cared for can be exhibited in the UK provided that they have been fitted with closed rings, thus proving their year of birth.

During the moult, baths can be offered daily and any bird that shows any of the characteristics required in an exhibition specimen should be caged by itself to avoid the possibility of another bird pecking feathers from it. With the exception of Lizard and frilled canaries, this is not too important where only the body feathers are concerned but if tail or wing feathers are lost, their replacements will be longer and of a different colour. This would give an unbalanced effect as the unmoulted feathers will still appear in their natural state. Occasionally youngsters will succeed in breaking off, along the bottom of the shaft, one of the wing or tail feathers, causing a loss of

Two birds enjoying a bath in a receptacle placed on the floor.

blood which not only badly stains the feathers but seems to act as a magnet for other birds to join in the pecking session. Should this be noticed, the bird should be removed from the cage, the bleeding stump pulled out and all traces of blood washed away. After drying, the bird can be sprayed with an anti-pecking preparation that can be purchased from most pet shops and it can then be returned to the cage. At this time the young males will begin to whistle and, if several birds of the same colour are being moulted in the same cage or flight, it is useful to catch the chick and note the ring number in the breeding register to facilitate recognition later.

Some breeders allow their females to raise a third brood but this is asking a lot, particularly if the female has already raised two broods. If she shows signs of wanting to build a third nest, facilities should be provided to allow her to do so but, when she has completed laying her clutch and has sat for 2 or 3 days, the nest pan should be removed and she should be placed in the flight with the youngsters.

Normally, adult birds will start to moult in midsummer and will finish in early autumn. The males can also be placed in the flight when their services are no longer required.

SHOW TRAINING

Training

All canaries need to have some training if they are to present themselves properly on the showbench. The amount of training varies greatly from bird to bird, some being natural showmen, others needing more encouragement to exhibit themselves to best advantage.

Show training starts immediately after the young birds have been transferred to flight cages for the moult. It is best started by fixing a show cage to the front of the breeding cage so that the bird has ready access to both cages. At first it may be necessary to put some titbit in the show cage to encourage the bird to enter. Within a short time, however, it is usually found that it will happily hop in and around both cages. Specific show cages are used for each variety and the beginner should seek clarification from an experienced breeder of that variety so that he can be sure of purchasing the correct type of cage.

After a week or two, the bird will have sufficient confidence to be shut into the show cage. At first this should be for a short period but the time spent in the cage should be gradually increased until the bird shows no form of fright or distress, however long it is left there. In the UK it is illegal to leave a bird in a show cage in the birdroom for longer than 1 hour at a time. When the bird is first introduced to a show cage, it should be watched carefully to determine whether it can locate the seed and water, particularly if the receptacles are different or are not arranged in the same way as in the flight cage.

Although visitors should be politely discouraged from entering the breeding room when incubation and rearing is taking place, they should be encouraged during show training so that the birds become used to being viewed at close quarters by a variety of people. Birds that have never encountered, for example, people with spectacles or hats, or even other birds with a white ground colour, will sometimes show panic on confrontation. It is, therefore, advisable for them to be subjected to as many different experiences as possible before being sent to an exhibition. At this time an accurate ring register should be prepared. In addition to the number of the ring, the register should show the sex, feather type and ground colour of the bird, together with details of any melanistic pigment present, any visible mutations and any other mutations carried by the bird. A note should also be made of the parent birds and space allowed to note, if necessary, the name of the breeder to whom it is sold. Often, one needs to reintroduce stock from a specific strain and, if records are kept of where birds have been placed, this simplifies the search.

Once the moult has been completed, the breeder can review the results of his efforts and begin again the difficult task of stock selection. Certain of the young will show the points for which he has been searching; others will be disappointing. Before any assessment is made of the quality of the stock, it should be decided how many pairs are to be kept for breeding in the following season and what varieties/mutations are to be involved. All males should then be placed in show cages and compared with each other to determine which of them carries the highest number of desirable qualities; care should also be taken to note faults. Reference to the breeding register should, if the records have been correctly kept, show any peculiarities associated with a particular bird. A similar exercise should be undertaken with the females. If a specific defect is apparent throughout the stud, it should be noted so that new stock can be introduced to correct the fault.

The Show Season

Prior to the start of the show season, a breeder is well advised to check the condition of his show cages and to carry out essential repairs, touching up areas where paint has been chipped etc. It is pointless placing a bird in a cage which is dirty and/or damaged as this will detract from the overall presentation.

If a breeder intends to exhibit every week, two teams of birds should be selected prior to the start of the show season, so that the teams can be alternated and the birds will not become unduly tired. Advice should be sought not only on the type of show cage to be used but on the type and location of seed, type of floor coverings, perch sizes etc., as these points will be taken into consideration when the bird is being judged.

The schedule of a show should be read very carefully before the entry form is completed to ensure that the bird is entered in the correct class. The beginner, if he has any doubts whatsoever, should ask an experienced breeder for advice. There is no greater disappointment than to arrive at a show, full of expectation, and then to find that the judge has disqualified the bird.

In the week leading up to a show the birds intended for exhibition should be sprayed with cold water daily until 2 days prior to the show. For this purpose, a small handspray obtainable from a garden centre is most suitable. Alternatively many fanciers, when preparing birds for shows, will handwash them. This is particularly helpful with the longer-feathered varieties such as the Norwich. Before it is washed, the bird should be examined carefully and the claws should be clipped if they are overgrown (see p. 36). A tried and tested method of handwashing is illustrated the sequence of photographs shown on p. 62. The equipment necessary is shown in (a) and this should obviously be prepared in advance. The small light-coloured bowl on the right contains a solution of baby shampoo. Care should be taken not to make the solution too strong and a mixture of about 1 tablespoonful of shampoo to 1 pint (30 millilitres to 1 litre) of tepid water is recommended. The bowl in the middle contains 1¾ pints (1 litre) of tepid water to which 2 teaspoonsful (10 millilitres) of malt vinegar has been added. This is used for the primary rinse. The large white bowl on the left contains tepid water and to this the recommended amount of a proprietary plumage spray is added; this is used for the final rinse. Other items required are cotton wool, a shaving brush, strips of absorbent linen and nail clippers.

In (b) the bird is being gently but firmly held in the left hand so that the lower part of the body, wing and tail are exposed. The bird is then immersed in the shampoo mixture up to the neck then, with the shaving brush, the feathers of the tail and those around the vent are lathered, followed by those of the lower wings and rump. This process is gradually extended until all of the bird's plumage has been lathered, finishing at the head. On the head, particularly early in the show season, small 'pin feathers' may be found and the lathering process will encourage the sheaths to be broken, thus allowing the feather to open out when dried.

The first rinse after the shampooing of the bird is shown in (c). The bird is totally immersed up to the neck and then withdrawn from the water; cotton wool is used to rinse the shampoo from the bird. The cotton wool, well-rinsed, should then be used to wipe down the plumage, care being taken to follow the natural growth pattern of the feathers.

The procedure adopted in (c) is repeated in (d) but this time using the solution containing plumage spray. Great care should be taken at the final rinse stage to ensure that all traces of shampoo are cleaned from the bird's plumage. Failure to do so will result in the feathers

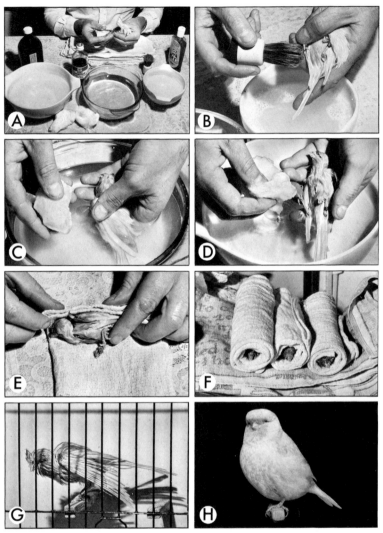

Handwashing: a) equipment, b) applying shampoo mixture, c) rinsing the bird, d) final rinse with plumage spray, e) wrapping the bird in towelling, f) canaries rolled in towelling, g) bird transferred to dry cage, h) dry bird.

sticking together after the bird has been dried.

Once the bird has been completely rinsed, excess water should be gently squeezed from the plumage by running the thumb and index finger from head to tail. The bird should then be transferred to a

62

length of towelling wide enough to cover the entire length of the bird and approximately 12 inches (300 millimetres) long. The bird is placed at one end of the strip and then the towelling is wrapped round the bird (e) to give the same effect as a rolled-up carpet (f). The birds are then transferred to a warm place, such as a hospital cage or an airing cupboard where they should be left for approximately 5 minutes.

In (g) the bird is shown after being transferred from the towelling strip into a clean cage. The cage needs to stand either in a room with a temperature of 80°F (25°C) or with a heat source directed on it to raise and maintain the temperature at this level.

It will take about 2 hours for the bird to become fully dry (h) and, during this period, the bird should be removed from the cage two or three times and its plumage 'brushed' with a silk cloth. This encourages the feathers to lay close to the body when the bird is totally dry.

If the temperature used to dry out the bird (80°F/25°C) is higher than that of the birdroom, it should gradually be reduced to that of the birdroom before the bird is returned to a clean stock cage.

Handwashing should take place 7–8 days prior to a show to allow the natural oils in the feathers, removed in the shampooing process, to be replenished by the natural preening of the bird.

At this time no greenfood should be offered. On the morning prior to the show, a final check should be made to ensure that the feet, tail etc. are not soiled and, if they are found to be dirty, they should be gently sponged with warm water.

In the UK all show cages have to be purchased by the exhibitor. In other countries, clubs own show cages and the exhibitor can transport his birds to the show in a carrying cage. If show cages are being transported, they are normally packed in a carrying box specially manufactured for the purpose. This allows for circulation of air but does not allow the cages to move about.

It is recommended that, whenever possible, birds are taken to the show the evening prior to judging. This allows them to become accustomed to the different surroundings and to overcome any nervousness prior to judging taking place.

In the UK, many clubs welcome volunteers to assist with stewarding duties at a show and this is an excellent way of learning about show procedures as well as allowing the beginner the opportunity to discuss the quality of his birds with the judge once judging has been completed. This may be impossible when visiting a show so, after judging has taken place, a beginner, if his birds have not won their classes, should study those that have beaten them very closely to see in what way they were superior. If this is not obvious, the advice of a judge or an experienced breeder should be sought and an effort made to discover which type of stock should be introduced into the stud to attain greater improvement in the following year.

When the birds are returned from the show, if the birdroom is in darkness the birds should be left in the carrying cage overnight, the lid being opened to allow ventilation. They can then be returned to their cages the following morning. A bath should be offered to all birds that have been to a show and a small dish of rearing food given. Preparations can then start for the following week's exhibition.

Breeding canaries can be the most frustrating of hobbies but equally it can be the most rewarding. As with most things, the more time, effort and attention to detail given to the canaries the greater will be the rewards.

CLUBS

Inevitably a newcomer to the Fancy will discover that a cage-bird society exists in his locality and the joining of such a club is recommended. Most clubs hold regular monthly meetings at which guest speakers lecture on a number of subjects relevant to the hobby; alternatively slide shows or quizzes take place. Here also a great deal of informal discussion takes place, with experienced breeders being only too willing to pass on helpful pieces of advice.

Equally, societies exist, certainly in the UK, which are aimed specifically at one section of the Fancy, even to the extent of being broken down to cater for the specialist breeder of a single variety. Whilst meetings of these clubs are infrequent, yearbooks and/or magazines are usually produced which offer much good advice to the newcomer and provide the names and addresses of breeders with similar interests. Other benefits of joining a specialist society are that the rules and regulations regarding the close ringing and exhibition of each of the breeds are determined by the membership of the specialist societies at Annual General Meetings and their findings are publicised in their magazines. It is also customary for members to be able to purchase close rings, colouring agents, etc. at reduced prices from these associations.

· CHAPTER 2 ·
NUTRITION AND DISEASE

A.J. PEARSON   BA, Vet. MB, MRCVS
Jill Pearson graduated from Cambridge University's Veterinary College in the UK in 1976, since when she has been employed in general practice in Cambridge. Over the past 5 years, recognising the overall lack of specialist knowledge in generally non-commercial species, she has concentrated her efforts on the nutritional needs, prevention and control of diseases in reptiles and caged birds. As well as performing her duties as a working veterinary practitioner, she also teaches on a part-time basis at the Veterinary Anatomy Department of Cambridge University.

INTRODUCTION

Whether you have one canary or hundreds, and whether you have been breeding for 50 years or have just purchased your first young stock – never pass up an opportunity to look at someone else's birds. There is nothing like it to help assess the level of health and vigour of your own.

The canary is now a fully-domesticated species, but don't forget its origins. The wild canary lived in woods and scrubland, ranging considerable distances for a wide variety of foodstuffs, active for most of the day. We have taken the canary, confined it in a cage or aviary, and restricted its food to that which we choose to give. We also force it, unless we are very careful about cleaning out, to live in close proximity to its droppings for often quite considerable periods of time. We also choose for our canary the company it must keep and the numbers of birds to be kept together. Of course, most birds live healthy, active and productive lives in captivity, but the following should be borne in mind:

1) A less than perfectly-balanced diet will lead to unfit birds.
2) Lack of exercise can produce unfit birds that fail to breed.
3) Low levels of hygiene encourage the spread of diseases, either bacterial infections or parasites which are passed from bird to bird via the droppings.
4) Overcrowding can produce behavioural problems such as excessive aggression and, again, breeding difficulties.

All these problems may manifest themselves by very sick or dead birds or simply by birds that are less than 100% healthy. So – look at other people's birds. Talk about birds with other fanciers, not to score points, but to find out what they feed to their birds and how often, whether they give vitamin supplements, how many they keep in a cage, whether or not your birds are in the very best condition possible.

There are a thousand different ways of housing and feeding canaries and most of them will keep birds fit and healthy. But there is always something still to be learned.

NUTRITION

What every canary needs for good health is, like us, the right balance of protein, carbohydrate, fat, minerals and vitamins, together with clean, fresh water. Of course, most of the above can be supplied by a proprietary seed mix – if it is of good quality and stored properly in a dry, airtight container. On no account should it be left in a paper sack on a damp floor, where it will go mouldy, get eaten by mice, waste your money and pass disease to your birds.

The seeds found in a standard canary mix can be divided into two groups, those which are rich in fats and those in which carbohydrates predominate. The millets and canary seed contain about: 4% fat, 60% carbohydrate and 10–15% protein. Hemp, maw, rape and niger contain: 30–40% fat, 10–20% carbohydrate and 15–20% protein.

Most caged birds are overweight in any case, so too great an amount of the second group will make the situation even worse and possibly lead to liver disease. The very fatty seeds are useful in winter for aviary birds that need large amounts of energy to keep warm, but should otherwise be fed sparingly, although some birds will always show a marked preference for them – especially for maw.

Vitamins

Vitamins are substances that are essential for various chemical processes within the body. They are divided into two groups: the fat-soluble and the water-soluble vitamins. The water-soluble vitamins (which include the Vitamin B complex) are usually found in sufficient quantities in good-quality seed. The fat-soluble vitamins (Vitamins A, D and E) are found in only small quantities in dry seed, and so deficiencies may occur in birds fed on a constant diet of seed mix only. These deficiencies are easily prevented by giving regular greenfood, sprouted seed and/or vitamin supplements. Suitable greenfoods include chickweed, dandelion and chicory, all of which should be gathered from a garden where no pesticides or weed-killers have been used; all should be washed thoroughly before use. They can be supplied daily, or once or twice weekly. Vitamin supplements are best given in the drinking water and a complete vitamin supplement designed for cage birds is the best type to use.

Proprietary softfoods and rearing foods are also vitamin-rich and so can be used as a supplement to the seed diet.

Minerals

There are two groups of essential minerals: those needed in relatively large quantities for health, and the 'trace elements'. Those needed in relatively large amounts are as follows:

Calcium This mineral is essential for the formation of healthy bones, for egg production, and for the proper functioning of the heart, muscles and nerves. Although there is some calcium in seeds, a supplement should always be provided in the form of crushed oystershell, cuttlefish bone etc. This is particularly important during the breeding season, when an additional commercial calcium supplement may be added to the seed or softfood.

Phosphorus Like calcium, phosphorus is present in oystershell, cuttlefish bone etc. as well as in greenstuff. It is also involved in bone formation. Deficiencies of phosphorus, and calcium, will result in soft, brittle bones and the birds may lay soft-shelled eggs.

Sodium and Chlorine These are generally found in combination as sodium chloride or common salt. Deficiency does not often occur. Both are found in all the usual foods. A low-level deficiency can give rise to infertility problems and to skin irritation causing feather plucking. If it seems necessary to supplement the salt in the diet never put it in the drinking water. Given in this way, it can kill the birds. Instead, sprinkle just a very little on the food. Be aware that the birds will usually need to drink more while the salt is being given, so do make sure that the drinking vessel is never empty.

Potassium and Iodine Both these minerals are found in cuttlefish bone and in bonemeal and they are important in growth and reproduction. Deficiency is rare.

Trace Elements Are essential in very small amounts and include: manganese, iron, copper, zinc, selenium, fluorine, cobalt, sulphur, and bromine. Deficiencies of any of these are rare in cage birds.

Important Dos and Don'ts of Feeding

DO use good quality seed and store it properly.
DO make sure water is clean and plentiful.
DO give oystershell and/or cuttlefish bone regularly.
DO give vitamin and mineral supplements at the *recommended* dose rate – twice as much is not twice as good!
DON'T use greenfood from roadsides or from gardens where chemicals are used.

RECOGNITION AND CARE OF SICK BIRDS

Recognising a Sick Bird

A healthy bird has a bright eye, a healthy appetite, is lively, moves from perch to perch, and has tidy, sleek plumage. A sick bird may be fluffed up, sitting on its own on a perch or on the floor. Its eyes may be half closed, the plumage may be untidy, the feathers round the vent may be matted with faeces, and it may be breathing more rapidly than usual or have discharge from its eyes and nostrils.

Isolation

Any bird that seems ill should be isolated. This is done for three reasons: firstly so that it can relax away from competition for food, perching sites, etc; secondly, so that it cannot pass on any infectious disease and, thirdly, so that it can be kept warm.

A 'hospital cage' is a very useful piece of equipment, well worth having if you keep a number of birds. It is designed to provide heat and seclusion for the sick bird, and can be one of two designs (see p. 70).

In the cage shown at the top of the figure the heat source is under the floor of the cage and it is essential to have a thermometer in the cage to ensure that the bird does not become overheated (a temperature range of between 75° and 85°F (24° and 30°C) is reasonable). In the other cage, the heat source is an infra-red lamp, positioned at one end of the cage so that the bird can regulate the amount of heat it receives by selecting a perch either in front of the lamp, or, as it starts to feel better, further away.

Both of these hospital cage designs are available commercially (made in metal and therefore easy to disinfect) or can be made up at home.

Use Your Veterinary Surgeon

Take any sick birds to your vet. Any vet. will treat a bird in an emergency, but if you have a number of birds, then ask around other birdkeepers and find out where they take their birds. There will quite often be a veterinary surgeon in the area who takes a particular interest in birds.

If a bird has diarrhoea, take with you a fresh sample of droppings in a clean container. A single bird is best seen in its cage but be sure to cover the cage well, with a thick towel for example, before travelling, especially in winter. Do not clean out the cage just before going. It is useful for the vet. to be able to see recent droppings and to note how many seed husks are around. If you have a number of canaries, and one or more dies, then a post-mortem examination may be useful to discover the cause of death and so, hopefully, prevent further fatalities. Some vets do their own post mortems, while others have them carried out at laboratories; there are some commercial laboratories prepared to do post mortems and issue reports direct to breeders.

If you have a bird to be post mortemed, it is best to wrap it in at least two layers of plastic and keep it refrigerated (not frozen) until it can be taken to the vet. or sent to the laboratory.

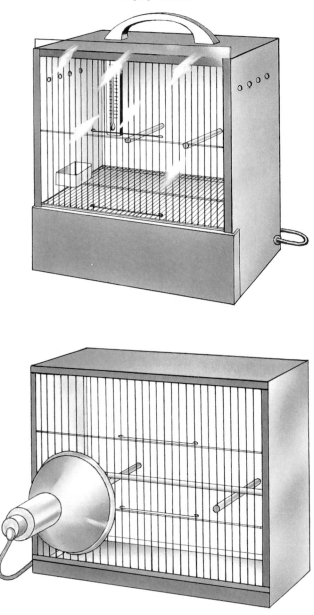

Two designs of hospital cage: with underfloor heat source (top), with infra-red lamp heat source (bottom).

DISEASES OF THE GASTRO-INTESTINAL TRACT

Any part of the gastro-intestinal tract may be affected by one problem or another. We will start at the top and work our way down.

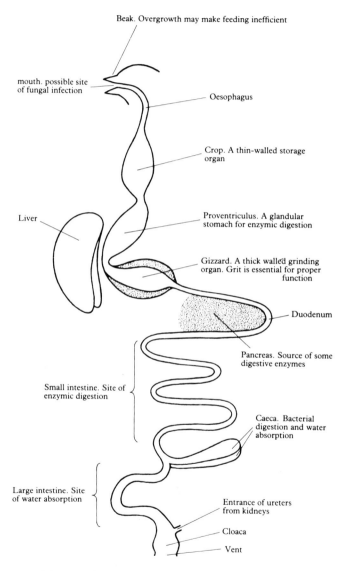

Beak. Overgrowth may make feeding inefficient

mouth. possible site of fungal infection

Oesophagus

Crop. A thin-walled storage organ

Liver

Proventriculus. A glandular stomach for enzymic digestion

Gizzard. A thick walled grinding organ. Grit is essential for proper function

Duodenum

Pancreas. Source of some digestive enzymes

Small intestine. Site of enzymic digestion

Caeca. Bacterial digestion and water absorption

Large intestine. Site of water absorption

Entrance of ureters from kidneys

Cloaca

Vent

Anatomy of the gastro-intestinal tract.

71

Beak

Overgrowth of the beak may prevent the bird from eating sufficient food. Sometimes nestlings start to develop beak deformities. This may be due to an inherited defect but more often occurs when the parents fail to clean the chicks properly and accumulated food debris distorts the young growing beak (p. 79).

Crop

Crop impaction is not common in cage birds.

Sour crop is also uncommon, but may occur. The bird may be dull, miserable and off its food, and may regurgitate foul-smelling crop contents. Sour crop may be due to the bird eating mouldy food, to chilling, undue disturbance, or an underlying infection.

Gizzard

Grit is essential for the proper functioning of the gizzard as a grinder and crusher of hard seeds. If the correct size of grit is not available, the gizzard cannot grind the seeds properly, so the food passing into the intestine may not be properly digested.

Small Intestine

Bacterial enteritis or worms may occur in this part of the gut. If the small intestine is severely inflamed, the reddened loops of intestine can be seen through the body wall in the abdominal region. A heavy burden of worms may cause a partial or total blockage of the intestine.

Large Intestine

This is where water is absorbed, leaving relatively firm faeces. Diarrhoea occurs when the water is not absorbed for one reason or another. It may be because the bowel is over-active, and the contents are moving along faster than normal (maybe due to inflammation of the small intestine), or it may be because the bird is taking in more water than normal. A bird may drink more than usual, because its surroundings are warmer than usual, or it may take in more fluid if there is a sudden increase in the amount of greenfood in the diet.

Water must *never* be restricted in an attempt to control diarrhoea, as it could lead rapidly to dehydration and death.

Caeca (one caecum; two caeca)

These are two blind-ended sacs which branch off the large intestine. Specific problems with the caeca are not common in canaries.

Cloaca and Vent

Sometimes, the cloaca may get impacted, either by faeces or by urinary matter. 'Pasting of the vent' may be associated with diarrhoea or it may occur when urates are not voided normally but accumulate on, and stick to, the feathers around the vent (p. 77). When this occurs, check general hygiene, build up of excreta on perches, in nests and around food bowls before looking for a specific disease that might be the cause of the problem.

Liver

The liver is a large gland associated with the small intestine and it is involved in the digestion of food and the storage of food products. Any severe infectious disease may affect the liver, but the commonest liver problem seen is fatty degeneration, usually due to a combination of incorrect diet and lack of exercise. It is most often seen in caged birds, especially pet birds in small cages and in birds allowed too many high-fat-content seeds. The diagnosis of liver disease is usually only made at post mortem.

DISEASES OF THE RESPIRATORY SYSTEM

In the lungs, air comes into close contact with blood vessels and oxygen is transferred to the blood and carbon dioxide is removed.

The air sacs are very thin-walled structures within the body cavity. In mammals, a dead-end breathing system operates. Inspiration draws the air into the lungs, expiration pushes it out and oxygen exchange takes place only on inspiration.

In birds, a circular system involving the air sacs operates and enables oxygenation to take place on both inspiration and expiration. This is essential for the high-oxygen-demand exercise of flying.

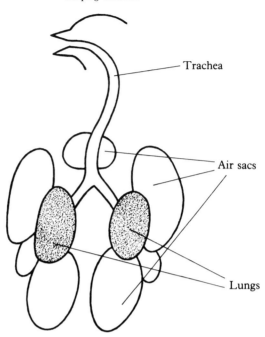

Anatomy of the respiratory tract.

Most diseases of the respiratory tract show themselves by one or more of the following signs: watery eyes, sneezing, discharge from the nostrils, gasping with open beak, fast shallow respirations, distress on exercise – for example, when forced to fly or when chased round the cage, weight loss.

Upper Respiratory Tract

Infection of this region is often called cold, coryza or rhinitis. This shows itself by discharge from the eyes and nose, and sneezing. In serious cases the birds will be lethargic and stop eating. It may be caused by viruses or bacteria, or may by brought on by a change of environment, such as the cage being placed in a draught. In the latter case, if action is taken promptly, the problem may settle if the bird is kept warm (possibly in a hospital cage) and out of draughts. However, infectious coryza can be a serious problem as it is very infectious and may spread rapidly through a flock housed together. In this case, antibiotics may be necessary and it can be helpful to give

74

vitamins as well because a marginal Vitamin A deficiency may make a bird more likely to get rhinitis.

Lower Respiratory Tract

All diseases of the lower respiratory tract tend to give similar signs and a definite diagnosis can often only be made at post mortem.

Infection of the lungs (pneumonia) tends to be a severe and rapidly fatal disease in small birds, whereas disease of the air sacs – whether due to bacteria, fungi or air sac mite – tends to produce a long drawn-out disease process during which the bird may go on living and feeding almost normally for a long time. In these cases, the problem may only be seen when the bird is stressed, when it flies or is chased round the cage. At these times it will wheeze and the respirations will be fast and shallow. Such birds may also lose weight, and be noticed as mildly poor 'doers'. What is known as 'asthma' amongst birdkeepers is simply the collection of signs such as wheezing and gasping that may be caused by any of the above problems.

DISEASES OF THE REPRODUCTIVE SYSTEM

Disorders of the reproductive system are mainly the concern of the serious breeder of canaries as, by and large, (except for the occasional egg-bound female), the problems that arise do not cause disease or death in the pet bird.

The Male

The male reproductive system is rarely affected by disease. Some males may be infertile and others will not mate – sometimes with particular hens. Occasionally, the set-up of cage or aviary stops a proper mating taking place. This may happen if there are no firm, stable perches – or if the perches are so high up that the cock hits his head on the roof!

The Female

In birds, there is only one ovary, which corresponds to the left one in mammals. The ovary produces the germ cells, or ova. Outside the breeding season, the ova are small and inactive. As day length increases in spring, and the breeding season arrives, the ova start to grow and mature and then, one at a time, the ripe ova are released into the infundibulum, the entrance to the oviduct. The mature ovum is the yolk of the egg. As it travels down the oviduct, firstly the 'white' or albumen is secreted onto it, then the shell membranes surround it and, finally, the shell itself is formed in the shell gland towards the base of the oviduct. The egg is then laid.

Needless to say, problems may occur at any stage of the process!

1) The ovum may be released into the abdomen instead of the infundibulum. This may cause a peritonitis or it may be resorbed without causing trouble.
2) Infection may travel up the oviduct from the cloaca and infect the egg at any stage of its journey. This may cause an infertile egg, a soft-shelled egg or, if the embryo goes on to develop, a dead-in-shell chick.
3) An egg may be retained at the top of the oviduct. In this case infection, and sometimes death, of the hen may follow.
4) The hen may not pass the egg. This 'egg binding' may be due to exhaustion, the egg being deformed, too cold an environment, or the hen simply being unfit.

Whether or not it is the breeding season, any laying hen which sits, fluffed up and lethargic, often on the floor of the cage or flight should be suspected of being egg bound. The bird's vent will often be swollen and sore, and the egg can be felt just behind it. A few hours in the warmth of a hospital cage, as well as a little moist heat in the form of steam (from a kettle or saucepan) often helps the hen to shift the egg. But *be careful*! It is all too easy to scald or suffocate a canary. Make sure that your hand is in the steam with the canary and that your face is over it too. Then you will know if things are getting uncomfortable as you *gently* massage the egg towards the vent. However, sometimes even this will not work and, in these cases, a vet. may have to apply lubricant actually within the vent to help to move the egg.

Soft-shelled Eggs These may be the result of a calcium/phosphorus deficiency or imbalance in the diet, or a result of infection in the oviduct.

Infertile Eggs   There are a number of causes of infertility, some of which have already been mentioned: infection of the reproductive tract, infertility in the cock or hen, the hen laying without mating, the hen not brooding her eggs, nutritional deficiencies (e.g. calcium/phosphorus).

Dead-in-shell Chicks   Possible causes of dead-in-shell chicks include: infection, nutritional deficiencies, the hen not brooding constantly – for example, if frightened off her eggs at night, too low a humidity for hatching, hereditary abnormalities.

DISEASES OF THE URINARY SYSTEM

In the normal bird, the kidneys filter waste products from the blood to produce urine in the form of a thick whitish paste (urate), this, together with the faeces, is passed from the cloaca as the familiar droppings.

In canaries and other small birds, disease of the kidneys is often not diagnosed in the live bird. Sometimes it is only one of a number of possibilities in a bird that is vaguely fluffed up and off colour for a period of time but then seems to recover; this may happen several times before the bird is eventually found dead one morning.

Nephritis   Nephritis means inflammation of the kidneys. It may be due to infection, a nutritional imbalance (Vitamin A deficiency) or excessive cold. Sometimes as the disease progresses the bird may pass abnormal, often watery, urate but, in many cases, no such signs are seen.

Pasting of the Vent   Blocking of the vent by thick urate, which dries onto the feathers and stops the bird passing faeces or further urate, may be seen in nephritis, or sometimes when the bird is unwell for other reasons. If this occurs, the blockage should be cleared away by a combination of bathing with warm salt solution and clipping feathers if necessary. If the blockage extends well inside the vent, then it is probably best dealt with by a vet.

Gout   Although not common in canaries, gout is seen occasionally. It is usually the result of a poor diet, either very low or excessively high in protein, over a long period of time. Gout occurs when waste products, instead of being excreted via the kidneys, are laid down in joints and in the body cavity. The symptoms generally are stiff, swollen joints in the legs.

SKIN, FEATHERS, BEAK AND FEET

Skin and Feathers

The Moult Every year after the breeding season, as the day length is decreasing, all birds undergo a complete moult, losing and replacing all their feathers (except for same-year chicks, which lose all but the main flight feathers). This, although a normal process, is inevitably a period of stress and problems can arise if the diet is deficient in essential proteins for feather production, or if the bird is stressed during the moult. A moult may also be disturbed or prolonged if the environmental conditions are unnatural. In birds kept indoors with artificial light in the evenings, for example, the moult may be prolonged, with new feathers growing but then falling out again. Sometimes in such cases, bald patches may be left on the head and neck. This prolonged moult may also occur when hens are allowed to go on breeding late in the season, so that chick rearing runs on into the moult.

Feather (Follicular) Cysts These are dry crusty lumps which develop on the wings during the moult. They are formed when a feather fails to develop properly and, with the follicle in the skin, forms a cheesy mass with the accumulated follicle secretions. Feather cysts can often be gently removed but will usually re-form.

Feather Plucking A bird may pluck its own or another bird's feathers. Feather plucking may be due to a number of reasons:

1) Nutritional deficiencies (protein or vitamin).
2) Skin or feather parasites.
3) Stress.
4) Some hens may pluck their first batch of chicks when preparing a nest for the second clutch.

Preen Gland This gland is situated just above the tail. It is the source of the oils which a bird uses when preening to keep its feathers in condition and waterproof. Occasionally the gland may become blocked or impacted, so stopping the supply of oil for preening. Gentle massage and bathing with warm water is usually sufficient to free the blockage.

Scratching   This is usually due to the presence of skin or feather parasites. It may also be due to general poor feather condition – especially in birds not given bathing facilities.

The Beak

This is a living part of the body and grows continually. In some birds, it may become overgrown, in which case careful trimming is required, taking care not to cut back as far as the blood vessel in the beak. The canary cleans its beak on its perches. If perches are allowed to get soiled the bird cannot clean its beak properly and accumulations of food on the beak may cause it to become distorted and deformed (especially in young birds) and may also lead to mouth infections. Infestation with the mite *Cnemidocoptes* may cause scaliness around the base of the beak, and also on the legs.

The Feet

Arthritis   This may be seen in canaries. The leg becomes red and sore, the joints may be swollen and the bird may move stiffly and slowly, or hold the affected leg up. Arthritis may also affect the wing joints.

Bumblefoot   Infection of the soft tissues of the toes, causing swelling, redness and often areas of ulceration of the sole of the foot is known as bumblefoot. It is sometimes caused by secondary infection of an initial, often very small, wound, especially when the living quarters, especially the perches, are not kept clean.

Overgrown Claws   The claws of a canary should be at most a quarter circle (see illustration on p. 37). Overgrown claws can be carefully trimmed with sharp scissors or nail clippers. Take care not to cut the blood vessel by cutting too short.

Scaliness Of the skin of the feet and legs is usually due to *Cnemidocoptes* infestation.

Undershot Claw Is a condition seen in young birds as they leave the nest, where the hind toe, instead of pointing backwards, is dislocated forwards so that the toe lies between the front toes, leaving the young bird unable to perch properly. Treatment consists of gently moving the toe back to its proper position and then gently supporting it there with a small rubber band or piece of tape. The support must be firm enough to support the toe, but not so tight as to cut into the leg and damage it.

PHYSICAL INJURIES

Physical injuries in birds in captivity can be kept to a minimum by providing them as far as possible with safe surroundings. Look out for bits of wire that stick out and could injure an eye, tear thin skin or injure a foot. Small gaps can result in toes, and even legs, getting trapped and broken when the bird tries to pull away. Nesting materials can be unwisely chosen – long unbreakable threads can get wound around feet and cut off the blood supply. Pet birds let out of a cage for exercise may fly into windows, breaking the beak or indeed fracturing the skull on the glass. For this reason, curtains are best kept closed until the bird is used to the idea of glass. Birds should *never* be left free in a room without supervision. Birds have been known to fly up chimneys, into fires, into cupboards, behind sideboards...!

Fractures

Skull Such fractures are usually fatal, either immediately or within a few hours. They are usually sustained by either 'night fright' as the birds panic and fly upwards in an aviary in the dark, or by flying into glass.

Wing These are very difficult to fix in small birds. Some individuals take very well to close confinement and gentle strapping of the wing in the normal resting position, but others refuse to eat, peck constantly at the strapping and make no progress. In this case, they are best simply confined to a small cage. In cases of severe compound fractures, where the bone has perforated the skin, birds are sometimes better destroyed.

Legs Simple fractures in the upper part of the leg, that are well supported by muscle, are best left well alone in small birds, apart from keeping the bird closely confined, either without perches or with only one perch not far from the ground. If the lower part of the leg is fractured, it should be immobilised, possibly by one of the following methods, although any vet. who has been faced with the problem has usually found a satisfactory solution with the materials available:

1) A longitudinally-split drinking straw, suitably padded.
2) Two small pieces of adhesive tape, laid adhesive sides together, with the leg in a normal perching position held between them. The tape is usually rigid enough to support the limb in a small bird.

Sometimes, when the fracture is very severe, the leg is best amputated. Most small birds can cope quite well with only one leg.

Toes Although toe fractures usually heal on their own, sometimes the toe is left very stiff so that it interferes with proper perching.

Frostbite
Aviary birds which roost outside in freezing weather may get frostbite. The toes start off red and sore. They may recover when brought into a warmer environment but, in severe cases, gangrene may set in and the bird may lose the affected toes.

Wounds to Soft Tissues
Keep cuts and bruises clean with warm salt water. If large or deep, check with your vet. – a cut may require a stitch and/or antibiotics to keep infection at bay. Note that, in trying to decide how severe a wound is, it can be helpful to imagine how big it would be if the canary was as big as you. Is it big enough to worry about is the question.

NERVOUS SYSTEM AND BEHAVIOURAL PROBLEMS

All kinds of nervous signs may sometimes be seen in small birds – twitching, shivering, leg or wing paralysis, fits, blindness, to name but a few. All these signs are the product of some interference with the normal functioning of the brain and spinal cord, which may be due to:

1) Trauma (e.g. skull fractures).
2) Tumours.
3) Vitamin deficiency.
4) Pressure on one or more nerves due to an injury such as a sprain, or a healed fracture.
5) Various infectious diseases.

Behavioural problems in canaries are very often due to either stress or a nutritional imbalance. Overcrowding in cage or aviary birds, or constant disturbance in cage birds, which results in them having insufficient time to eat and sleep may produce stereotyped behaviour and feather plucking (of self). Excessive aggression may also be seen. Feather plucking, either of self or of other birds, may also be due to dietary problems.

POISONING

Poisonings seen commonly in canaries are as follows:

1) Fumes from gas stoves and boilers, from car exhausts (carbon monoxide), and also from electric rotisserie grills. All these may be very rapidly fatal.
2) Insecticides or weedkillers sprayed onto greenstuff which is then used for food (e.g. lettuce, chickweed). *Always* know the source of your greenfood so that you can be sure it is not contaminated. As a further precaution, wash it well under running water before feeding it to your birds.

PARASITES

Parasites may be internal (worms, Coccidia) or external (fleas, lice etc.). In any group of birds kept in close contact with one another –

either on one patch of land or in one group of cages any parasite present will tend to build up its numbers and cause a problem if not kept under control. Every birdkeeper should be aware of likely parasite problems and guard against them, rather than waiting for trouble to occur and then trying to cure it.

Internal Parasites

Coccidiosis This disease is caused by protozoan organisms (*Eimeria* and *Isospora*) in the intestine and caeca. Both these parasites belong to a group of protozoans called Coccidia – hence the name of the disease. Many species are susceptible to coccidiosis (e.g. cattle, rabbits, sparrows), but each species hosts its own variety of the organism and cross-contamination does not seem to occur. In canaries, Coccidia are often found at post mortem, but are not necessarily a cause of severe disease or death. When coccidiosis does occur as a disease, the signs are diarrhoea, often watery and sometimes bloody, and weight loss.

Roundworms There are many types of roundworms, but the ones most likely to affect canaries are as follows:

1) Threadworms (*Capillaria*) are mainly found in aviary birds or in birds kept in unhygienic conditions. Large numbers of threadworms in a canary will cause yellow, slimy droppings and a very dull, anaemic bird.
2) Large roundworms (ascarids) may occasionally be seen in canaries, but are more commonly a problem in parrakeets.
3) Gapeworms are often blamed for causing wheezing and gasping in canaries, but this is in fact highly unlikely, especially in caged birds, because the roundworm has to pass through an intermediate host, in this case an earthworm, before it can be passed onto the canary.

Diagnosis of all roundworms is by examination of faeces under a microscope.

Tapeworms All tapeworms have to pass through an intermediate host, usually an insect, rather than being passed directly from one canary to another. They are not commonly seen in canaries.

External Parasites

Feather Mange This causes feather loss and scabby skin on the affected parts of the bird, which is usually the neck and body. The main flight and tail feathers are not usually affected.

Fleas These parasites feed on the blood of the host bird, but they lay their eggs and the larvae develop in cracks and crevices in the environment. Fleas are not normally a problem in canaries, but they are occasionally seen. Fleas are insects, flattened from side to side and are easily visible to the naked eye.

Lice Lice are common in all types of birds. They live all the time on the host and lay their eggs on the feathers. Different types of lice may either feed on skin debris or suck blood. Infestation with lice may cause birds to continually scratch and preen, and may lead on to feather plucking. The birds may also be restless, not sleep or eat properly and lose weight.

Northern Mite Northern mite is much the same as the red mite, except that it comes from the tropics and so is more likely to be a summer problem. It differs from red mite in that it spends its whole life on the bird, laying its eggs on the host, and so control is easier.

Red Mite Red mites are very common parasites. They live in crevices in woodwork and perches, and come out at night to attack birds by sucking blood. As in lice infestations, loss of sleep, poor plumage and feather plucking may result. Treatment for red mite must include both birds and the cages.

Air Sac (Respiratory) Mite This mite may be present throughout the respiratory tract of canaries – the lungs, the air sacs and the trachea. The life cycle of this parasite is not known, but it tends not to spread through a group, instead, it will simply attack a few individuals.

Scaly Leg/Face Mite (Cnemidocoptes) This is more commonly seen in budgerigars, but can and does occur in canaries, producing dry whitish crumbly matter on the unfeathered parts of the bird – the legs, the base of the beak, and round the eyes. It can spread through a group, but may also crop up in isolated birds.

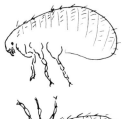

Flea – flattened body, dark brown colour. Six legs. About 1.5 to 2.0mm long

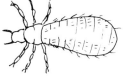

Louse – about the same size as a flea, but moves much more slowly

Red mite about 0.5mm long. Eight legs. Northern mite is very similar

Air Sac Mite – usually only seen at post mortem in airsacs and trachea

Scaly-leg mite – eight legs. Not visible to naked eye

Some external parasites.

INFECTIOUS DISEASES

Most of the research into bird disease so far has involved the species of major economic importance – poultry, game birds, to a lesser extent pigeons, and, more recently, parrots and birds of prey. Many diseases that are well recognised in these species also occur in canaries with varying frequency. However, many cases of 'ill canary' come and go with no specific disease being diagnosed for one of two reasons.

Firstly, rather than being due to a specific infectious agent, an infection of the bowel, liver, lungs etc. may be due to a naturally-occurring organism that gets out of control and starts to multiply fast within a weakened bird, thus causing disease. The bird may be out

85

of condition because of stress, weakened at the end of a breeding season, suffering from a slight nutritional deficiency or the effects of accidental trauma, or it may be kept unhygienically, so that the level of environmental bacteria has built up. In the latter case, bacteriological tests may show a mixture of organisms involved in the disease process – and treatment must consist not only of treating the sick bird, but also of eliminating the factors that brought on the problem in the first place.

Secondly, some disease may go undiagnosed, or be wrongly diagnosed as opportunist infections, simply because the disease in question has not yet been identified. We still have a great deal to learn about disease in canaries!

Viral and Bacterial Diseases

Some specific viral and bacterial diseases that may affect canaries are as follows.

Avian pox (Avian Diphtheria) This is a viral disease. Different strains of the disease affect different species – for example pigeon pox, canary pox. This disease most often affects the skin of the head of the bird, producing blisters, which rupture and then scab over. They occur mainly round the eyes and eyelids, the beak, and often inside the mouth as well. Scabs may also be seen on the legs and feet and, in rare cases, it may spread to the internal organs. The disease may be fatal, but any bird that recovers will then be immune to the disease. Pox viruses may survive in scabs in the environment for a long time. In severe outbreaks, vaccination may save many birds.

Chronic Respiratory Disease (CRD or Mycoplasmosis) CRD produces all the signs of infection of the upper and lower respiratory tract – nasal discharge, wheezing, poor condition. This is a highly-infectious disease that is common in pigeons and may occasionally be seen in canaries.

Colibacillosis A bacterium called *Escherichia coli* is normally present in the gut, but may cause disease if the balance of organisms in the bowel is upset, or if it gets into some other part of the bird, such as the oviduct. Commonly, it causes a pale, watery diarrhoea, especially in nestlings (nestling diarrhoea) and is very often fatal.

Fowl Pest (Newcastle Disease) This is a highly infectious viral disease, not often seen in canaries. The signs of the disease include wheezing, diarrhoea and sometimes fits. Affected birds usually die within 2 or 3 days. Chickens are usually the source of the infection.

Ornithosis (Psittacosis) This is an important disease because it can affect human beings causing serious or even fatal disease. It is most commonly seen in parrots and in pigeons, but may occur from time to time in canaries. Diseased birds may have diarrhoea, or show signs of respiratory disease, but in many cases a bird may carry psittacosis without showing any signs, and pass it on to other birds or to man.

Pasteurellosis (Avian Cholera) This is caused by a bacterium called *Pasteurella*. It is not a common disease in canaries, but if introduced into a non-immune population it may cause many deaths in a very short time. It has an incubation period of about 10 days.

Salmonellosis This bacterial disease is caused by various types of *Salmonella*, many of which can affect man. *Salmonella* is most likely to be a problem where there is a high density of birds, poor hygiene, and often the possibility of contamination of food by rodents (often the original source of the infection). Salmonellosis may cause enteritis in adult birds, or be a cause of deaths in chicks, either before or after hatching.

Other bacterial diseases that may occur in canaries include tuberculosis and pseudotuberculosis. Both of these are usually only diagnosed at post mortem and usually affect only an occasional bird.

Fungal Diseases

Aspergillosis A very common and important disease of cage birds, aspergillosis is caused by the fungus, *Aspergillus*, which grows as a mould on dusty, old or damp seed. It usually causes fungal infection of the lungs and air sacs, but may affect any or all of the internal organs. It may be a fast-developing disease, or it may cause gradual debilitation over a long period. It is almost invariably eventually fatal.

Candidiasis   A fungal infection usually of the crop of the bird, this is not often seen in canaries.

Favus or Ringworm   Caused by *Trichophyton*, this disease is very rare in canaries.

PREVENTION OF DISEASE

Prevention is much more important than treatment as far as disease is concerned. Most disease in canaries is at least partly due to poor management or marginal nutritional deficiency. Only a small proportion of disease seen is due to unavoidable infectious conditions.

Good Feeding

This is important in the prevention of disease. Birds deficient in any essential nutrients will be more susceptible to disease, whereas fit healthy birds will be able to fight disease. Spend money on good quality seed. Don't be content with second best.

Good Hygiene

Clean surroundings and a clean atmosphere will cut down on both the build up of parasites and bacteria and the spread of airborne infection. Whenever you can empty a cage, disinfect it thoroughly. Leaving cleaned cages empty from time to time will cut into the cycle of parasite or bacterial build up. Sunlight is a good disinfectant – anything that can be put outside to dry after cleaning will be the better for it.

Keep floors and surfaces clean, sweep up and dispose of feathers and seed husks. Ventilate birdrooms as much as possible – extractor fans and ionisers may both help to keep the atmosphere as clean and free of dust as possible.

Quarantine

If at all possible, any new birds brought into a collection should be kept separately from the rest, in a separate room, for at least 10 days in case they are incubating disease. Routine treatment against worms and external parasites can also be undertaken at this time. Good observation, and isolation of any bird as soon as it is seen to be ill is not only best for the bird, but will also lessen the possibility of disease spread.

Routine Disease Prevention

Regular spraying against external parasites. Regular worming, and/or checks for worm eggs in faeces. Use of dietary supplements (vitamin/mineral preparations), especially at times of particular stress.

TREATMENT OF DISEASE

Because of their size, canaries are best given medication by mouth (often in the drinking water or directly by dropper into the beak) rather than by injection, although this route will need to be used from time to time. In the UK, most of the drugs described below are only available on prescription from a veterinary surgeon. These are known as 'POM', or 'prescription-only medicines', and the vet is only allowed to prescribe them for animals under his care. All antibiotics fall into this category, but most insecticides and wormers are available on request. There are certain basic principles which should be adhered to when using drugs:

1) Read the label and follow the instructions carefully.
2) Use only at the recommended dose rate and for the recommended period of time.
3) Do not combine treatments unless told to by your vet.

If any of these principles are not followed then the drug, especially if it is an antibiotic, may end up causing more problems than it solves.

Dose rates are important. Too little may be ineffective and too much may be harmful. If a course of antibiotic treatment is not completed, but left off after a day or two, then the organism may start to develop resistance to the drug. Excessively-long courses of antibiotics may predispose to enteritis or to fungal infections, because the balance of normal bacteria in the gut is upset.

Mixing drugs may make them ineffective.

A number of drugs are particularly useful in caring for canaries and a selection is listed below. However, these are not by any means all that are available! Some may only be obtained from a vet.

1) *Anti-Parasitic Agents*

Anti-Mite® (Johnson's)	Useful against all mites, fleas and lice on the bird.
benzyl benzoate	Apply with a cottonbud direct onto *Cnemidocoptes* (scaly leg) lesions.
Panacur® (suspension 2.5% – Hoechst; fenbendazole 25 milligrams/millilitre)	For routine worming at 25 milligrams/kilogram body weight! (a canary weighs 25–40 grams). Can be given in water.
Nemicide® (levamisole 7.5% – Coopers)	For routine worming. Can be given in drinking water.

2) *Anti-Bacterial Agents*

tetracyclines	Useful and relatively safe in non-specific respiratory problems and enteritis. Drug of choice if treating ornithosis.
ampicillin	Often useful in respiratory tract infections
furazolidone	Sometimes used in salmonellosis and colibacillosis.
chloramphenicol	Eye ointments containing chloramphenicol and chloramphenicol suspensions can be used in canaries.
sulfadimidine (sulfamethazine solution 33⅓% – ICI)	Useful in cases of coccidiosis, non-specific enteritis and pasteurellosis.

3) *Anti-Fungal Agents*

There is no drug very effective against aspergillosis. Nystatin (Nystan® oral suspension – E.R. Squibb & Sons Ltd) can be used against candidiasis should it occur.

4) *Vitamin and Mineral Preparations*

Vionate® (Ciba-Geigy)	A powder, it can be given on the seed, but is better given on moist greens or rearing food, as then it tends to stick, and not be lost with the husk. An all-round vitamin/mineral preparation.
Abidec® (Parke-Davis)	A vitamin supplement available from chemists. It can be given in water.

Minivit® (Univet)	A vitamin supplement formulated for cage birds.
Collo-Cal D® (C-Vet)	A Vitamin D/calcium supplement made for dogs and cats, but can be given to canaries when a specific calcium deficiency has been diagnosed.

There are many more supplements available covering vitamins or essential minerals, or both. Some are very good and others less useful. If in doubt, ask your vet. as to the suitability of any supplement.

· CHAPTER 3 ·
INHERITANCE

INTRODUCTION

The study of inheritance in depth can be very difficult. For the serious student of genetics, a large amount of complex information can be acquired and related to whatever subject is under scrutiny. However, for the practical canary breeder, who has no wish to understand the detailed scientific aspects, all that is necessary is the commitment to memory of a few specific inheritance patterns and an understanding of those rules which are relevant to canary breeding. Whatever the approach, any serious breeder must acquire some background knowledge so that the production of specific kinds of yound birds is planned rather than achieved as a matter of chance.

There a five main factors involved in type canaries, with a sixth being added in some coloured canaries.

1) Sex of the bird: male (♂) and female (♀).
2) Feather type: intensive (yellow), non-intensive (buff), or dimorphic.
3) Head: plainhead or crest.
4) Ground colour (lipochrome): gold, dominant white, recessive white, red, plus the ivory factor which can be applied to each of the four.
5) Classic colours (melanins): green (bronze is the equivalent in red-ground birds) or brown (cinnamon). (In coloured-canary circles the mutated agate gene and the isabel are also considered to be classic colours, making four in all.)
6) New colours (melanins): pastel, opal, ino, satinette, topaz.

In each instance the appearance of a particular feature in the offspring of a pairing is due to the transmission of the relevant gene by pre-determined inheritance patterns.

SEX INHERITANCE

All sexual reproduction starts with the germ cells or *gametes*. A gamete (or sperm) from the male joins with a gamete (egg or ovum) from the female (fertilisation) and forms a new cell which is termed a *zygote*. The most important part of a germ cell, or indeed any cell, is the nucleus. This contains a fixed number of threadlike units (*chromosomes*) on which are located genes which control the hereditary characteristics. These genes, again fixed in number, appear on the chromosomes like beads on a string. Germs cells differ from body cells (known as somatic cells) in that they have only one each of the pairs of chromosomes that exist in the body cells. There is only one pair of sex chromosomes whereas there are a larger number of somatic chromosomes. (Various reports give the number as being between eight and twenty-two in canaries.) In all bisexual species, all chromosomes except the sex chromosomes are similar in both male and female. In birds in general (unlike mammals where the reverse applies), the male sex chromosomes are alike and designated XX. Those of the female are not alike and are designated XY.

Each germ cell is formed from a parent cell which has the full number of chromosome pairs all bunched together. When the parent cell divides to form two germ cells, these chromosomes unravel and one of each pair goes to each germ cell. Thus when a sperm and ovum fuse, the resulting zygote has a full complement of chromosomes.

The movement of the chromosomes on separation is completely at random as can be seen by examining the inheritance pattern of the sex chromosomes:

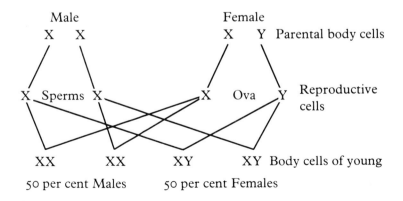

93

This can also be represented by using an arrangement known as a *Punnet Square*:

♂ \ ♀	X	Y
X	XX	XY
X	XX	XY

The single genes in the reproductive cell (ovum) of the female are represented along the top of the Punnet Square. Those in the reproductive cell (sperm) of the male are shown on the left side of the square. When the sperm and ovum unite, a gene from each makes up the pair of genes in the zygote, which will develop into a baby bird.

We know that the male bird has two sex chromosomes the same (designated XX) whilst those of the female (designated XY) are different. We also know that these chromosomes separate when germ cells are being produced and link with a chromosome from the other parent to form a zygote. Thus one of the X chromosomes from the male can join with either the X or Y chromosome from the female. If it joins with the X chromosome, a male is produced; if with the Y chromosome, a female results. From the chart above, we can see that, theoretically, 50% males and 50% females should result from a pairing. As practical breeders, however, we know that it is not uncommon to produce all males or all females in a nest, due to the laws of chance.

Thus, the inheritance pattern of the first of the factors previously mentioned is explained.

MUTATIONS

The production of male and female offspring is determined by the presence of the whole chromosome. As with all other chromosomes, the sex chromosomes carry a pre-determined sequence of genes, each of which is responsible for a specific characteristic. Occasionally accidents occur which affect the action of the gene; two forms are known: the first, a *crossover*, will be studied later (p. 100); the second, a *mutation*, is a spontaneous reaction changing the normal functions of the gene. Mutations do not affect the position of a gene on the chromosome but the mutated gene produces a different effect. Most mutations have some obscure effect and, when mutated, a gene can be more, or less, effective than its unchanged counterpart. Most mutated genes are less effective, in which case they are said to be *recessive*. In certain instances, however, they are more effective and are referred to as *dominant*. Once a mutation has taken place, the gene exists in two forms: the original one, which produces a known effect, and the mutant one which produces a new effect. Two different forms of the same gene are called *allelomorphs*, the original being known as the *wild* allelomorph and the new one as the *mutant* allelomorph.

If a bird has a pair of identical genes, it is said to be *homozygous*. When they are different the bird is said to be *heterozygous*. A bird can be homozygous for some factors and heterozygous for others.

Sex-Linked Mutations

When a mutation appears in one of the genes situated on the sex chromosome, the inheritance pattern of this mutation is said to be *sex linked*. All sex-linked mutations known to date are able to express themselves only when they are present on both sex chromosomes of the male or on the single sex chromosome of the female. They are, therefore, less effective than their unchanged wild allelomorph and are referred to as recessive – or, in this instance, *sex-linked recessive* – factors. As these mutations are situated on the sex chromosome they have to follow the inheritance table illustrated below to determine sex expectations. The mutations known to exist at present which fall into this category are the brown (cinnamon), agate, pastel, satinette and ivory.

The brown (cinnamon) mutation is the one relevant to all breeds of canary and this will, therefore, be used as the example of the inheritance pattern:

♂ \ ♀	X	Y
XB	XBX	XBY
XB	XBX	XBY

THE LETTER B IS USED TO DENOTE THE MUTATED GENE FOR BROWN

From the above illustration we can see that the female is a non-brown (i.e. green), whereas the male has both of its pair of chromosomes mutated and is, therefore, a visual brown. It can also be seen that all the females produced carry the mutated gene on the only X chromosome they possess and are, therefore, visual browns whereas, in the males, only one of the two X chromosomes carries the mutated brown gene and they are, therefore, visual greens. As will now be shown, however, these males are capable of producing brown youngsters.

For this example, we will take one of the young males and pair it to its sister:

♂	♀ XB	Y
XB	XBXB	XBY
X	XXB	XY

It can be seen that such a pairing can produce brown females (XBY), green females (XY), brown males (XBXB) and green males (XXB). The last mentioned heterozygous male (i.e. the green with its wild allelomorph suppressing the visual effect of the mutated allelomorph) is said to be a green split for, or carrying, brown. With sex-linked mutations, a female cannot carry the mutation because her sole sex chromosome is either mutated or wild (i.e. normal or natural).

The other possible pairings to be taken into account when considering the effect of a sex-linked mutation are illustrated below:

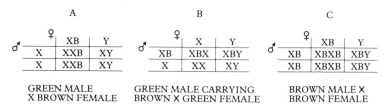

A		
♂	♀ XB	Y
X	XXB	XY
X	XXB	XY

GREEN MALE
X BROWN FEMALE

B		
♂	♀ X	Y
XB	XBX	XBY
X	XX	XY

GREEN MALE CARRYING
BROWN X GREEN FEMALE

C		
♂	♀ XB	Y
XB	XBXB	XBY
XB	XBXB	XBY

BROWN MALE X
BROWN FEMALE

Thus, from pairing A all female youngsters produced will be green and all males are visually green but are carrying brown. From pairing B half the females on average will be brown and half will be green. All the males will be green but half of them will be capable of producing browns. In this case, the visual appearance (or *phenotype*) of all the males will be the same. Genetically, however, they are different and so the birds are said to have different *genotypes*. In the offspring of pairing C, the genotype and phenotype will be the same.

Exactly the same principles can be applied to the study of the inheritance pattern of any other sex-linked mutations and also when considering a multi-factor bird.

♂ \ ♀	XP	Y
XR	XRXP	XRY
XRB	XRBXP	XRBY

THE LETTER R DENOTES THE PRESENCE OF THE MUTATED GENE FOR THE PRODUCTION OF ROSE B FOR BROWN AND P FOR PASTEL

Our pairing, therefore, is of a rose bronze male carrying brown and a bronze pastel female. The theoretical expectation of youngsters produced from such a pairing is as follows: all the young males are bronze, all of them carry pastel and rose and half of them also carry brown (the difference can only be determined by test mating the birds). Also rose bronze and rose brown females can appear in equal numbers.

Thus the use of a single box can simplify the explanation of the sex-linked inheritance pattern and can render unnecessary the memorising of expectation tables for all of the mutations mentioned. The only thing that must always be remembered is that the mutated gene needs to be present on all available X chromosomes for it to be evident.

Heterozygous Dominant and Homozygous Recessive Mutations

The reader is now in a position to understand the inheritance of sex and also the sex-linked mutations but there are still several characteristics mentioned in our original list of six factors to be considered.

Two other forms of mutation may occur within the genes of the somatic chromosomes. In some cases, the phenotype of the bird alters when one of the pair of genes mutates. These are known as *heterozygous dominant mutations*. When each of the pair of genes must mutate before the phenotype alters, the mutation is said to be a *homozygous recessive mutation*.

Heterozygous Dominant Mutation Examples of this are the intensive (yellow) feather, the crest and the dominant white mutation. As the intensive feather is common to almost all breeds, this will be used as our example. Exactly the same formula can be used as for the sex-linked mutations but it must be remembered that we are now studying variances on the somatic chromosomes. The female and the male each have two sets of somatic chromosomes, and only one of a pair needs to have the mutated gene for the new phenotype to be evident. We will use the capital letter *I* to denote the normal allelomorph and the small *i* for its mutated allelomorph.

	NON-INTENSIVE COCK OR HEN	
	I	I
INTENSIVE COCK OR HEN		
I	II	II
i	iI	iI

Thus, from an intensive male or female paired to a non-intensive partner, theoretically, 50% of the young will be intensive (*Ii*) and 50% non-intensive (*II*), regardless of sex. The same results apply when the inheritance pattern is related to either the crest or dominant white mutations. By pairing together two intensive birds it can be seen that 75% of the resulting young will be intensive and one third of these will be homozygous intensives. This pairing with crest to crest, or dominant white to dominant white, is not recommended, however, because there is a suggestion that when the factors are present in double dose, the bird becomes non-viable and is unable to reach maturity.

	INTENSIVE COCK OR HEN	
	i	I
INTENSIVE COCK OR HEN		
i	ii	iI
I	Ii	II

It will also be seen that 25% of the progeny from such a pairing will be non-intensives. Intensives cannot be produced from a non-intensive to non-intensive pairing.

Homozygous Recessive Mutation   The remaining mode of inheritance, the homozygous recessive mutation, is only relevant to coloured-canary and Lizard-canary breeders at the present time, and covers the remaining known mutations referred to on the list of six factors. These are the recessive white ground colour and the lizard, opal, ino and topaz mutations. Again, it must be remembered that both males and females have paired sets of somatic chromosomes but, in this instance, both of the pair of genes concerned must have mutated before the altered phenotype is visible. Also, in this instance, a female can carry the factor. For the example we will use the opal factor, with the capital O representing the wild or normal allelomorph and the small o its mutated equivalent.

	OPAL COCK OR HEN	
	o	o
NORMAL COCK OR HEN O	Oo	Oo
O	Oo	Oo

From this pairing of a male or female normal to an opal partner, it can be seen that, in all instances, only one mutated gene can be present in the progeny of either sex and therefore their phenotype will be normal, although they will all carry opal and be capable of producing the visible opal factor when paired to a suitable mate.

For the second mating, we will pair together brother and sister from the above pairing:

	NORMAL CARRYING OPAL	
	O	o
NORMAL CARRYING OPAL O	OO	Oo
o	oO	oo

As can be seen, 25% of the offspring will be opals, 50% will be normals split for (or carrying) opal and 25% will be homozygous normals. This result follows the Mendelian ratio of 1–2–1, the theoretical expectation of progeny produced from two first filial offspring. The third pairing is the most widely used when breeding for these mutations, i.e. pure opal to normal carrying opal.

	OPAL	
	o	o
NORMAL CARRYING OPAL O	Oo	Oo
o	oo	oo

The expectation is the same whichever bird is the male; i.e. 50% pure opals and 50% normals carrying opal.

Thus we have examined the three possible inheritance patterns and, by applying the correct one to examples of each of the six factors, we can arrive at the theoretical expectation of the sex, genotype and phenotype of the offspring from any given pairing.

CROSSOVER

Earlier, we spoke of a phenomenon known as *crossover*. Although it is quite feasible, and, in fact, highly probable, that this phenomenon occurs in all breeds of canary, it is only where two mutations are sited on the same chromosome that its effect is noted. The classic illustration of crossover is the explanation of the appearance of the isabel canary, which is not a separate mutation but a combination of the joint effect of the agate and the brown mutations.

The brown canary was well established when the agate appeared and was recognised as something different. Breeders' thoughts went to the possibility of joining the two factors to give a dilute brown as well as the dilute green (the agate). Following the sex-linked inheritance pattern previously described, this would seem to be impossible. The two pairings available are shown below. D denotes the gene for dilute and B for brown.

	AGATE FEMALE ♀				BROWN FEMALE ♀	
	XD	Y		XB	Y
BROWN MALE ♂ XB	XBXD	XBY	AGATE MALE ♂ XD	XDXB	XDY
XB	XBXD	XBY	XD	XDXB	XDY

In both instances the male progeny have a green phenotype and carry both the mutated brown and agate genes – this bird is known as a passe partout. This would appear to be just the male we need to produce isabel females, which would be designated XBDY, and as practical breeders we know that such a female can appear. By following our charts, however, this does not seem possible. Although of no particular significance, we will use an agate as the female of the pair. This gives us a table as follows:

	AGATE FEMALE ♀	
	XD	Y
GREEN MALE ♂ CARRYING BROWN AND DILUTE XB	XBXD	XBY
XD	XDXD	XDY

The result is green passe partout males, agate males, brown females and agate females. Regardless of how we re-arrange our pairings it is impossible to create the sought after XBDY formula. The answer lies in the crossover.

It has already been stated that, when the parent cell divides to form two germ cells, the paired chromosomes in the parent cell separate and one goes into each gamete. What was not mentioned was the fact that, prior to separating, the chromosomes become entwined and, on separation, sometimes exchange pieces. If the chromosomes are identical no effect will be noted but, if two dissimilar chromosomes are involved, the effect could be as follows:

The result depends upon whether one or two crossovers have occurred.

To illustrate the matter more clearly we will introduce another method of charting inheritance tables. For this, we will use the following key to denote the genetical make-up of the canary:

B = brown
Z = black
z = absence of black
O = oxidation factor
oa = diluting factor.

All of these symbols are enclosed in a box which represents the chromosomes.

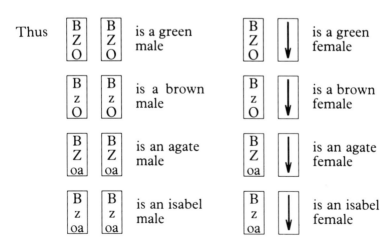

101

Using this new system to re-illustrate our last tables we find:

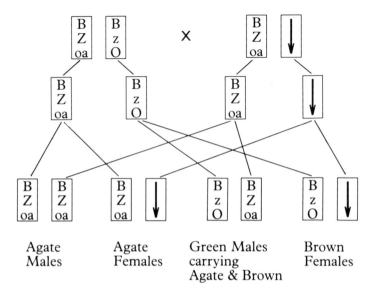

Agate	Agate	Green Males	Brown
Males	Females	carrying	Females
		Agate & Brown	

Using the principle of the crossover we can now see how the isabel can appear. The green male passe partout could on separation appear as:

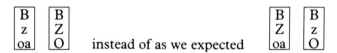

Thus, when this chromosome joins with the empty Y chromosome of any female, an isabel female would be produced, i.e.:

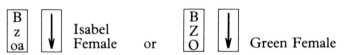

EXAMPLES OF INHERITANCE PATTERNS

This chapter is completed with written lists of examples of each of the inheritance patterns used. In each instance the percentages, where applicable, are theoretical.

102

1 Sex-Linked

The example to be used is the brown (cinnamon). Remember, however, that by substituting the word ivory (rose), pastel, agate or isabel or satinette for brown, the table can be used for these mutations.

Pair 1: brown male × brown female will produce all brown young.

Pair 2: brown male × green female will produce green males carrying brown and brown females.

Pair 3: green male × brown female will produce green males carrying brown and green females.

Pair 4: green male carrying brown × brown female will produce brown males, green males carrying brown, brown females and green females.

Pair 5: green male carrying brown × green female will produce green males (homozygous), green males carrying brown, green females and brown females.

2 Heterozygous Dominant

We will use the example of the crest but, as with the previous tables, by substituting the word intensive (yellow) for feather type, or dominant white for ground colour, the possible breeding expectation can be worked out for these mutations.

Pair 1: Only one true pairing applies, i.e. crest × plainhead, which will give 50% crests and 50% plainheads.

Pair 2: The second possible pairing is crest × crest, which will give 50% heterozygous crests, 25% homozygous crests and 25% plainheads.

3 Homozygous Recessive

The example used here is the ino but equally opal, topaz or recessive white could be used. The inheritance pattern of the lizard is explored in the section on hybrids and other experimental pairings (p. 315).

Pair 1: ino × ino will produce all ino young.

Pair 2: ino × normal will produce all normals carrying ino.

Pair 3: ino × normal carrying ino will produce 50% ino and 50% normal carrying ino.

Pair 4: normal carrying ino × normal carrying ino will produce 25% ino, 50% normal carrying ino and 25% homozygous normals.

Pair 5: normal carrying ino × normal will produce 50% homozygous normal and 50% normals carrying ino.

PART TWO

CANARY VARIETIES

· CHAPTER 4 ·
TYPE CANARIES

SMOOTH-FEATHERED VARIETIES

BELGIUM FANCY

For a breed that has such a major influence in the creation of a great number of the breeds of canary now in existence, remarkably little is known about the precise ancestry and early history of the Belgium Fancy canary. Its presence is noted in documentation relating to the Fancy as early as the start of the nineteenth century and it is thought to be a descendant of the Old Dutch canary.

W.A. Blakston, who wrote the canary section of the monumental Victorian work *The Book of Canaries and Cage Birds* (1877), attributed the development of the Belgium Fancy canary to town guilds in its native country, which were originally set up for the extension of trade and the protection of commerce. As time passed, these societies became more social in their aims, having set as their object the advancement of art, music or simply pleasure. Thus, painting, sculpture, music, rabbits, pigeons and canaries etc. came to be encouraged and, once adopted, the particular interest was promoted by all the members of the society. In the 1840s, Courtrai was first of all Belgian towns for 'Canaries of Position', the others, in order of importance, being Brussels, Antwerp, Ghent and Bruges.

The Belgium Fancy was probably then at the height of its popularity and standard of excellence, with dealers travelling to the continent to acquire good specimens for British fanciers. By the latter part of the nineteenth century, however, it was in decline; partly due no doubt to changing tastes, but also to the extensive use made of Belgiums in the creation of the Yorkshire canary, and as an outcross with Scotch Fancies. This latter practice was detrimental to both breeds and Claude St John (1911) in *Our Canaries* observed:

'... that the blending of the two breeds (Belgium and Scotch) has been brought with evil results to the general welfare of both is never largely recognised. It has undoubtedly contributed in no small measure in various ways to the decline of both breeds in popularity, by bringing them into such close juxtaposition as to overlap each other and to bring about such a confusion of type as to leave little or no strongly-marked dividing line to show where Belgium ends and Scotch Fancy commences. The confusion has been carried so far that crosses between the two breeds have, at times, been awarded the bulk of the honours on the show bench and might also be found exhibited, as opportunities occurred, as either variety.'

A bad Belgium can never be a Scotch Fancy, nor an indifferent Scotch Fancy a Belgium, and a first cross should never be permitted to become either.

Up to 1914, pure-bred stock were imported into the UK from Belgium, but two World Wars fought across that country greatly reduced number and quality.

The essential points of a Belgium Fancy are 'shape and position' derived from its broad high shoulders, which give it the French name of Bossu Belge (Belgium Hunchback) and its elongated neck. Although the distribution of points in the standard of excellence has altered over the years, the description of the ideal has not changed for 100 years.

Primarily the bird is a posture canary and thus the way it presents itself whilst being judged is of major importance. As a consequence, the need to familiarise the bird with differing conditions, handling of the show cage by people other than the breeder etc. must be a prime consideration. The ability to display the required position is an inborn quality that cannot be taught. Some birds will, however, adopt the required posture at will; others need constant encouragement in the form of show training before displaying to perfection. A bird which cannot assume the required stance, to at least some degree, is not a Belgium.

The most important features of a Belgium canary are the high, broad and prominent shoulders which should be well filled in. When in show position, the long, broad back, tapering through a long body into a long, rigid and narrow tail, should fall down perpendicularly. This can only be achieved by the bird firmly gripping the perch and 'pushing' upwards, whilst at the same time extending from the shoulders a long and slender neck with a small neat head.

The modern standard states:

'*In show position the bird "pulls itself together" gripping the perch firmly, stiffening its legs and reaching up with its shoulders to attain its tallest height, the line from shoulder to tail then being completely perpendicular. At the same time, the head is depressed and the neck stretched out to its limit until the beak is pointing directly downwards.*'

The Belgium is a bird of angles and modern specimens tend to adopt a position with the neck and head held at right angles to the body. Illustrations of exhibition Belgiums of the Victorian era, however, depict the neck and head pointing downwards, as though the bird was trying to touch its toes with its beak.

The head is required to be small and oval in shape. Running down the front of the bird, a prominent well-filled chest should gently taper in towards the top of the legs. It is inevitable that, when holding the show position, the bird will display a fair amount of thigh; this should, however, be at a minimum and should be well covered by tight feathering.

The Belgium Fancy exists in both intensive (yellow) and non-intensive (buff) forms. Colour is unimportant but smooth feather is essential and roughness or frilling will spoil a bird for exhibition. An overall size of 6¾–7 inches (170–180 millimetres) is now stipulated. It seems certain, however, that, at the height of its popularity, the Belgium was a big canary and the aim with present stocks should be to maintain or increase size. It is usual in all breeds to have far more average-quality birds available for breeding than top-quality birds. Many fanciers make the mistake of pairing a top-quality exhibition specimen to an average one, rather than looking for a good stock bird. Such a bird may have rough feathering, which spoils it for exhibitions, but if it possesses superb shoulders and position it could be invaluable for breeding purposes. With relatively few breeders available from whom it is possible to purchase the top-quality outcrosses, we all need, at times, to turn our thoughts to other species suitable for an outcross. Care must, of course, be taken to ensure that undesirable features are kept to a minimum and, for this reason, the possibilities are restricted to three varieties: the Scotch, Yorkshire and the Southern Dutch Frill (all direct descendants of the Belgium).

Not having attempted these crosses himself, the author is loath to be dogmatic, but he is informed that Belgiums imported into the UK from the continent in 1970 were extremely small birds, no more than 4½–5 inches (114–127 millimetres) in length. They were, however, capable of adopting and holding an excellent posture with an angle between neck and body of 90° and were extremely prolific. The only difficulty in their management was the ability of young birds, because of their overall size, to escape through the cage drinking holes. At the time the Scotch Fancy was also in the process of being 'improved' and the very few typical birds with regard to shape that were available, carried a great deal of loose feather. They were not, therefore, particularly suitable as an outcross and a rather fine-headed yellow Yorkshire was used. The resultant offspring were, as expected, rather heavy in the head and short necked and did not display. However, when mated back to the pure Belgium stock, an improvement was evident after 2 or 3 years of selective breeding. Unfortunately, few fanciers have persevered with the breed and many more are needed if the variety is to regain its former eminence. The same position seems to exist in Europe, where an excellent outcross in the form of the French Frill is readily available. The French Frill is, of course, a heavily-feathered bird, but it possesses the clean narrow head, long neck and above all, posture, of the Belgium and would appear to be admirably suited for the purpose.

The training and general management of Belgiums is similar to that for other varieties of canary. Young birds are, however, rather 'stilty', both when in the nest and on leaving it. A deep nest pen is, therefore, desirable, whilst perches in the nursery cage should at first be placed low down. It is preferable to keep adult Belgiums in a high position in the birdroom as this encourages them to adopt their traditional stance and is the first step in training them for exhibition.

BERNER

The origin of the Berner canary dates back to 1880 when a Mr Wyss from Steffisburg, a suburb of Thun in the Bern of Oberland (Switzerland), is credited with their creation. Their origin is credited to the pairing of the Yorkshire with a canary referred to as the 'Land canary'. Whether this was the Old Dutch canary is not certain but the possibility cannot be ruled out. Little was heard of the new breed until 1910, when the first ones appeared at an exhibition in Berne, the town from which they take their name. An association was formed to promote the bird and a standard was set. This standard has continued unchanged to the present day. Modern-day breeders state that the Berner is difficult to breed, and those problems generally associated with the larger breeds are experienced. The most obvious of these problems is the reluctance of the female to feed her offspring. The use of smaller breeds as foster parents is, therefore, recommended. The Berner appears in both intensive (yellow) and non-intensive (buff) feather types, with individual classes normally being provided at exhibitions for each, in both clear and variegated forms. No colour feeding is allowed and any birds showing signs of an orange ground colour are disqualified.

An exhibition-quality Berner stands very erect to show off to the maximum its 6½–7 inches (160–175 millimetres) length. Its head, which needs to be held firm and erect, should be small but broad with a flat top. The back of the skull should stand out and form a slight curve into a short thick neck. The breast should be full and well rounded, flowing down between the legs. The back should be long and slightly rounded. The wings of the bird should be long, curved well over the back in a bow shape held well into the back of the bird and should not cross. The wing joint, where the wings join the body, should be clearly visible and not masked by overhanging feathers from the neck or chest. A long tightly-formed tail completes the plumage. Thighs should be well feathered but barely visible, with the legs slightly bent allowing the vertical stance. Although a large bird from long-feathered ancestors, the Berner should carry tight neat plumage.

Few examples of the Berner are seen outside its native country except at World Shows. Perhaps its popularity is now due for a lift and the breed will soon be seen in countries throughout the world.

BORDER CANARY

A.J. Ellison
Alan Ellison is a retired civil servant. He was sent with his RAF Squadron to Scotland from his native Yorkshire in 1943 and has remained in that country – noted for the number and quality of Border canary breeders – ever since.

He has been a breeder of Border canaries for over 30 years and has a leaning towards clear and lightly variegated examples, with which, over the years, he has had his share of success on the show bench.

Alan Ellison, although having been a judge for some 10 years, is somewhat critical of the tendency nowadays to annex major prizes to the largest birds rather than to smaller examples with a greater overall quality.

In trying to trace the ancestry of the Border canary, I have found no mention of it in any writings before 1889, yet the variety had been in the making for many years before that date. J.B. Evans, in a letter to *Cage Birds* on 25 October 1902, says that in the border towns of 60–70 years ago there were old Border fanciers. This takes us back to about 1832 but presumably the variety had started to evolve a little earlier than that.

It is fairly clear that, in the UK, from the early nineteeth century, at least one new variety of canary was in the making in the counties of Cumberland, Dumfries, Roxburgh and Selkirk. There may have been two. C.A. House, writing in 1889, records that the birds in Cumberland were like diminutive Yorkshires whereas, further north, the birds were more squat and low set, features indicative of a small Norwich. Strangely enough, in volume II of the 1902 edition of *Cage Birds*, page 821 shows a picture of a yellow Border and a buff Border and both are like the Norwich in type and stance. However, up to 1880, 'local-type' birds were being bred in the counties mentioned and, in 1882, Cumberland fanciers decided to call their bird the 'Cumberland Fancy'. This incensed the fanciers in the Scottish border counties as they maintained that they themselves had created the new variety. (It has been mentioned earlier that two varieties may have been in the making and there is evidence that Scottish birds had gone to Cumberland.) James Patterson of Chirnside, for example, tells us that the type of bird being bred in the Borders was first introduced into Cumberland by a shoemaker from Langholm in Dumfriesshire, who moved permanently to Cumberland and took his birds with him. The possibility is that, in the 1870s and early 1880s, a common variety of bird evolved, hence the furore when the Cumberland Fancy was launched. C.A. House claims that the Cumberland fanciers asked him to assist in setting up a standard but no action seems to have been taken, possibly because the fanciers had agreed on a meeting at Hawick in July 1890. The outcome of that meeting was the birth of the Border Fancy Canary Club with a membership of 643. The following year, a Mr Bell of Jedburgh and Mr Davidson of Dumfries were delegated to create a model. For their model, they took a bird shown by Mr McMillan of Langholm. So, from 1891 onwards, a Border Fancy canary has officially existed. It was another 10 years before the question of

A typical top-quality Border canary.

colour feeding was settled but it was banned in 1901 and has remained so ever since.

It will not have escaped notice that, at the birth of the Border Fancy Canary Club, the Scottish fanciers took control and, for some time, this was clearly an error of judgement. By 1905, the Border had made no progress south of the Border but, in Scotland, had become a very popular canary. As a result, in 1905, the English and Welsh Border Fancy Canary Club was formed with S. Hadwin as secretary. It was from this point that the Border started to grow in general popularity in the UK and gradually displaced the Norwich and Yorkshire. To digress, although the Yorkshire type existed some time before the Border, it did not officially become a variety until 1894, about 4 years after the Border.

Having established the Border Fancy, and a model, there is little more to say about the historical aspect except that, 39 years after the first model was created, there came a change of model (1930) and 37 years later (1967), a third model was produced. And now, in 1987, a fourth model has been adopted. This of course is natural progress. The Fancy cannot be allowed to stand still; when anything stagnates it dies. It seems to the author that there is a case for a review of the model every 15 or 20 years.

Looking back to the early Borders some points stand out. Originally it was s small bird – 'the pigmy of the fancy' C.A. House says – and fanciers will recall it was christened 'the wee gem'. It seems to have remained a rather diminutive bird up to World War 2; thereafter size tended to increase.

Fanciers of yesteryear gave much attention to quality of feather. They wanted it to look like polished wax. In fact, they did polish their birds by means of a piece of silk which had been impregnated with paraffin. With silky boxy feathers this does give a good shine, but most of the modern Borders would not benefit; in the pursuit of size, feather has lengthened and softened and thus quality has been affected.

Technical markings were highly prized by the old fanciers and they gave much thought and time to producing 4- and 6-pointers. It might be noticed that the model is always portrayed as a 4-pointer! Nowadays, fanciers are loath to make an effort to produce good markings. Perhaps there is a case for a well-marked bird to be placed higher in the order of merit (all other points, of course being considered).

Although much is to be learned from the fanciers of years ago, it

114

would be a mistake to turn the clock back. For the author's money, the present-day Border is a much more attractive bird than its forebears, although it is still capable of improvement.

Do not be misled into thinking that throughout the years 1890–1930, the Border fanciers stuck meticulously to one standard of excellence. A study of pictures of winning birds in this period, will show by how much they vary over the years. Fanciers must have had as much discussion in 'judges' opinions' as they do today. Everyone cannot be pleased all the time!

It is interesting to note that the fanciers of the past tended to favour double buffings, but within limits. They felt it did no harm if done carefully, e.g. with good-quality birds. One of their beliefs was that double buffing increased size! Double yellowing tended to be unpopular.

Size in Borders is a very ticklish subject. A bird 5½ inches (140 millimetres) long is not a small bird and, to maintain it at this length is not easy. Prolonged inbreeding and, in many cases, simple line-breeding will see a reduction in size. The author believes that, to maintain size, hybrid vigour must be introduced, backed by an element of luck. Alternatively the Mendelian theory can be adopted. The problem here is that few breeders have sufficient space, nor are willing to operate, a programme that can take years. Which breeder has the patience required to undertake observations, note-taking and planning? Arising from all this, it is fairly obvious that large, coarse birds will always be much sought after as stock birds, which means quality of feather may deteriorate further.

Colour is also a point offering problems. Good colour cannot be obtained from poor parent birds. A breeder wanting to improve colour has these options:

1) To purchase good-coloured birds.
2) To try double yellowing and introduce the offspring into the following breeding season.
3) To use some cinnamon blood, but never to cross cinnamon variegated with green variegated.

A 60° postural angle, it is said, can be achieved by training, a point with which the author disagrees. Good position can only be obtained by breeding. Be wary of using birds which tend to squat; show birds should be a bit leggy and, remember, they have to be good movers, which short-legged birds never are.

Above all, never lose faith in your birds. All fanciers tend to think that other fanciers' birds are better than their own – and the other fanciers think the same! It is very encouraging to hear fellow fanciers speaking well of other birds, but a good fancier does not need to be told when he has produced a good bird. Everyone knows that far more satisfaction is to be gained from winning with a home-produced bird than winning with one bought in. Don't forget that people will only get as much from the Fancy as they put into it. Keep trying, and good luck.

The author is loath to give advice on any subject but perhaps the following will be heeded. If a fancier's method of breeding has been successful in the past then he should stick with that method and not be tempted to copy another fancier. If a breeder finds himself getting greedy for numbers, he should remember the law of diminishing returns, i.e. the greater the number of birds kept the lower, comparatively speaking, will be the results. For instance, eight youngsters might be bred from one pair but eighty will never be bred from ten pairs. Finally for about a month before pairing up the birds, make sure that they get an occasional dose of Epsom salts!

Technical markings, as opposed to the haphazard marks on variegated birds, are clearly defined and form a distinct pattern. Birds carrying them are usually referred to as 4-pointers, 5-pointers or 6-pointers. A 4-pointer is one with small oval marks surrounding each eye and with three dark feathers forming a mark towards the outer edge of each wing. A 5-pointer is a 4-pointer with dark feathers which form a mark down the centre of the tail. Birds with good markings are not often seen nowadays, as fanciers tend not to breed for them specifically but, a good type of Border with the 4-pointer marks is a most attractive bird. Whereas, long ago, the marks were expected to be perfect, present-day rules are relaxed to allow 'broken eye marks', which means that a bird can have rather uneven spreads of variegation around the eyes.

Double buffing simply means the pairing of buff (non-intensive) to buff (non-intensive) rather than the traditional yellow (intensive) to buff (non-intensive) pairing. From a double buff pair, all the offspring should be buffs but, occasionally, it is heard that a yellow has been bred from such a pair. The author, personally, has always doubted such claims. Continuous double buffing should be avoided as it can lead to an affliction called 'lumps'. This was very bad in Norwich canaries some years ago and it has been heard of in connection with Glosters.

116

The main advantage of double buffing is said to be increase in size. It may seem to do this but this is largely due to an increase in both the thickness and length of feather. The author has seen good birds bred out of double-buff pairings but, if it is to be attempted, ensure that both birds have a good quality feather.

Double yellowing is the reverse of double buffing, i.e. both birds in the pair are yellows (intensives). It is much less popular than double buffing as it tends to thin the feather and, if overdone, it can result in the offspring lacking feather on the breast and thighs, or even having bald patches on the back of the head. Buffs will be bred from a double-yellow pairing.

Long ago in the UK, double yellowing was common amongst fanciers breeding mules. They continuously double-yellowed so as to produce canary females which would increase the number of clear or lightly-marked mules bred! This cross has the disadvantage of producing many poor-colour birds. The yellow tends to look washed out and, instead of being a deep shade, it is more of a 'lemon' shade. For anyone interested in breeding greens, the 'lemon' shade of bird can be useful as it tends to reduce the bronziness in the green colour.

In livestock circles, Epsom salts are regarded as being a good conditioner and a help in increasing the gloss in the coat. They are an aid to bringing females into breeding condition and are beneficial throughout the breeding season. Don't overdo the use of the salts; about enough to cover a 1 new penny piece or a 1 cent piece per bird a couple of times a week, dissolved in water, should be sufficient.

The best show birds are naturals and, once they have become accustomed to the show cage, all they need is to be handled occasionally. Such birds have a quiet temperament, possess good position and are good movers. They do not panic when handled. Many fanciers think birds can be trained for showing. Putting a bird in a show cage as often as possible and handling it at every opportunity may generate some response but be wary of over-optimism. There are many good birds that are not good show birds because they lack the correct temperament. Frankly, this asset has to be bred into the stock. A common fault with many birds at shows is that they are in too high a condition. A bird needs to be about 20% below top condition for showing. Once the birds have been through the moult they should be moved onto plain canary seed and so fed until they are no longer required for showing.

It is impossible to make a silk purse out of a sow's ear! Neither can good Borders be bred from poor or mediocre stock. But once a breeder is satisfied that he has reasonable birds, he must appraise them critically so as to recognise faults; these must be bred out. Never pair two birds which both have the same fault, e.g. poor heads. Never carry passengers, i.e. sickly birds or poor specimens.

It is often said that 'like produces like'; frankly, it rarely does. As an example, if a good male bird is purchased, it should not be expected to throw images of itself; it is more likely to give images of its parents. That is really over-simplifying the situation as it takes two to make a pair. Therefore the number of permutations expected from one pair of birds is very high. If six young birds are produced from one pair and only one of them is a good show bird, this is an achievement. Breeding 100 birds and getting ten to fifteen to make up a show team can be counted as a successful season.

A breeder should always be critical of his own birds but should not lose confidence in them. When new stock is bought, it should be bought wisely. Improvement is the aim. The first lesson in breeding is to ensure that the females are in the peak of fitness. After Christmas, make sure that they have the maximum exercise and let them bathe as often as possible. A novice should use his time wisely. Winning is far less important than accumulating good experience.

A breeder cannot talk about 'good Borders' without knowing the standard of excellence and having a model in his mind's eye. He should visit as many shows as possible and study the winning birds at close quarters. Initially he may feel that the winning birds do not match the 'model' but he should not forget that the model may be out of date and that fanciers have improved on it.

A good Border is a bird of position, gay and jaunty, not more than 5½ inches (140 millimetres) in length, with feather of a quality that at its best looks like polished wax. The head should be neat and round, the body having a nice rise over the shoulders, the chest well rounded and fairly prominent; the roundness of the chest then tapers off in to what is called a 'strong draw' to the root of the tail. The tail should not be too long and should be closely packed. Overall, the Border is a well-balanced bird in all respects and, if any part is out of balance, it stands out like a sore thumb. Frankly, a 'good bird man' will soon know a good Border – a beautiful bird.

FIFE FANCY

Whereas most breeds of canary have been created by pairing together a combination of two or more varieties, in many ways the

Fife Fancy arrived by accident. The Border Fancy canary (see p. 111) was originally a relatively diminutive bird. Following World War 2, stocks of Border canaries, like those of so many breeds, had fallen and the Fancy in general had to undergo a rebuilding exercise in order to restore the numbers of quality stock that had existed prior to the commencement of hostilities. This is not to say that top-quality examples did not exist; the problem was that these birds were relatively scarce and, in order to expand in numbers, outcrosses were made to small Norwich canaries which resulted in the production of larger birds with rounder heavier heads.

Unfortunately, some of these birds were awarded prizes on the showbench, causing dissatisfaction in some quarters. Finding this quite unacceptable, a group of breeders applied themselves to the breeding of birds to the old Border shape and concentrated on the reduction of the overall length to 4½ inches (115 millimetres). When this aim was achieved, the birds were exhibited in Miniature classes or Any Other Variety classes.

Eventually, the pioneers were approached by other fanciers for stock and a small group formed to start a specialist club to promote the birds. As an originator, and being a native of the Kingdom of Fife in Scotland, Walter Lumsden was invited to name the bird and so it was called the 'Fife Fancy'. Slowly the Fife gained popularity until a bird exhibited by Mr Lumsden at the National Exhibition of Cage Birds in London, in the late 1970s, achieved the ultimate award in English canary circles – Best Canary. Following this accolade, the popularity of the breed in England and Wales has progressed at an unprecedented pace so that, today, it rivals most of the longer-established breeds at exhibitions throughout the UK. Because of its ancestry, and the fact that the accepted show standard calls for the same standards of excellence as those found in a top-quality Border canary, albeit in a more diminutive format, it has been relatively easy for breeders to acquire outcrosses to improve specific faults in their birds. Today, with Fifes proving prolific breeders, such outcrosses are rendered unnecessary and many first-class examples are offered for sale each year.

Quality of feather is an attribute sought in many breeds of canary but it is of paramount importance in a Fife. Any bird showing less than perfection in this area has no chance of winning major awards at exhibitions and, because of the dangers of proliferating the fault throughout a stud, it should be culled.

The shape sought consists of a small round head with a small neat beak and the eyes in a central position. A well-defined neck should blend into a well-filled and rounded back, the breast being full but not too prominent. The outline of the body should flow straight and clean between the legs. The wings should be carried closely to the body, meeting at the tips (but not crossing) just below the root of the tail. The tail itself should be short, close packed and well filled in at the root. The legs need to be short and to show little or no thigh, holding the bird at an angle of 60° to the perch. No colour feeding of Fife Fancy is allowed and a natural rich, soft, even tint is called for.

As with most small breeds, the Fife is an active bird and is required to present a gay, jaunty appearance when it is being judged. There being, as yet, no long history of inbreeding, the Fife Fancy does not normally display nervous tendencies and is, therefore, relatively easy to train to present itself properly when in a show cage. The systems covered elsewhere in this book (p. 59) on show training can be adopted for this breed.

As mentioned elsewhere, the Fife is a very active and prolific breed requiring no specialised treatment in consequence, the methods outlined in Chapter 1 can be adopted with confidence. Indeed, so easy is the bird to breed that it is often used as a foster parent for more difficult varieties. The pairing of intensive (yellow) to non-intensive (buff) is recommended.

IRISH FANCY

A breed still bred and exhibited only in its native country is the Irish Fancy canary.

As with the American Hartz, the Irish have for many years provided classes at their open shows for a canary that did not fit into any of the definitions of the various type canary breeds. Originating from the singing Roller canary, these birds, which, one suspects, were not solely purebred but also outcrossed Roller canaries, were brought in large numbers to shows in a vast variety of show cages, ranging from manufactured box cages to literally unpainted wooden boxes with wire fronts nailed on. Possibly as an aid to the indestructable Irish pleasure for friendly but animated discussion, no points standards were created. This enabled judges and fanciers alike to decide both what resembled the ideal bird and also the class placings, so that subsequently endless discussions and arguments ensued.

The Irish Fancy canary was originally known as the Irish Roller canary and was shown as a type canary initially along the east coast of southern Ireland, particularly in the town and county of Wexford.

As time passed, however, its popularity has spread throughout the country. This resulted in the name being changed to the Irish Fancy canary to avoid confusion with the true Roller canary, which is a bird bred for, and contested entirely on, its song.

As a natural progression, judges and breeders started to reach agreement on a standard of excellence for the exhibition Irish Fancy canary. In February 1975, a number of interested fanciers formed the Irish Fancy Canary Society, their major aim being to attract serious consideration and recognition for the bird as a separate type species. To this end, a scale of points was laid down and a distinctive show cage designed (see p. 164).

As can be seen, several differences exist in this standard from those required for most type canaries, the most striking perhaps being the shape of the head. Here, instead of the almost universal demand for a broad round appearance, as in other breeds, a narrow, snipey shape is desired.

The bird exists in both yellow (intensive) and buff (non-intensive) variations and, when breeding, the normal system of pairing one with the other applies.

Classes are provided at major shows not only for clear specimens but also for ticked, lightly-variegated, heavily-variegated, three-parts dark and foul/self examples. The bird also appears with a white ground colour which allows for many further variations.

As white examples of the breed are dominant whites, the normal rules regarding the pairing of this mutation apply, i.e. only in the most exceptional circumstances should white be paired to white. Normally a white should be paired to a yellow-ground bird, thus giving a theoretical expectation of 50% white and 50% yellow-ground offspring. This rule applies to all parent birds, from clears right through to full selfs (green in the yellow-ground series and blue in the white-ground series).

The old fallacy of pairing a white-ground bird to a buff (non-intensive) yellow-ground bird must be discounted in this day and age as having no scientific basis. The colour of a bird's plumage has nothing to do with the feather type and white-ground birds consequently appear in both yellow (intensive) and buff (non-intensive) feather types; close examination of the plumage allows the differentiation to be detected. Once this is clarified it is possible to proceed within normal pairing constraints, i.e. yellow (intensive) to buff (non-intensive).

As with all small canary breeds, the Irish Fancy canary is an easy bird to keep and is most prolific. No special management techniques are required and, if followed, the details listed in Chapter 1 should ensure success.

Colour feeding of the breed is not permitted. The birds, if given proper care during the moult, and a well-balanced diet, will present themselves to the best advantage, showing the desired rich and brightly-coloured natural plumage.

Given the relatively short time in which the breed has been stabilised, its popularity has increased dramatically, with examples now being found in all areas of both southern and Northern Ireland. It can only be a limited time before examples of the breed are to be found throughout the UK and, it is to be hoped, also in mainland Europe. One can only hope that the hard work of the pioneers will be truly rewarded when the breed is recognised by the COM following its successful representation at three consecutive World Shows.

JAPANESE HOSO

One of the more recent type canaries to be accepted by the COM as a separate race is the Japanese Hoso. As we will discuss, this breed is one not only of type but of position, i.e. its show position is different from that which it normally holds and, in consequence, breeding and training are very important.

At first glance, one might mistake the Japanese Hoso for a minia-ture Scotch Fancy and, as that species represents one half of the breed's lineage, this similarity is to be expected. The other half of the breed's ancestry can be found in the Belgium Fancy, itself probably the only ancestor of the Scotch Fancy.

The process of creating the Japanese Hoso has been going on for many years, using the breeds mentioned above and, in Japan, where the breed originated, two versions exist: the Tokyo Hoso, which is the bird known in Europe as the Japanese Hoso, and the Ethigo Hoso, a bird similar in all respects but with a shorter neck. The latter version, so far as can be ascertained, has never been exported from Japan.

Normal breeding techniques are recommended, i.e. pairing buff (non-intensive) to yellow (intensive), with either bird, providing it meets normal exhibition criteria, being accepted on the showbench.

The bird is also accepted as an exhibition example whether it is clear, ticked, variegated or self.

In order for a bird to assume a non-natural position, it is necessary for it to grip the perch firmly and force itself into the required show position. Such is the case with the Japanese Hoso, which has to form itself into the semi-circular show position.

A long thin neck, ending in a small oval-shaped head and a small neat beak, should blend into the shoulders which are held tightly together and should themselves blend into the back without trace of the 'hunchback' effect seen in the bird's Belgium Fancy ancestry.

The front of the neck should blend in a semi-circular pattern into the chest which itself should link up with the tail in an unbroken line.

The wings should be held tightly to the back, not crossing, with the tips laying over the back of the tail.

The tail itself is required to be long and curving under the perch to form the semi-circular show position.

Legs should be held rigidly to assist the bird in assuming its show position, with well-feathered thighs clearly visible.

With an overall length of 4¼–4¾ inches (110–120 millimetres), the Japanese Hoso is one of the smallest breeds in existence and, in consequence, with its nearest equivalent – the Scotch or Belgium Fancies – being almost one and a half times as big, outcrossing to correct faults in a stud is difficult. Care must therefore be taken in selecting breeding pairs; a bird with too stiff a back, for example, should be paired to a mate showing perfection in this characteristic.

The breed itself is not noted for being difficult in any respect and therefore the management systems explained in Chapter 1 should provide acceptable results.

In Europe, only yellow-ground birds are seen and therefore accepted as show specimens. Correspondence from Japan, however, confirms that the Hoso is seen on the showbench in that country in many of the variations accepted here as coloured canaries.

LIZARD

Any attempt to trace with accuracy or certainty the origins and much of the subsequent history of the Lizard canary is fraught with great difficulty. A breed of canary that vaguely meets the description we now recognise as the Lizard is documented as far back as the mid-eighteenth century. Further reports from contemporary sources concentrate on the now extinct London Fancy canary, a breed which was closely related to the Lizard.

Because of references in eighteenth-century books to canaries of the 'spangled sort' or French Canary birds, it is not unreasonable to assume that the Lizard was introduced to England by French refugees. By selective breeding, fanciers then fixed the unique characteristics which we will examine in due course. It would appear that both the Lizard and the London Fancy canaries existed in the perfect form that we seek today as early as 1846. This is confirmed by an article in the *Illustrated London News* of that year and the existence of both is established by their mention in a booklet, *The Bird-keepers Guide and Companion*, by Thomas Andrew, a Soho cage-maker, which was published some years earlier. It is interesting to note however that there was no mention of a canary breed which could be interpreted as the Lizard in the latest complete list of Hervieux (thought to be Inspector of Canary Breeding to the Duchesse de Berry), which was published in 1713. A variety resembling the now-extinct London Fancy (Serin Panaché de Noir-Jonquille et Regulier) is mentioned, however, which perhaps suggests that the Lizard and London Fancy were closely related. This is a point that could be debated almost indefinitely without any positive resolution.

It is however fair to say that the Lizard, unlike the majority of canary breeds, has continued for at least a century and a half in more or less the same form, although it is probable that, overall, modern-day Lizards are superior to their predecessors.

The original wild canary (*Serinus canaria*) is the ancestor of all the existing and the many now-extinct breeds. Changes have occurred in the phenotype for three reasons:

1) Domestication, i.e. the selective breeding of birds showing an unusual or unexpected characteristic, thus establishing and developing an appearance different from the normal.
2) Mutation.
3) Hybridisation, using a compatible related wild finch.

The creation of the unique feather patterns now recognised in the Lizard canary were probably originally caused by the second option, i.e. mutation, and then fixed and improved upon by the first option. Some discussion on the methods of inheritance of the 'Lizard factor' and some of its idiosyncrasies have been studied further on pp. 319–322.

The Lizard canary is unique in that it is now the only canary to be bred and exhibited for its distinctive plumage. Because of the number of specific points that need to be considered, and because of the fact that it is principally a one-year show bird, it has never attracted large numbers of breeders, although it must be said that its beauty is greatly admired by many.

When studying the Lizard, eight main areas need to be concentrated upon: 1) the spangle, 2) rowings, 3) the cap, 4) ground colour, 5) feather quality, 6) type, 7) beak, legs and claws, 8) wings and tail. These will be considered individually.

THE SPANGLE

It is not difficult to understand how its name was earned, as the pattern of feathering on the back, 'the spangle', resembles in appearance the overlapping scales of the reptile of that name. Whilst in many breeds showing melanistic pigment, a form of spangling is evident, in exhibition examples of the Lizard canary, this characteristic is the most important feature and should be very evident. In the feathers of a normal green canary the central area is black with the top edge coloured brown. The spangling on a Lizard can best be described as an extension of the web on each side of the midrib by a light edging, suggesting the presence of the optical blue/reduction of brown factor (a factor that is examined more closely on p. 238). The spangling should be very distinct in both gold (intensive) and silver (non-intensive) versions, although it is fair to say that the wider feather of the silver form, which has a paler ground colour, lends itself more readily to producing the perfection required.

Whilst the spangle is the most sought-after aspect of the Lizard, excess of spangling, causing a small moon effect, is to be avoided. This will, by its very nature, impinge on the dark area of the feather, thus destroying the means by which the spangle is viewable, resulting instead in a hazy impression. Conversely, too little light edging will allow no break in the melanistic stripes, leaving the black spots to run into each other and giving the tram-lines effect seen in normal green birds.

It is interesting to note that no trace of spangle is evident in a young bird prior to its first moult. The chicks are similarly marked to other green series birds at this stage of their development and it is not until the first moult is completed that an accurate impression of the bird can be obtained and comparison made with the ideal. Also, at the second and subsequent moults, it is not unusual for the spangle to increase in size, giving the hazy appearance already described. Provided that it is only at these later moults that this fault becomes evident, no consideration need be given to it when looking for potential breeding pairs.

Being well spangled is, however, not the total requirement, as this spangle must be well distributed, not only across the back but down the saddle and on the small feathers at the back of the head, and also on the head in the case of a broken- or non-capped bird.

ROWINGS

This feature describes the stripes along the flanks and around the breast of the Lizard and the term is unique to the breed. Rowings should be distinct and ideally should pass right to the centre of the chest. In reality this is difficult to achieve and usually only silver hens approach the ideal. As a feature, however, it would seem to have improved considerably over the last decade and, in time, perhaps further improvements will be viewed.

THE CAP

Next in importance to the spangle is the cap of the Lizard. This is an area of clear feathers located on top of the bird's head. For many years, only clear-capped examples were adjudged fit for exhibition purposes but this has now changed with classes also being available for both broken- and non-capped birds. For exhibition, and therefore show-classification purposes, clear-capped birds and nearly clear-capped, i.e. birds with no more than 10% dark feathers, are exhibited together, other classes being provided for non-capped, i.e. birds showing no light feathers or less than 10% light feathers, and broken-capped, these being birds that obviously fall between the two extremes. Notwithstanding this, the clear cap is still regarded as the ideal Lizard and, all other things being equal, the clear cap will be placed higher in esteem than its broken- or non-capped contemporary.

The ideal clear cap should extend from the top of the beak to the base of the skull and, whilst the best examples are oval-shaped, many resemble the shape of a thumbnail. The cap should be bounded by a line commencing at the top of the beak and passing over the top of the beak and over the top of the eyes, round to the back of the head in the same plane. An eyebrow of clearly-defined black feathers should separate the eye from the cap. The cap should not extend into the neck, described as overcapped: nor should it extend below the beak or eye, categorised as being bald-faced. The

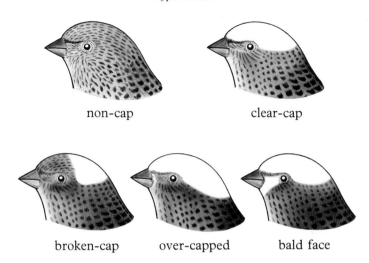

non-cap   clear-cap

broken-cap   over-capped   bald face

The varying caps of the Lizard.

latter fault will cause the bird to be disqualified from exhibition whilst the former is considered a fault.

When dark feathers appear in the cap to the extent of 10% or more of the clear area, the bird is termed broken-capped and, where the dark area is large enough to be well defined, this pigmentation should display clearly-defined spangles.

Examples also appear of birds showing no light feathers whatsoever. These birds obviously should show well-defined spangle all over and are called non-capped.

To confine the light feathers within the area of the cap, it is usual to pair clear cap to broken cap, and this will give an equal percentage of each type of cap in the young. Clear cap to clear cap will quickly result in overcapped young and birds displaying patches of light feathering on the body and white flight feathers in wings and tail, which render them useless for exhibition or breeding.

GROUND COLOUR

In the UK, Lizards are colour fed for exhibition and this has the effect of turning the golds to a rich golden chestnut colour and silvers to a warm silver grey. Any tinge of green is a serious fault, whilst patchy colour caused by incorrect feeding or plucking is detrimental to a bird's show career. It is normal always to mate gold to silver (i.e. intensive to non-intensive).

127

FEATHER QUALITY

A most important feature of the Lizard is that it should have tight fine feathers and this should be looked for as a matter of prime consideration. A loose- or coarse-feathered bird obviously cannot display the feather pattern to advantage.

TYPE

Unlike most breeds of posture canaries, the shape of a Lizard canary is not essential for it to exhibit to the maximum its unique features. It is desirable, however, for it to have a cobby shape with a broad back and skull, so that the spangle and the cap can be fully displayed, and also to have a full round chest for the rowings to be best seen.

BEAK, LEGS AND CLAWS

As with all green canaries of whatever breed, these features should be as dark as possible; jet black being the ideal, sooty black being more realistically achievable and dark grey being more usually seen. Any kind not having black beak, legs and claws will have points deducted, depending upon the degree of dilution; birds possessing flesh-coloured horny areas are the most penalised. There is a difference between a flesh-coloured nail and a white nail, however, the latter being a form of variegation. Those with white claws should not be used for breeding as there is a tendency for them to produce foul feathers in some of their progeny.

WINGS AND TAIL

These should always be black, carrying only a very narrow light edging. A pure white flight is a serious fault and disqualifies a bird from exhibition. Such birds should not be retained for breeding purposes. In unflighted birds, no trace of the grey or grizzled effect should be evident and, should this appear in the young of a well-established stud, it is worth examining the diet being offered to the nesting hens. The black colouration is a form of melanistic pigment which is derived from the protein in a bird's diet and a protein deficiency could be at the root of the problem. After the first full moult, it is usual for tail and wing feathers to take on this grizzled appearance. If odd feathers are accidentally lost during the first year of a young Lizard's life, the replacements will also normally appear grizzled, thus upsetting the presentation of the bird and effectively reducing its chances of winning major prizes at shows. When placed in overcrowded cages, much feather plucking invariably ensues and care must be taken to ensure that this does not happen. Ideally, youngsters should be caged singly for moulting purposes and kept apart until the show season is completed.

Being a small and active bird, the Lizard can be reared successfully using the methods described in Chapter 1. Once bred, however, great care should be taken with the young birds until after the first show season. In the UK, Lizard canaries have to be colour fed to reach the ground colour expected on the showbench. In some other countries this is forbidden and any fancier proposing to start keeping and breeding these beautiful birds with the ultimate intention of exhibiting them should check with the rules of the association within the country in which he lives. The ground colour of a bird can only be affected when new feathers are growing within the feather sacs, to replace either feathers lost through the natural annual moult or those lost accidentally.

It is at this time that colouring agents should be offered. Traditionally, Lizard canaries were offered cayenne within a softfood but, in more recent times, most fanciers have changed to offering a 10% canthaxin based product marketed in the UK by Roche Products Limited under the trade name Carophyll Red®. The advantage of using this product is that it can be offered in either dry or wet form by mixing with either softfood or the drinking water. Once the moult is complete, it is sufficient to offer colour food once a week to ensure that any feathers lost accidentally are replaced in the same hue. When the show season is completed, the practice can be discontinued until just before the commencement of the next full moult. With first-year babies, colouring agents should be offered once the chicks are 6 weeks old in the way described.

Young Lizards should be treated with particular care to ensure that no accidental loss of tail or flight feathers occurs. During the first moult of any canary the flight and tail feathers are not dropped. As stated earlier these feathers should be very black but frequently they start to take on a grizzled effect after the first full moult.

The Lizard is not a bird of posture and, in consequence, little show training is required. The bird does, however, need to present a steady image on the showbench and it is advisable to get it used to a show cage before sending it to a show. This is best accomplished by initally attaching a show cage to the cage in which the bird has been placed for moulting purposes, aligning the doors so that it can move freely between both cages. To encourage the young bird to enter the show cage, various titbits should be placed in it. After a week or two, the bird will become accustomed to entering the show cage voluntarily and the cage can then be handled as casually as it would be at a show.

MUNCHENER

To determine exactly when the Munchener canary came into being is difficult, as also is the identification of which existing species were used in its creation. Certainly, at the turn of the century, two forms of the Munchener existed, one with frills and the other without. The former has now disappeared and frilled feathers of any description are regarded as being a major fault in modern day examples. This leads one to think that possibly the Northern Dutch Frill and/or the Belgium Fancy were involved and, as with so many other varieties, by selective breeding, a different variety was created with a separate standard. In this instance it is also not difficult to assume, in view of the bird's name, that breeders in or around Munich in West Germany were responsible.

The Munchener is a bird of type and posture, i.e. it has a specific shape and is required to adopt a set stance when being judged. The bird is required to have an overall length of 6½ inches (160 millimetres) with a ⅕ inch (5 millimetre) tolerance.

Most standards for type canaries call for a full round head but, in the case of the Munchener, this is not so, a very small, oval-shaped flat-topped head being the ideal. A round head is a major fault.

The head is carried on a long thin neck which blends into narrow shoulders. When buying birds, the breeder is advised to avoid stock carrying either a short or thick neck on wide shoulders, as these faults can spread throughout a stud.

From the narrow shoulders, a small slightly-rounded chest should naturally follow, flowing elegantly through the legs to where the body joins the tail.

The wings, as with the tail, should be long and held tightly to the body. As uniform colour is required throughout the bird, including both wings and tail, additional lutein needs to be included in the diet at the time when the flight and tail feathers are being formed. This will ensure that they will not be visibly paler in the unflighted bird than in the adult, as is normal with all breeds of canary. This can most easily be achieved by ensuring that leaves from plants of the brassica family are included in the diet offered to the feeding hens. The tail, in addition to being long, should be as piped as possible with the V-shaped tip being as small as possible. An open spread or short tail or one with a large V ending is to be avoided.

To complete the picture, the legs should be long and, when the bird is in show position, should be slightly bent. Faults to look for here are short legs and legs held straight or overcurved, allowing the thigh area to be masked.

The feathering throughout the bird should be short and tight and the colour should be bright and even over the whole bird. This is an encouragement to establish a characteristic different from many other species, where bulk is an essential requirement. The fancier should pair birds in the normal manner, i.e. intensive (yellow) to non-intensive (buff), with short-feathered buffs being particularly sought. The greatest danger results from the use of too many short-feathered birds over a long period which adversely affects the overall length. This should be avoided, as any Munchener under 6 inches (150 millimetres) long will be disqualified from competition.

It is well known that variegation can be a boon when attempting to retain or improve colour or vigour and, as birds in this form compete with clear examples as equals on the show bench, their use is strongly recommended.

Having dealt with the 'type' of the Munchener we return to the all-important area of posture or stance. To be judged properly, it is important that examples of the breed not only stand correctly but maintain their position. Thus show training is an important feature and, in addition to following the suggestions found elsewhere in this book on general show training (p. 59), it is of paramount importance that the bird becomes totally conversant with a show cage and that it is accustomed to the cage being handled and set down by persons other than the breeder.

Regular and frequent bathing is also recommended. Experience shows that regular bathing of birds not only renders unnecessary the unwelcome task of hand washing before a show but results in the bird holding its feathers tightly to its body, which is a prime requirement for the variety.

The stance of the Munchener is of a slightly curved nature, similar to that of the Scotch Fancy but less rounded, with the whole contour from beak to tip of tail over the back being in a continuous, even and unbroken curve. The legs should be erect but slightly bent.

From this description it is not difficult to determine faults, i.e. too erect a stance or one too diagonal to the perch; the tail dipping under the body, or the neck curving upwards.

131

As with all lively varieties, the Munchener, given proper conditions and diet, is a ready breeder and can prove an interesting challenge to both experienced fanciers and newcomers alike.

NORWICH

C.S. Goodall
Chris Goodall has been a breeder of Norwich canaries for 20 years, having previously assisted his father – Sam Goodall – a well-known breeder and judge – for at least 10 years prior to starting his own stud. Chris, in partnership with his father, has many birds that have annexed major awards at all the important British exhibitions. They are particularly noted for their fine stud of cinnamon and green examples, although all-round strength is apparent in all sections.

In addition to his breeding and exhibiting prowess, Chris has for the last 10 years proved himself a most capable judge.

As with most breeds, it is difficult to be precise about the date when the Norwich canary originated. Hervieux, as far back as 1713, speaks of a clear orange/yellow canary and we know that, up to around a century ago, the Norwich canary was primarily bred for its colour. Without justifying his comments with hard-based facts, John Robson, in his book *Canaries, Hybrids and British Birds in Cage and Aviary*, thought to have been published in the early years of this century, dates the cultivation of the Norwich canary as a speciality to the latter quarter of the sixteenth century, when the Flemish, driven from their country by the Duke of Alva, settled in the UK. Many of these refugees settled in Norfolk, where they worked as weavers, and it is thought that it was they who introduced and then started to perfect the canary named after the city in or around which they worked.

Exhibition-quality Norwich canaries of today are unrecognisable from those of the early days and have, in fact, evolved tremendously during this century. Today's Norwich needs to be a cobby bird of 6–6¼ inches (150–160 millimetres) in length with a well-filled-in broad back showing a slight rise transversely. The chest needs to be deep and broad with an expansive curved front which sweeps under in one full curve to the tail. The head should be proportionately bold with a full forehead, rising from a short neat beak, well rounded over and across the skull. The cheeks need to be full and clean featured,

A good example of a Norwich Canary.

with a well-placed unobscured eye. The neck should be short and thick, running from the back of the skull on to the shoulders and from a full throat into the breast. The wings should be short and well braced, resting lightly, but closely, on the rump and meeting at the tips. A short close-packed tail should be well filled in at the root. It should be rigidly carried, giving an 'all-of-one-piece' appearance with the body. The legs should be well set back, allowing the bird to stand at an angle of 45°.

This contrasts greatly with Norwich canaries of yesteryear which, if drawings of the time are to be believed, varied from the size and type seen today in coloured canaries to that of the Border canary. Records also show that, around the 1850s, the Norwich and Lizard were birds of similar stature, the crossing of both breeds often taking place to improve colour and feather quality in the Norwich. Robson states that the bird should be about the size and shape of the German bullfinch (*Pyrrhula pyrrhula*) and it seems probable that the size and shape seen today is due, in part, to outcrossings with the crestbred and Lancashire canaries many years ago.

Up to the turn of the century, colour was the most important feature of the Norwich, accounting for 45 points out of 100, with an additional 20 points for extra good sheen and brilliance. Size and shape were considered of secondary importance with 8 and 6 points only being awarded for these features. Variegation, when present, had to be evenly marked. Today, of course, this constriction has been removed and birds with varying amounts and distribution of variegation are being judged and subsequently awarded prizes based on their shape, colour and feather quality.

Much mystery surrounded the colour of the Norwich canary. Where, for example, did this orange hue originate? Keeping in mind the problems associated with travel and communication, 'secrets' could be restricted to a small geographical area, their mystery compounding as the distance from their source increased. It was many years, therefore, before it was generally known that the lipochrome colouring of the Norwich resulted from it being offered cayenne pepper as part of a softfood mixture immediately prior to, and during, the moult. Such practices continue today. In fact, it is essential for any exhibitor intending to show his birds in the UK that the bird should have been colour fed. It is understood that it is not universally obligatory for this to happen and non-UK breeders of Norwich canaries would be well advised to seek guidance from an experienced exhibitor before commencing colour feeding.

Nowadays, many breeders have stopped the traditional method of using cayenne pepper as their colouring agent, preferring instead to offer Carophyll Red★. The author uses both in the following system. One part of red pepper is mixed some 3 months previous to use with six parts of the softfood chosen. Prior to the commencement of colour feeding about ¼ ounce (10 grams) of Carophyll Red® is blended with about 1 pound (0.5 kg) of softfood. One part of this mixture is then mixed with five parts of the mixture containing the cayenne and this is fed to the birds on alternate days at the rate of a heaped teaspoonful (5 gm) per bird. By using this method, it is found that the birds moult out evenly and richly coloured. Emphasis is made on the even colouring as it is pointless for any exhibitor to send to a show a bird which is unevenly coloured.

Many people, particularly those seeking stock, fail to realise that the 'perfect' bird does not, has not and, in all probability, never will exist. What breeders must seek to do is to produce specimens that are as close to the written standards as possible. When purchasing stock, breeders should seek birds which display the qualities absent in their own stock. At the same time, these birds should not display too many other faults, particularly ones which will compound problems already existing in the breeder's stock.

Those faults considered most problematical by the author concern the head and overall feather quality; all other faults can usually be corrected quite easily. With regard to the head, the two most serious faults are a flat top or a 'pinched-in' front accentuating the beak. Regardless of any other qualities which the bird might possess, a prospective buyer is advised to avoid such an acquisition. Also, should such an example be produced in the progeny of a particular pair, neither the parents nor the offending bird should be used for future breeding. The Norwich canary should have roundness proliferating all around its head; no straight lines should be visible, regardless of the angle from which the bird is viewed.

A long or thin neck is also to be avoided, although a bird with such a feature need not necessarily be culled from a strain if bred. Such birds will need to be paired back to short- and/or thick-necked partners during the next breeding season for the problem to be corrected in successive generations.

Feathering problems are usually centred on signs of frilling

★ Roche Products Ltd

135

around the neck, inevitably caused by coarse-feathered birds being paired together. This is relatively easy to correct if finer-feathered mates are offered for the next breeding season. Dropped secondary flight feathers do not usually occur in young birds; their presence normally indicates that the bird is advanced in years. In the event of this fault appearing in young birds, they should not be used for breeding. If evident in a known older bird, providing that its progeny do not themselves exhibit the fault, there is no reason why it should not be used for breeding purposes. One irritating fault that does seem to be genetically transmitted and, therefore, when located, one that needs to be removed from a strain, is that of the 'robin tail', i.e. a tail that hinges up from its base rather than following the contour of the body. Nothing spoils the overall

The method employed in trimming excess feather around the vent of heavily feathered breeds prior to the commencement of the breeding season.

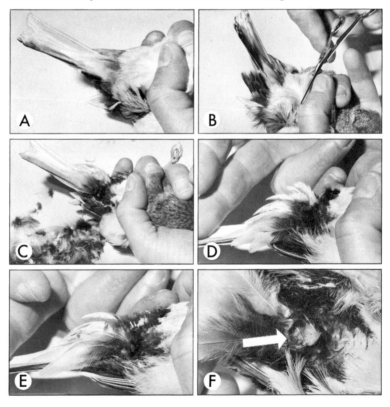

impression of a Norwich canary more than this; hence the advice not to persevere with birds possessing the fault in the hope that it can be corrected.

Whilst the general management and breeding techniques described in Chapter 1 can, in most instances, be related to breeding the Norwich canary, the author, having achieved consistent success in breeding what is considered to be a most difficult breed, will list one or two methods that he specifically follows in the hope that other breeders might share his success.

About 13 weeks prior to the commencement of the breeding season, all males are placed in single breeding cages with the females left in flights and/or flight cages. Six weeks prior to breeding, the heavy feathering around the vents of the birds is trimmed. Folklore dictates that the 'feeler' feathers of the males should not be touched. However, the author once owned a superb-quality male which failed to fertilise eggs over two nests, and, noticing that the 'feeler' feathers were extremely dense, in desperation and with nothing to lose, he trimmed down these feathers to the bare skin. The next nest contained all fertile eggs and this practice has been continued ever since.

Some 4 weeks before the breeding season, prospective mates are introduced to each other. They are left in their eventual breeding unit for 2 weeks, at which time they are split up again for 2 weeks before eventually being paired up again and the normal breeding techniques started.

There are breeders who will always attempt to line-breed their birds in the belief that this improves their chances of producing more youngsters which approach the ideal. The author's experiences have failed to confirm that this is the best method and he selects pairs based on the phenotype of the individuals, ensuring that a particular fault in one bird is compensated for in its mate.

Two unflighted birds are rarely paired together as it is considered more advantageous for at least one of the pair to be adult and, therefore, experienced in the breeding cycle. There are seldom two experienced fanciers who will agree precisely on breeding techniques etc. and there is no doubt that the methods described here will be received sceptically by a great many people. The only answer to this is that the results achieved by the author, both in quantity of youngsters produced and the quality obtained, are good.

Apart from a brief aberration in the 1985 breeding season, the use of a secondary stud of a smaller breed to assist in feeding the youngsters has not been pursued. Norwich canaries have a reputa-

A Norwich canary feeding her young.

tion for being poor parents but this has not been substantiated with the author's stock and one must wonder whether poor results in other breeders' birdrooms can be attributed to the failure to adopt necessary and realistic management techniques.

Whilst the pairing of flighted to unflighted birds is considered to be beneficial in obtaining quantity, quality is obtained by always pairing together clear stock with variegated examples and, whilst occasionally a double buff (non-intensive) pairing may be made in place of the almost universally-used yellow (intensive) to buff (non-intensive), never is a double yellow (intensive) one used.

It is important, when writing about Norwich canaries, not to ignore the issue of lumps. Whilst many theories have been put forward on the cause of lumps, no one is yet able to be dogmatic about it precisely. It is known that two soft-, wide-feathered birds paired together more frequently produce progeny with lumps than a pairing of hard- to soft-feathered bird. This apart, no guarantees can ever be given and it has to be accepted that, from time to time, breeders of Norwich canaries will produce birds possessing this undesirable characteristic. When this occurs, the bird should not be used for breeding. Often, such examples are gratefully accepted by breeders interested in hybridising the canary with native species and here they cause no lasting harm. Although traditionally the yellow (intensive) feather is considered to be hard and the buff (non-

A typical lump on the chest area.

A selection of lumps in different forms taken from a Norwich canary.

intensive) soft, this is not necessarily so and a simple exercise can be implemented to determine whether a bird possesses hard or soft feathers. Simply wash the bird and then note the time it takes for the plumage to dry completely. If the bird possesses hard feathers, it will take around 2 hours; if soft it will take 6 or 7 hours.

Whilst green and cinnamon canaries now exist in most varieties, up to the turn of the century they were considered separate breeds and then slowly became associated with the Norwich. Today green and cinnamon Norwich are kept only by a few specialist breeders as the majority prefer to keep only clear and variegated examples. The author gains pleasure from keeping a mixed stud and has gained equal success with his green/cinnamon strain as with his normal plainheads. The breeding of these dark birds and the clear varieties is identical but the author prefers, when breeding for cinnamons, to pair green to cinnamon, believing that this pairing helps maintain the size, shape and feather quality.

RAZA ESPANOLA

For a variety that has only recently become relatively widespread throughout Europe, the Raza Espanola has been in existence for a considerable amount of time.

The Union de Canariculture de Barcelona was founded in 1931 and its members decided to create a breed of canary quite different from any in existence at that time. They set as their criteria that the new bird should be a miniature canary of smooth feathering and that song should be of no consequence. This bird was named Canario del Pai (Canary of the Country).

Bad times, caused by the Spanish Civil War, existed between 1936 and 1939; many of the birds that had been bred were lost and those remaining were left in the hands of very few breeders. By the mid to late 1940s, stocks had again built up and at the 4th Spanish National Exhibition held at Madrid in 1948, a standard of excellence was drawn up for the breed and the name was changed to the Raza Espanola. At the 4th Congress of the CIC (the Confederation Internationale d'Amateurs et Eleveurs de Canaries – the forerunner of the Confederation Ornithologique Mondiale or COM), which was held in Barcelona in 1956, the Raza Espanola was accepted internationally as a new breed of type canary.

A feather lump on the wing butt, an area frequently troubled by this problem.

When the CIC and the Association Ornithologique Mondiale (AOI) joined together, the COM was founded and a standard fixed for the Raza Espanola. Spanish breeders did not, however, participate at World Shows for a number of years and it was not until the World Show of 1976, held in Valencia, that the new breed was presented to a wider public. Because of administration errors, however, the birds were not accepted as a recognised breed which, obviously, caused some consternation and bad feeling. The standards were, however, resubmitted and, at the World Show the following year, held at Genoa in Italy, the breed was officially recognised. Just prior to this exhibition, a specialist society was set up to foster interest in the Raza Espanola, both nationally and internationally.

The author has been unable to determine which breeds were used in the experimental stages leading up to the presentation of the Raza Espanola. It is not impossible, however considering the bird's size, to imagine that, possibly, the song canaries of the time – probably German Rollers, which themselves are not normally overlarge – were hybridised with one of the members of the Serin family. It is highly probable that the European serin (*Serinus serinus*) was used because:

1) It is known to readily cross with canaries and provide fertile hybrids.
2) Large numbers are to be found in Spain.

Half of the available 100 points used to judge the variety are awarded for size and slimness, which serves to emphasize the importance of these features.

The size is set as an ideal at 4⅓ inches (110 millimetres), no penalty points are deducted should the bird exceed this limit by ⅕ inch (5 millimetres) but points are deducted if the bird is larger than this, up to the maximum permitted size of 4⁹⁄₁₀ inches (125 millimetres). If the bird exceeds this length, it is disqualified from exhibition. No lower limit is set.

The back and breast of the bird is required to be flat and slim, no hint of roundness being required.

A short thin neck extends from the body on which there is a small oval-shaped flat head, similar to that of a Lizard. When judged, the head is required to point forwards, with the beak thrust so as to give an overall impression of a pencil with a sharp point.

The wings are required to fit tightly to the back, laying perfectly, with no trace of crossing and the tail being short and held tightly together. The end of the tail should be V-shaped but must not be wide.

The legs of the Raza Espanola should be as short as possible, just over ½ inch (14 millimetres) being considered the ideal size from the 'ankle' to 'knee' joints. When in the working position, the thighs should not be seen. The feet need to be small, dainty and in perfect condition.

Feathering needs to be perfect in every consideration, short but dense and lying perfectly. No roughness nor absence of feather is permitted.

As the bird is required to be constantly in motion – it is noted as being of an extremely nervous nature – the show position, and, therefore, the one where it is evaluated, is held only for a brief period of time at the point where it actually lands on the perch. At this time, it is in a crouching position with the ideal angle against the perch set at less than 45°.

No colour feeding is accepted, richness of colour being required to be bred into the bird rather than fed.

Although of a nervous disposition, the Raza Espanola is not noted as being difficult to breed. Regardless of their tiny stature, the birds should be bred in normal-size cages and the general rules of management apply.

In an attempt to keep the size of the Raza Espanola down to the prescribed level it is very common to find intensive (yellow) to intensive (yellow) pairings being used. The dangers of this system are well debated elsewhere in this book (p. 257). It is perhaps worth re-emphasising, however, that, whilst the over use of non-intensive (buff) to non-intensive (buff) pairings creates problems with overfeathering and the subsequent appearance of lumps, the indiscriminate use of intensive (yellow) to intensive (yellow) pairings will result in thin, sparse feathering which could prove extremely counterproductive.

SCOTCH FANCY

As its name suggests, the Scotch Fancy is the national canary of Scotland, although it is fair to say that its heyday is long past and few breeders of the variety are to be found in Scotland or elsewhere.

The Scotch Fancy came into being during the early years of the

143

nineteenth century and, without doubt, it is a direct descendant of the Belgium Fancy, but whereas the Belgium Fancy stands in an angular statuesque position with its neck and head thrust sharply forward, the Scotch Fancy is a bird of curves and stands in a semi-circular or half-moon posture. The breed was particularly popular in the Glasgow area of Scotland and has been known at times as the Glasgow Fancy and Glasgow Don. In the first edition of his *Canary Book* (1879), R.L. Wallace writes:

'The old fashioned Dons appear to have come from Glasgow. One of the first and most respected fanciers in Scotland informs me that he has known the breed for the past forty years and describes them as "small birds" with "plenty of action" and "cranked necks" and "crooked tails"; but where the birds really originated or how they became the possessors of such peculiarities my informant deponeth not. But this is, so it seems, how they came to be named the "Glasgow Dons", but they are now better known as Scotch Fancy canaries. The old fashioned Don of the period just alluded to, is rarely to be met with, as much improvement has been made in the breed, first by crossing them with the Dutch canary, a large strong bird resembling the old-fashioned Belgium canary in shape, but with a heavily frilled breast and back, and deficient in shoulders; but lately they have been still further improved by crossing with Belgium canaries of a more modern type, but round in form and having tails included to curve inwards.'

By the 1870s, the breed had reached the height of its popularity and there are records of an entry at a Glasgow show of 850 Scotch Fancies from a total of 300 exhibitors. Sixteen judges, eight from Glasgow and eight from other towns, were appointed to officiate. Yet, within a comparatively short period, the breed's popularity had started to wane.

The causes for the decline are examined in the section on the Belgium Fancy (p. 107). There seems little doubt that the practice of outcrossing with the Belgium led to Scotch Fancies being produced and exhibited which carried the Belgium's stiff square shoulders and were no doubt deficient in the characteristic action of the old Scotch Fancy. By the beginning of the twentieth century, illustrations show a bird with high shoulders and neck and head pointing forward and sidewards, a considerable departure from the 'half moon' shape of the mid-Victorian era.

Though kept in ever-decreasing numbers and rarely exhibited, this type of Scotch Fancy, often displaying a great deal of loose breast feathers, was favoured until the formation of the Old Varieties Canary Association in 1970, when a decision was taken to return to the 'half moon' smooth-feathered type of bird. In that time, progress has been made and Scotch Fancies of the type favoured over 100 years ago are now appearing on the showbench in increasing numbers.

The modern Scotch Fancy, like its mid-Victorian counterpart, is a bird of type, movement and posture. To categorise it as a rounded Belgium is to oversimplify the difference. The head of a good specimen differs from that of the Belgium in that it is slightly rounder. A small enough point one might think but nevertheless an important one in that, whilst one thinks of the back of the bird curving in a convex manner, equally the front of the bird should form a perfect concave curve. Thus the slightly more rounded head, with filled-in throat and little or no break from head to neck, allows for this to happen. The shoulders should be prominent but narrower than the Belgium and well filled in, giving a rounded appearance in direct contrast to the square Belgium shape. There should be good depth through from the point of the chest to the peak of the shoulder, albeit the pointed tendency should not in any way break the concave of breast and body. The neck of the bird should be long and slender, tapering into the head at one end and gradually expanding into the breast and shoulders. The back from the shoulder should be narrow and rounded, of good length and well filled in; the wings should be long and carried tight to the body. The tail should be long and closely folded, sweeping well under the perch at the tip, giving a continuation of the curve of the back. The lower coverts and vent feathers play an important part in the continuance of the unbroken curve of body and tail. The body, long in size, should taper away from the breast to the vent, giving a fine symmetrical finish to the concave curve. Faults to be avoided in the Scotch Fancy are a large coarse head or a short thick neck; neither should it have broad angular shoulders. It should not have a chubby chest nor should the feathering show any tendency to frilling. Its tail should be neither short, broad nor fan-shaped, nor held straight and inflexible.

When holding the show position, a Scotch Fancy should not stand 'over the perch', nor should it hold any position that destroys the perfect curve. At no time should the bird be small. 6¾ inches (170 millimetres) is considered the minimum.

As well as presenting a perfect show position, the bird is required to hold this position whilst hopping continuously from perch to perch. The bird must perform this action without in any way opening its wings or ruffling a feather.

This 'action', or 'travelling the perches', is of great importance and R.L. Wallace observed that 'unless a bird is a rapid and graceful mover its chances as a prize taker are more to be greatly impaired'. He also placed great importance on the free and easy movement of the bird's tail which he described as being 'souple' i.e. 'supple'.

Whenever a bird travels from one perch to another, the action of its tail is critically observed, and, unless it is perfectly free and glib, it is reckoned a fault. To a great extent the modern Scotch Fancy fails in this respect.

Colour and markings are of little importance for exhibition, clear, ticked, variegated and self birds all being considered equally. It is interesting to note that not all fanciers used the normal terms for canary markings, but referred to clears as 'clean', ticked as 'flecked', and variegated as 'piebald'.

The Scotch Fancy show cage is similar in shape, though slightly larger, than that used for the Border Fancy canary, but whereas all Border show cages are of exactly the same type, exhibitors of Scotch Fancies have used cages incorporating a high degree of individual craftmanship. This usually takes the form of inlaying the wooden sides to the base with marquetry work and some very beautiful and intricate designs are produced.

Whilst nowadays a full standard of excellence has been written, with points allocated to the various exhibition features of the bird, together with its size, general condition, showmanship etc., in the early years of its existence no such standard was considered necessary. The general criteria were retained in the minds of breeders and judges and passed on by word of mouth. ·

During this period, Scotch Fancy canaries were often judged in pairs by two judges standing opposite each other on either side of the judging bench; the birds were transferred from judge to judge with the better bird of the two being retained for comparison with the next bird until an eventual winner was found.

The Scotch Fancy appears and can be exhibited in intensive (yellow) and non-intensive (buff) forms. In consequence, normal pairing criteria should be employed, i.e. intensive being paired to non-intensive.

Thought might also be given to retaining a few pairs of a more reliable variety – Borders or Fife Fancy for example – to act as foster parents. It is important, however, that females of all species are given the opportunity to incubate and rear chicks. With this in mind, two possibilities exist. Firstly, the exchange can be made when the eggs are set; secondly, poor feeding hens may often be seen to ignore newly hatched, weak offspring but, on being given a nest of strong, healthy chicks aged 3 to 5 days, will find it impossible to ignore their cries for food and will rear such a nest normally. Regular observations should, of course, be made at every step, from hatching to weaning, to ensure growth is normal and no chick is failing to mature at the same rate as its nest mates.

YORKSHIRE

E. Henshall.
Edwin Henshall started to breed and exhibit Yorkshires in 1946, having bred Borders as a boy before the outbreak of war in 1939. For several years he specialised in whites in an attempt to re-establish their popularity and later moved on to include the normal colours.

Since then he has won major prizes at most of the leading specialist Yorkshire shows and also at several World Shows and other International Exhibitions in most European Countries. He is also a National Judge of Yorkshire Canaries and International Judge of all posture canaries and as such has often judged in Europe as well as at the World Show.

The modern Yorkshire as we know it today has come about as a result of many years of selective breeding and, in some respects, is a far different bird from the legendary Yorkshire, which some would have us believe could pass through a wedding ring. Personally the author finds this a little difficult to accept but, suffice to say, it must indeed have been a very slender bird.

No doubt, during its evolution, use has been made of other breeds, notably the Lancashire Plainhead, the Belgium and the Norwich, in order to introduce certain desired characteristics which these breeds possessed. It is thought that the first Yorkshires were exhibited around 1860 but this cannot really be verified.

Most readers will no doubt be familiar with the appearance of a typical Yorkshire but, for the benefit of newcomers to the Fancy, the illustration on p. 148 will show not only what the modern Yorkshire looks like but also the basic changes which have taken place during the last 100 years or so. Unfortunately it is not possible to put exact dates on the changes.

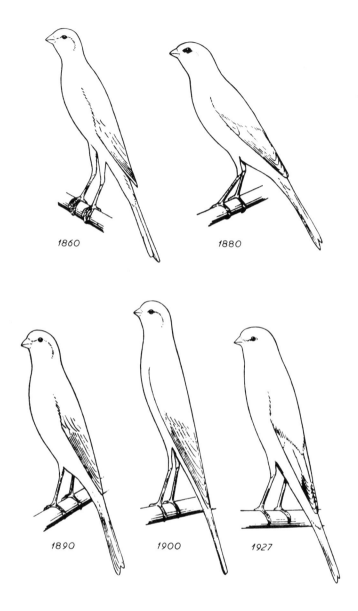

The varying standard of excellence of the Yorkshire canary from 1860–1927.

148

It will be seen straight away that, in certain respects, the bird has not changed at all, as it is still essentially a long bird and still maintains an upright position.

The scale of points for judging as published more than 100 hundred years ago stated: 'Size, for length with corresponding symmetrical proportions'.

Today's official Yorkshire Canary Club (YCC) standard states on the subject of size: 'length approximately 17.2 centimetres with corresponding symmetrical proportions'. Mark the words 'corresponding symmetrical proportions' carefully as they are most important, deliberate emphasis has been placed on these words as they are the key to understanding what a good Yorkshire should look like; always keep them in mind when assessing a particular bird.

The reader may be wondering why the description of the Yorkshire canary has commenced with its size or length, whereas the scale of points normally starts off with the head, size coming next to last. The reason for doing this is to identify the areas which have not in essence changed. The value of the points allocated may have changed slightly but it is worth noting that the words used to describe the birds have changed but little in more than a century. The oldest records state: 'Attitude, Erect with fearless carriage'. Today's standard on the same subject is identically worded. In reference to feathers, both standards read: 'feather short close and tight'. Legs are also described in the same words for both standards: 'long without being stilty'. In both standards wings are referred to as long and evenly carried and the tail as compact and closely folded.

So, in effect, the Yorkshire canary, for at least 100 years, has been a long upright bird, with long wings set on a compact and closely-folded tail, with legs that are long without being stilty, and clad in feathers which ideally would be short, close and tight. So far so good, but there the similarity ends.

The areas where the principal changes have taken place are the head, which is now much larger in all respects, and the neck, which is no longer moderately long and straight. The neck in today's YCC standard is not referred to directly as it was a century ago. The standard now states; 'Breast full and deep, corresponding to width and rise of shoulders and carried up full to base of beak which should be neat and fine'. The body too should be well rounded and gradually tapering throughout to the tail.

Birds having the qualities just referred to are spoken of as having 'good top ends'. This is a phrase which is most frequently used when the merits of particular birds are discussed. Indeed it would be a very poor Yorkshire if it did not have a good top end.

To summarise the features of a good modern Yorkshire: essentially it should be a long upright bird some 6¾ inches (172 millimetres) in length, standing at approximately 60°. The head should be nice and round with a neat fine beak – quite often an otherwise good bird can be spoiled by having a large coarse beak – the eye should be set in the centre of the head. The bird should also have a very full neck – not nipped in – and the neck should merge into a deeper round chest and back with a hint of rise at the shoulder. The roundness should be apparent whether viewed from the side, above or from any other viewpoint. The bird should now taper gradually from the full round chest throughout to the tail. This tapering effect should also be evident from every angle. It sometimes happens that a bird may have a very nice profile when seen from the side but, when seen from behind or above, it may appear to be devoid of any taper and, instead, be the same thickness all the way down from the shoulder, thus spoiling an otherwise good specimen.

On the subject of negative features it is perhaps worth mentioning that no fancier has a room full of perfect specimens. Indeed he would be most fortunate if he had but a few. All serious breeders of any form of livestock have a similar goal in mind, and that is to produce specimens which are as near as possible to the ideal for the breed.

To return to the description of the ideal show bird, it should stand on a long pair of legs, positioned in such a way that an imaginary line, if continued upwards, would pass through the shoulder. The legs should not be short nor should they be set too far back, both of which are common faults.

We now come to the wings and tail. The wings should be proportionately long and evenly carried down the centre of the back and firmly set on a compact and closely-folded tail. 'Piped tail' is a term often used to describe such a tail.

There are some common and serious tail faults: 'dropped tail', which makes the bird look 'hoopy', and 'fish-tail', which is when the tail feathers spread out at the ends. There are also a couple of wing faults. 'Scissor wings' refers to wings which cross part-way up the back, which in my opinion is a bad fault. This should not be confused with wings which tip at the ends. Quite often a bird will do

Top-quality Yorkshire canary in show position.

this and judges know how to deal with such birds when this occurs. The other wing fault, which I do not like, is bad secondary flight feathers which stick out instead of lying flat.

The ideal bird should obviously be clad in feathers which should be close and tight with no evidence of coarseness or frilling. In other words it should appear to have been moulded in one piece. Quality is a term which is used to describe birds which have this moulded appearance.

Another term which the newcomer to the Yorkshire Fancy will often hear is 'character'. This is used when admiring a bird which has a nice rise at the shoulder and a hint of lift at the tail, giving the bird 'character'.

As mentioned already, the exhibition Yorkshire of 100 years ago was a very long slender bird and the first scale of points for judging was drawn up at about that time. To cater for the needs of the breed, the Yorkshire Canary Club was founded in 1894.

Unfortunately, as there are several regrettable gaps in certain records, it is impossible to confirm some of the dates when changes to the official standard took place. The last change took place in 1961 when S.R. Golding's much fuller and more streamlined model was accepted by all the leading specialist societies.

To move on to the acquisition of stock, it is most likely that newcomers to the Yorkshire Fancy will have gained some experience in breeding other varieties of canary and will probably have been attracted to the Yorkshire after visits to shows, or perhaps after admiring them in a friend's birdroom. Hopefully they will already be members of a local Cage Bird Society. If not, it is strongly recommended that they join one and decide to attend the meetings regularly where they should learn a great deal.

Where can good initial stock be purchased for breeding purposes? It would be a good idea to join at least one of the leading Specialist Yorkshire Canary Clubs where there will be a good opportunity to meet many other Yorkshire breeders and perhaps be invited to visit their birdrooms and inspect their stock. As a general rule, it is a good idea to purchase initial stock from one breeder. This guarantees the buyer a reasonable chance of pairing together birds which are slightly related and so increases the chances of producing chicks which, at worst, will resemble their parents or grandparents.

It would seem appropriate at this stage to touch on the subject of line-breeding, having just mentioned the pairing together of slightly-related birds. Line-breeding and inbreeding form a most complex subject about which there are a lot of popular misconceptions. The fact that it is so complex really places it beyond the scope of this chapter, so I will touch on it but briefly.

In essence the main difference between the two terms concerns the closeness of the matings. Inbreeding is a system whereby closely-related specimens are mated together, e.g. father to daughter, mother to son, or perhaps brother to sister. Line-breeding, on the other hand, involves the mating of less closely-related specimens. It is really a matter of degree.

Both systems theoretically increase the chances of producing offspring which closely resemble each other and/or their parents. Mating unrelated specimens means just the opposite, since each pairing (outcross) introduces 'new' genes into the stud. Many good birds are produced each year by all three systems. What is important to remember is that both inbreeding and line-breeding per se will not produce anything, either good or bad. The results depend on the genetic make-up of the birds. It is a popular misconception that both systems produce weakness or degenerate stock but this is not so. If such conditions do occur, it is because these tendencies were already latent in the stock and were merely brought out more quickly. Remember the phrase 'each outcross introduces new genes'. The opposite must also be true, i.e. that inbreeding and line-breeding reshuffle and reassemble the same genes (and their normal altern-atives), so that nothing 'new' is introduced. As far as the introduction of defects is concerned, it is a case of the undesirable genes consolidating and manifesting themselves more quickly.

What is absolutely vital to keep in mind before attempting to inbreed or line-breed is to ensure that the stock which it is intended to breed from is completely sound in wind and limb. Also both sets of parents and grandparents should display all the attributes which it is hoped will ultimately be seen throughout the stock. Always keep in mind that, just as the 'good desirable' features are able to mani-fest themselves when the genes have regrouped, so will the 'bad undesirable' features appear.

The foregoing is a simplification of the basic concepts of line-breeding and inbreeding but should serve to sweep away some of the mystery surrounding the subject. So whenever the purchase of new stock is contemplated, glance around the breeder's birdroom to see which features, both good and bad, are predominant in his stock, because these are the features which will be introduced into the buyer's stock. Two particular faults which should not be tolerated in a birdroom are 'dropped (or 'hinged') tail', which completely spoils the outline of the bird, however good it may be in other areas, and a twist or group of frilled feathers on the breastbone. Either of these faults is most difficult to eradicate and will proliferate in the stock.

One way to avoid serious faults is not to bring birds which possess them into the birdroom in the first place. Strictly speaking, this applies with certainty only to 'dominant' faults. It is not possible to tell whether a fault is dominant or recessive without knowing a great deal about the parentage of a bird or carrying out a programme of test matings, which is a long and tedious process. It is therefore necessary to rely on advice. If, despite the precautions described, some feature, good or bad, suddenly appears, then a breeder will know that recessive genes are responsible. For the sake of simplicity, it should be accepted that recessive (or hidden) factors normally manifest themselves only when each parent has contributed a gene responsible for a particular characteristic. A fuller understanding of the mechanism involved can be gained from reading Chapter 3 on inheritance.

Generally speaking, the management of Yorkshire canaries is little different to that of other breeds of canary and this is described in Chapter 1. Contrary to popular belief, female Yorkshire canaries are not as a general rule bad feeders. In the author's experience, if the commonsense precautions are taken to ensure that they (just as any other females) are feeding properly, there is usually nothing to fear. They are quite capable of rearing a nest of three or four chicks unaided if necessary.

The author has always been favoured with having excellent feeding hens and believes it possible to breed this attribute into the strain just like any other feature. Very few Yorkshire breeders of the author's acquaintance use foster mothers, or 'feeders' as they are known, and instead they allow their birds to rear their own chicks.

There are, of course, exceptions but, quite often when chicks are lost, it is the mother bird which is blamed. However it is possible for the chicks to be at fault, e.g. if they are sickly and fail to gape properly.

At around 7 or 8 weeks old, young Yorkshires, with the exception of white or white-ground birds and self or foul greens (see p. 158), can be started on colour food. The subject of colour feeding is dealt with more fully on p. 56, to which the reader is referred.

To start training young birds for show purposes, it is a long-established custom to hang Yorkshire show cages on the front of the

Training Yorkshire canaries to stand erect by placing cardboard partitions between cages covering the bottom three-quarters of the height.

cages in which young stock are housed. The normal way of doing this is to hang the show cage in such a manner that the doors of both show and stock cages are level. The young birds may than move freely in and out of both cages.

As soon as they are fully used to the show cages, it is a good idea to gently remove the show cage containing the young bird and to place it either on top of a previously-prepared staging, if space permits, or at some other vantage point from which the show potential of the occupant may be assessed. At first it is better to allow the bird to settle down before attempting to handle the cage, because a sudden fright at this stage is quite often responsible for causing the bird to extend its back claw, a condition that is difficult to correct. This can occur in seconds and will ruin an otherwise promising bird.

Most fanciers use a 'training stick' to assist in the training process. This is a flat piece of wood approximately ½ inch (10 millimetres) wide and 10–20 inches (400–500 millimetres) long. It is the author's practice to gently draw the slide across the bars of the show cage, causing the bird to alert itself and start to 'show off'. If the bird is on the bottom perch, a gently tap on the cage near to the perch will cause it to jump up to the top perch, where it can be seen to better advantage. The bird will soon learn what is required when the cage is tapped.

155

Whilst the author has no special way of encouraging young birds to 'stand' properly in the show cage, there are a couple of intriguing ideas which used to be in vogue many years ago. Some fanciers used to fix a small of mirror approximately ¾ × ¾ inches (20 × 20 millimetres) above one of the perches in the stock cage in such a way that the young bird, being inquisitive, would be encouraged to stretch in order to satisfy its natural curiosity. The other idea was to secure a piece of paper around the show cage again at such a height that the young bird would have to stretch itself in order to look over the top of the paper. The logic in these ideas is questionable, at least as far as modern Yorkshires are concerned, as the last thing fanciers want is for their birds to develop the habit of stretching. Many an otherwise good bird will ruin its chances of 'getting in the cards' if it has the misfortune to stretch itself whilst it is being judged. The modern Yorkshire is seen at its best when it is relaxed but standing properly on the top perch of the show cage.

As a general rule, not a great deal of training is required as the young birds tend to 'train' themselves. However, a few birds are quite nervous and great patience is called for when dealing with them. As soon as the birds are trained, they can easily be coaxed into show cages with the aid of the training stick. Quite often the mere sight of the stick will make them run into the show cage.

It is a good idea to use several show cages because this will accustom the birds to being 'staged'. The breeder should try his hand at judging the birds, rearranging the cages in order of preference, so that the birds will get used to being moved about, just as they will be at the shows. Don't forget to hang a show drinker on the show cage during the training stage. Quite often this is overlooked and sometimes young birds are unable to find their water and consequently are marked 'soft' at the shows.

When it comes to entering birds in a chosen show it is very important to study the show rules and schedule most carefully in order to avoid the possibility of having birds 'wrong-classed'. This is a most disappointing experience, especially if a good bird is being entered.

Whilst most judges dislike 'wrong-classing' birds, they are quite often obliged to do so, particularly at the large shows. A number of fanciers become confused when deciding how to classify their birds, in spite of the fact that the standard of markings is clearly stated in the handbooks of the Yorkshire-canary specialist societies.

The classification of Yorkshire canaries is, in certain respects, unique so it is suggested straightaway that readers with any experience at all of other breeds of canary should forget any ideas of what constituted a ticked or variegated bird in those breeds. This is very important in the understanding of the classification issue. If the classification reads: 'Clear, ticked or lightly variegated (only 1 technical mark)', then the deciding issue is the technical mark. The variegation is only considered if the bird does not have what is termed 'a technical mark'. A technical mark is, in effect, a dark feather or a group of feathers which actually touches the eye, or the primary or secondary feathers of the wing, or is situated on one side or each side of the tail, i.e. the outer feathers only. This explanation will be clarified as we progress by the use of examples. Some of these examples may seem to be rather extreme, but it is these extreme cases which tend to cause the misunderstandings and lead to birds being 'wrong-classed'. A very important point which should be mentioned is that the presence of dark feather on the thigh or discolouration of the beak, legs or feet, or any mark which is not discernible as the bird stands in its natural position in the show cage, is entirely ignored throughout the whole classification. Also it is important to remember the phrase 'without intervening light feathers' as this is one of the criteria which often decides some issues, as will become apparent.

We shall now consider some examples featuring the tail:

Example 1   A bird which is completely clear apart from an all-dark tail, for the purpose of the classification, is considered to have only 1 technical mark. If it also had dark feathers elsewhere, these would be ignored provided that they did not touch the eyes or the wings. However if one feather had touched just one of these areas, this would count as 1 technical mark and the bird would be classified as having 2 or more technical marks, i.e. heavily variegated.

Example 2   A bird which has a clear body and a dark tail but with just one intervening light feather would have more than 1 technical mark and would be classified as such, i.e. heavily variegated. It would be similarly classified if instead, it had just a single dark feather on either side of its tail.

Example 3   An otherwise clear bird may have a dark tail except for one clear feather on each side of its tail and this would still remain a clear bird.

To re-iterate, technical marks are dark feathers which touch the eyes/wings/or outer feathers of the tail. Any other markings should be completely ignored. If this is kept in mind, there should be no problems in deciding how to classify a particular bird.

The head or eyes will now be considered and it should be assumed that the following examples are, for the purpose of the exercise, 'clear' in all respects other than those mentioned.

Example 1   A bird with a mark which touches the eye will be considered as having 1 technical mark. It is as simple as that. It matters little whether the mark is large or small; even if one mark was to touch both eyes, it would still be considered as 1 technical mark. However, if there are any intervening light feathers completely dividing the mark, the bird would be deemed to have 2 technical marks.

Example 2   A bird which has dark feathers covering the head, neck etc., but stopping short of the wings is still be considered to have only 1 technical mark.

Example 3   At the other extreme, it does not matter how small the mark/s are. Two tiny marks, each touching an eye renders the bird 'heavily variegated' for the purpose of classification, even though it is completely free of dark feathers elsewhere on its body. This is because it has 2 technical marks.

When it comes to the wings, little remains to be said as it will be obvious by now that the size of the marks is of no consequence. Suffice it to say that any dark feather on the wing primary or secondaries constitutes 1 technical mark.

There is one final category which covers the self or foul classes. A self-coloured bird is one which shows no light feathers at all, i.e. an all dark bird.

A 'foul' on the other hand is one which may have light feathers in wing flights or tail – but not in both. Light feathers elsewhere render it variegated.

These extreme examples should be useful in classifying difficult cases and go someway to preventing the disappointment of having birds wrong-classed. This subject is most important because there are always instances of birds being entered incorrectly due to the failure of some fanciers to understand the standard of markings.

When birds have been correctly entered and sent to the show it is advisable to spend some time on arrival studying all the birds to see if you have any birds 'in the cards'. In particular, compare the winning birds with your own to see where they may fail.

As far as judges are concerned, it should be remembered that, when engaged, they are in effect being asked to pass an *opinion* as to the order of merit of the birds placed before them. Opinions differ so it is hardly surprising that some people may disagree with certain awards. Indeed, it may sometimes happen that the judge himself may wish the birds had been placed in a different order when he sees them an hour or so after judging (although this is not a frequent occurrence). When it does happen, it is usually because some of the birds may have settled down and appear quite different than they did earlier. Some Yorkshires will just not stand being handled.

This is where 'show birds' score but, although it might sound contradictory, not all good birds are show birds. Some very good birds look fine if they are not disturbed and quite naturally are 'in the cards' if they are on their best behaviour when judged. If, however, they are upset whilst being judged they can be beaten by worse birds. Show birds, on the other hand, always look the same and consequently can only be beaten by better birds. It is perhaps worth remembering this when you next hear judges being criticised.

Show Standards

BELGIUM FANCY

Body	25 points
Head/neck	12 points
Size	5 points
Legs	5 points
Tail	5 points
Condition and feather quality	8 points
Presentation in working position	40 points
Total	100 points

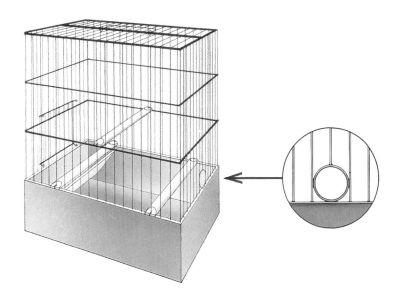

BERNER

Position	20 points
Head and neck	20 points
Body	20 points
Tail and wings	10 points
Feet and legs	10 points
Feather quality and colour	10 points
General condition	10 points
Total	100 points

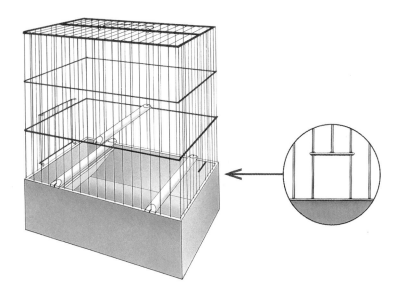

BORDER

Head	10 points
Body	15 points
Wings	10 points
Feet and legs	5 points
Feather quality	10 points
Tail	5 points
Presentation	15 points
Elegance	10 points
Colour	15 points
Size	5 points
Total	100 points

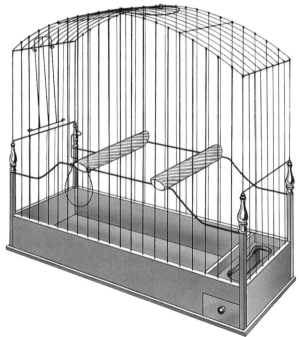

162

FIFE FANCY

Head and beak	10 points
Shape	10 points
Wings	10 points
Feet/legs	5 points
Feather quality	10 points
Tail	5 points
Presentation	10 points
Colour	10 points
Size	20 points
General condition	10 points
Total	100 points

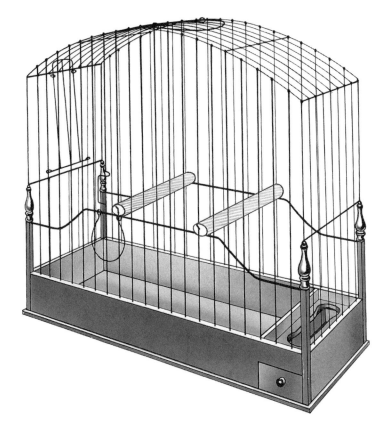

IRISH FANCY

Head	15 points
Eyes	10 points
Body	15 points
Tail	10 points
Feather quality	15 points
Position	15 points
Legs/feet	5 points
General condition	15 points
Total	100 points

JAPANESE HOSO

Shape	25 points
Size	10 points
Head and neck	10 points
Shoulders and body	15 points
Position	30 points
Tail	5 points
General condition	5 points
Total	100 points

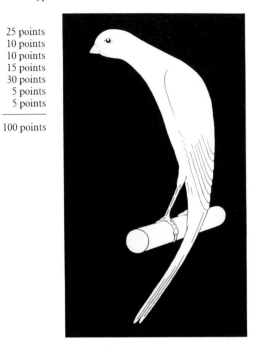

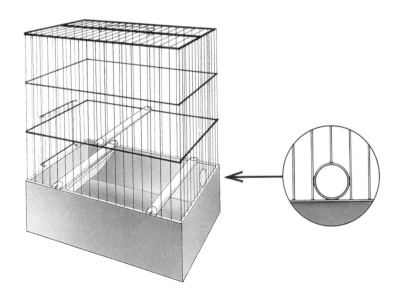

LIZARD

Cap	10 points
Ground colour	10 points
Eyebrows	5 points
Spangle on back	25 points
Spangle on chest/flanks	10 points
Wings and tail	10 points
Feather quality	15 points
Wing butts	5 points
Beak/legs/feet	5 points
General condition	5 points
Total	100 points

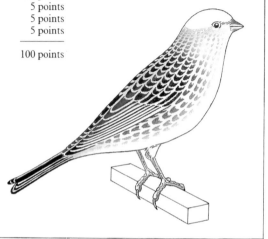

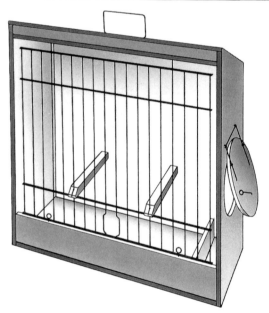

MUNCHENER

Presentation	20 points
Head and neck	20 points
Shoulders and body	20 points
Tail	10 points
Feet/legs	10 points
Feather quality and colour	10 points
General condition	10 points
Total	100 points

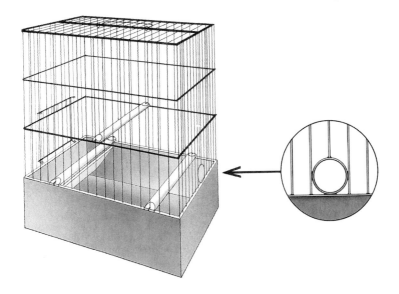

NORWICH

Shape	25 points
Head	10 points
Base of skull	10 points
Wings	10 points
Tail	5 points
Legs and feet	5 points
Condition	10 points
Feather quality	10 points
Colour	5 points
Overall presentation	10 points
Total	100 points

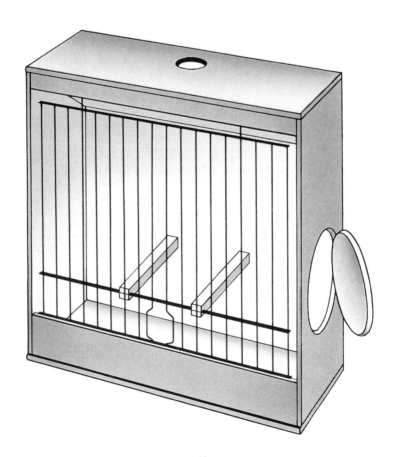

168

RAZA ESPANOLA

Size	25 points
Head and neck	10 points
Body	25 points
Wings and tail	10 points
Feet/legs	10 points
Feather quality	10 points
Agility	5 points
General condition	5 points
Total	100 points

SCOTCH FANCY

Shape	20 points
Size	10 points
Head and neck	10 points
Shoulders and body	20 points
Position/movements/style	25 points
Tail	5 points
General condition	10 points
Total	100 points

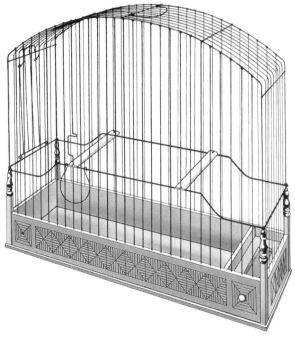

170

YORKSHIRE

Head	10 points
Size	10 points
Body	10 points
Presentation	25 points
Feather quality	25 points
Colour	10 points
General condition	10 points
Total	100 points

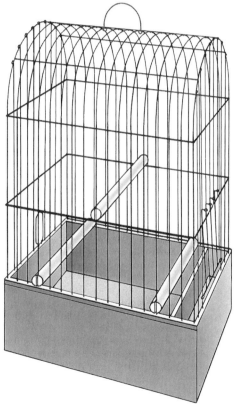

SMOOTH-FEATHERED CRESTED VARIETIES

COLUMBUS FANCY

A variety of Canary generally unknown outside its native country (USA) is the Columbus Fancy, so called, it is thought, because of its creation in or near the town of Columbus, Ohio, by a Mrs W.A. Phinney. Having viewed the birds at first hand, it is somewhat surprising that it has not found favour with type-canary fanciers outside the USA, despite the difficulties involved in importing birds from there. This could also be partly due to breeders, particularly in Europe, being unaware of its existence. It is hoped that this chapter may encourage someone, somewhere, to import the bird into Europe so that examples can be viewed at World Shows. The author is confident that a huge amount of interest will be created should this happen.

The Columbus Fancy was created in the 1930s by crossing small Norwich canaries with crested Hartz canaries. It must be remembered, however, that the Norwich canary of that time was much less cobby than today's examples, and was also somewhat longer. Also, the Hartz canary used initially was the genuine Roller canary, and should not be confused with those birds seen at today's exhibitions in the USA, where the term 'Hartz' is used to describe those canaries which fail to meet the specifications required for other type breeds.

The end result of the experimentation was the creation of smaller Norwich-type canaries with a crest (and a very sweet song). It is true to say that in many but not all respects, the modern-day Columbus Fancy fills the gap between the Gloster and Crest varieties.

To the uneducated, at first glance, the crested Columbus Fancy might be mistaken for a small Crest canary. If further examination fails to change this opinion, then the bird is not of good quality.

The standard of excellence for the Columbus Fancy calls for a maximum length of 6 inches (152 millimetres). The head should be rounded when viewed from all angles, the beak should be short and the eye central. When present, the crest should be neat, covering the eyes at the front but, unlike the Crest variety, not covering the eyes. The back of the crest should be like a hood of closely-packed feathers finishing off like a cap; the feathering here should be no longer than an ordinary non-crested or plainhead canary.

The neck and body of the Columbus Fancy should resemble a small Norwich, i.e. a short thick neck with a rounded cobby body. A

172

short neat tail and tightly-packed wings complete the description of the ideal specimen.

The head of the non-crested, called a smooth-head, should be round with brows being encouraged.

Colour is of extreme importance to the Columbus Fancy with a beautiful bright luminous yellow effect being call for. Colour feeding of any description is banned and birds showing any tendency to orange are disqualified.

Unlike many of the heavier breeds, feather quality is a much sought-after requisite and good-quality birds should display the tightness of feather one usually associates with the Border Canary.

The Columbus Fancy, for such a comparatively large bird, is extremely active and this is partly the reason for the generally good breeding results. The use of a secondary stud of smaller feeding females is unnecessary.

As with most breeds of canary, a crested bird should be paired to a non-crested and a yellow (intensive) to a buff (non-intensive).

The ideal Columbus Fancy is a clear bird with a dark crest but, being a bird of posture, the overall shape is of paramount importance. Clear, ticked, variegated and self varieties are bred and exhibited with some success in both green and cinnamon varieties.

The Columbus Fancy, as previously mentioned, is an active free breeder and, as such, the breeding and general management techniques covered in Chapter 1 should suffice for breeders handling the breed for the first time. Ideally, however, as with all crested breeds, to avoid the possibility of the crest being damaged during the moult by feather picking, crested examples should, whenever possible, be moulted singly.

An association, the International Columbus Fancy Association, has recently, if somewhat belatedly, been formed to promote interest in the breed, which has, over the years, neared extinction several times.

CREST

The presence of a crest on a canary was known for many years prior to the attempts to make this characteristic the central feature of a separate breed of canary. Certainly, the Hartz Mountain canary was well established and flourishing before thoughts turned to the production of birds of a specific shape rather than solely for their song. The existence of the crest is recorded in these birds and it is not, therefore, difficult to imagine its introduction into the UK as part of the consignments of canaries which are known to have been imported, from Germany, throughout the eighteenth century and, later, to meet the demand for singing canaries as pets. The formation of a distinct crest rather than the more usual effect of feathers all lying the same way must have been caused by a mutation rather than by the selective breeding that is thought to have brought about the various frilled breeds in existence. Selective breeding has, however, played an important part in improving the quality of the various Crests found today. It is now an established fact that the mutation responsible for producing the crest effect is a dominant heterozygous mutation, i.e. only one of the pair of genes responsible for the lie of the feathers on the top of the head needs to have mutated before the crest is evident. Thus one of any pair must be a Crest to reproduce Crests, i.e. two Plainheads paired together will never produce Crests, whereas two Crests paired together can produce Plainheads.

The two possible pairings are, therefore:

Pair 1: Crest × Plainhead which will produce, on average, 50% Crests and 50% Plainheads.

Pair 2: Crest × Crest which will produce 25% homozygous Crests, 50% heterozygous Crests and 25% Plainheads.

The second pairing, however, is not recommended because the 25% homozygous Crests will prove non-viable, i.e. they will not grow to maturity because of an inborn genetical defect which does not allow the bones of the skull to close together. Any pressure put on this area will result in the bird's death either in embryo or as a nestling. The author is unable to trace any positive confirmation of this hypothesis, but given the many thousands of crested canaries (Glosters, Crests and Lancashires) bred each year, and the complete absence of a true-breeding all-crested strain amongst any of them, it is a conclusion that must be accepted.

The mating of Crest to Crest may, however, be used to advantage occasionally, as a means of improving the length and density of the head feathers. Great care must be taken with this mating as there is a tendency for the resulting crested young to have 'mop crests', i.e. no properly defined centre of radiation of the crest feathers. Such birds, though quite unsuitable for exhibition, may prove invaluable as stock birds when paired to a suitable crestbred.

The precise history of the origination of the Crest of today, as with so many other varieties of canary, is clouded. It would seem that the

174

addition of the crest to Norwich canaries was a prime motivation. Certainly the term 'Norwich Turncrown' was applied to early examples, and in his *Book of Canaries and Cage Birds* (1878), W.A. Blakston, who contributed the section on canaries, devotes a great deal of space to the Norwich in both its plainhead and crested forms. The birds he describes are, however, medium-sized, lively canaries, valued chiefly for their depth of natural colour and quality of feather. The crested birds carried small, neat daisy-type crests, which did not obscure the birds' eyes or heads.

In 1871 the discovery that feeding cayenne pepper during the moult imparted a rich orange tint to the new plumage and made the colour of such birds increasingly superior – for exhibition purposes – to naturally-bred specimens, destroyed the old standards almost at a stroke. Within the next few years, the introduction of the massive Lancashire Coppy into both types of Norwich, also changes their character completely, and produced a much larger canary of short 'bullfinch' – like proportions. The most dramatic change, however, was to the head feathers of the crested Norwich; these were increased in size to such an extent that, in a good specimen, they would equal a crown piece (38 mm) in diameter. The resultant craze for 'the Crest' as it soon became known, swept through the Fancy, with prices equating to many hundreds of pounds at present-day values, being paid for winning birds. For a quarter of a century the Crest was known as the 'King of the Fancy' but, by the beginning of the twentieth century, its great days were over and, though it retained a faithful following who maintained a remarkably high standard of birds – a Crest took the award for best exhibit at the National Exhibition in London in 1960 – it is only as recently as the 1980s that it has reappeared in reasonable numbers.

Understandably the major point for consideration in the Crest is that characteristic from which its name is derived. A crest cannot be too large; in fact, all other points considered, the rule is the larger the better. Having made this point, the small central area from which the crest radiates is of major importance. If this is situated other than in a central position on the skull, it is impossible for the crest to lie evenly and an undesirable imbalance or lack of symmetry will arise. The absolute ideal is for the centre of the crest to be in a centrally-placed position just behind the eye. Although a flat crest may be accepted, providing all other criteria are met, preference is always given to one that has an abundance of long, wide and veiny feathers that rise upwards and then drop over the eyes and beak. The faults associated with the crest are as follows. It must not be horned at the back nor split in any direction. It must not consist of thin scanty feathers. The centre must be small and round, it must not be open or long or, as previously described, anywhere other than in a central position.

Whilst a bird with a large wide skull should carry the most impressive crest, this is not always the case. The length and width of the feathers determine the ultimate quality of the crest and, on a thin narrow head, they cannot express fully the desired effect. Conversely, a magnificent skull carrying small narrow feathers again cannot produce a top-quality crest. Notwithstanding this, such a bird may be invaluable as a stock bird if the breeder is in possession of broad, long-feathered stock lacking head qualities.

Although the author has not heard any such theory in discussions with modern-day breeders, it has been commonly thought throughout the years that the presence of a crescent-shaped clear area on the skin of young dark-crested birds in the nest will result in no feathers growing through this area of skin. The area described invariably resulted in a poor back to the crest. Such problems were often blamed on the bird knocking out feathers whilst sticking its head through the drinker/feeder holes in the cage front, but writers of 100 years ago were adamant that this was an excuse offered to disguise the fact that the bird was defective in this characteristic.

To elaborate further on potential faults, a good crest should not stand up in front nor should the front show any tendency towards a point. The ideal crest will be completely round, i.e. every point of the circumference should be equidistant from the centre. Whilst on the subject of the centre, this should be distinct but small and round. It should not appear as a line dividing one side from the other; nor should it be a point from which two lines or partings appear running backwards to right and left, destroying the appearance of perfect radiation. Equally, the crest should not be without a centre, having instead a tuft of feathers, as in a mop crest. Other faults to avoid are an oval crest where the corners, particularly at the front, seem to have been cut away; the sides, particularly behind the eyes, should not be pinched in or inclined to appear as 'horns'.

Although today, neither the actual colour of the crest nor the amount and distribution of variegation are of importance, during the heyday of the Crest, great importance was placed on the colour of the crest, with classes being provided for various combinations. The most sought-after were clear birds with a dark crest, the term dark crest meaning precisely that, no light feathers at all being allowed. Birds with an even wing variegation and a dark crest were considered to be easier to breed and, therefore, whilst sought-after, less important. These two variations were considered to be the zenith in crest breeding and, whilst other variations were accepted, their worth was considerably less. The five other classes were: unevenly marked, heavily variegated, grizzle crested, self greens and clear crested.

The crest is the most important characteristic of the breed but standards are written for the balance of the bird. Whilst the Crested Canary Club in the UK does not have a written points standard, the COM does allocate points to the various areas of consideration. Interestingly, such a standard did exist in the UK during the heyday of the Crest.

Today's standards call for the body of the bird to be well rounded and in proportion somewhat similar to the Norwich. Actual size is of secondary importance; in fact, all points being equal, the smaller bird should take preference at an exhibition. The back should be broad and well arched with the chest full and well circled. The tail should be short and narrow with the wings fitting close to the body, not crossed at the tips and not extending beyond the root of the tail. The bird should stand well across the perch on short legs with thighs and hocks well set back. A difficult condition to meet is that of feather quality. The feathers of the body need to be as short as possible, lying tightly to the body with no trace of loose feathers or frilling being evident. In practice, however, as it is necessary for the feathers of the head to be long to give the desired crest, the problem is evident. One method of controlling feather length is the use of intensive (yellow) birds as one of a pair and, whilst the frequent use of such birds will result in a loss of size in the crest itself, the pairing is recommended occasionally.

The crestbred is a very important part of any stud in that, if the necessary quality is absent from this bird, good-quality Crests will not ensue. In addition to being the vehicle from which good Crests are bred, the crestbred is an exhibition bird in its own right, having gained this distinction in 1888. The body, tail, wings etc. of the crestbred should follow exactly the same format as those sought in the crested example. The head is the most important feature in that it should be large and broad and the front of the skull above the base of the beak should be wide. The feathers should be so dense that they immediately rise from the base of the beak. This flow of feathers should gradually expand in width as the crest falls gracefully over the skull to the back of the head, its density causing it to fall over the eyes at the side. This fall of feather is known as 'browing'.

As with most of the heavy breeds of canary, the Crest has a reputation for not being a prolific breeder and it is advisable to have foster parents in readiness. This point apart, methods of management described in Chapter 1 should ensure relative success with this breed, although with heavily-feathered specimens the side crest feathers over the eyes, and the feathers around the vent, should be trimmed when pairing.

Little show training is required with the Crest but, as with all long-feathered birds, the bird normally benefits from being hand washed prior to an exhibition, with the crest itself being groomed. This is an area that perhaps is contentious, in that it allows for accusations of unsportsmanlike behaviour. The author, however, is of the opinion that the pulling out of an odd feather demonstrates the keenness of a breeder to present his bird in prime condition and is far more praiseworthy than entering a bird in a show with no thought to its presentation. It is not everyone, however, who agrees with this view and, taken to its logical conclusion, it can lead to all sorts of undesirable practices. It is a fact, however, that the old Crest fanciers went to extreme lengths to 'dress' their Crests, and C.A. House in his book stated that: 'a stage has been reached when the best Crests cannot be staged on the show bench, without a hairdresser being in attendance'.

GERMAN CREST

One of the greatest contradictions within the world of aviculture is the German Crest, the contradiction being that the show example is a crested coloured canary exhibited under type canary judges, who base their judging on shape and posture, whilst the Consorts, necessarily kept to breed the Crests, are exhibited as normal coloured canaries and are judged as such.

Although somewhat mysteriously mentioned in German avicultural literature as far back as the early seventeenth century, prior to the real recognition of coloured canaries, it was not until 1963 that a show standard was presented.

In simplified terms, the exhibition German Crest is a coloured canary – of any colour or mutation – carrying a crest. In consequence, the usual rules regarding the breeding of coloured canaries, which are described in detail in Chapter 5 should be applied. The sole difference is that consideration needs to be given to perfecting the crest and, in the case of lipochrome examples, ensuring that the crest is not only perfect in shape but also consists of dark or grizzled feathers or is totally clear. Variegation in the crest is not acceptable.

Taking the latter point first, within the concept of the COM judging standards, variegated birds can be exhibited only if they are symmetrically variegated, i.e. following the technical marks pattern described for Border canaries (p. 116) and then only in the special classes provided for them. Non-self German Crests can be exhibited, providing that they are symmetrically variegated but also, as previously mentioned, carry a dark, grizzled or clean crest. It is thus easy to see that the breeder of this species has a major challenge on his hands, more particularly so if he wishes to exhibit the non-crests in the coloured canary classes, as variegation on the head would result in the bird being disqualified.

In the self examples, regardless of mutation, no variegation whatsoever is allowed; one foul feather or a light claw will result in the bird's disqualification.

In an attempt to keep the breed separate from the main crested type breeds, the standards permitted include particular mention of the bird's general shape, which should follow that expected for coloured canaries, and the 'plus' factors associated particularly with the Gloster canary. This latter is probably nearest in shape to the German Crest, i.e. with short tail and legs, a round head and body and, very importantly, with the crest blending into the neck.

The ideal crest should start above the beak, continue over the top of the eyes and then round to the back of the neck in a complete crest, i.e. it should not blend into the neck. Unlike most crested examples, the German Crest should not carry a central point, but a small $7/100$–$11/100$-inch (2–3 millimetre) 'parting' from which the crest evolves.

The rear of the crest in a superb example should curl upwards (similar in shape to the tail of a male duck), thus displaying a small area devoid of feathering in the back of the neck.

From this description, it is not too difficult to determine that major faults associated with the crest are: loose feathering, a central point, an overlarge parting.

The length required is 5½ inches (140 millimetres) with a tolerance of ± ⅕ inch (± 5 millimetres).

GLOSTER

G.R. Wolfendale
Gerry Wolfendale has been breeding canaries for over 50 years. As a boy, born and raised in the north-east of England, his initial preference was for Border canaries and native British species. Although he had a slight flirtation with the Gloster just prior to World War 2, it was not until his demobilisation from the army, following active service, and his subsequent re-settlement into civilian life in the west of England that he took up breeding and exhibiting Glosters seriously. Over the years he has been responsible, with others, for setting up the first All Gloster Show, for founding the International Gloster Breeders Association and for joining together the various specialist Gloster breeders societies into the Gloster convention. As well as proving his prowess on the showbench, Gerry has judged extensively in the UK, as well as officiating and lecturing in South Africa, Canada, Italy and the USA.

Credit for the creation of this breed is given to Mrs Rogerson, a lady who admired all miniature things, as was illustrated by her garden and its contents. Assisted by a Mr Madigan, who supplied very small Border canaries, Mrs Rogerson crossed these birds with crested Roller canaries. Their debut on the showbench was in the Any Other Variety classes at the 1925 British National Exhibition, where the judge was John McLay. Mr McLay was a noted breeder of Crest canaries and brought the new breed to the attention of Mr A.W. Smith who was so instrumental in promoting the species. The bird appears in two forms: a crested version, known as a Corona, and a non-crested version known as a Consort. Mr A.W. Smith is credited with having given these names to the breed.

Other breeders in the Cheltenham area of Gloucestershire took up the challenge to develop this breed. As with all breeds, much time and dedication had to be given to attain consistency in the quality of the stock produced. Amongst these pioneers Messrs Mullis, Widdowes, Bowd, Lockstone, Thornton, Phillips and Bryant come particularly to mind as it was they who formed the original specialist club, which was set up to assist breeders and to promote the new variety.

This club was called the Gloster Fancy Canary Club. It was around 1949/1950 when the author was first introduced to the Gloster Fancy and also to these gentlemen and he has pleasant

A near-perfect crest on a Gloster canary.

memories of their enthusiasm. Bert Widdowes was particularly helpful to anyone needing assistance.

It is rewarding, having been involved with the breed since the late 1940s, to see how its popularity has developed. All-Gloster shows, promoted by various specialist societies, are held in many parts of the UK and also in other countries. At the 1984 English National Exhibition, 1,400 examples were on view and the support also given to the Scottish National Exhibition clearly illustrates the overall, non-regionalised popularity of the breed.

In the 1960s, the five specialist Gloster societies created the first Gloster convention. Their aim was to co-ordinate, formulate and regulate all things relevant to the Gloster Fancy. Today the convention is attended by representatives from twenty-three societies, which further emphasises the growth in popularity of the breed.

It is said by many people that it is more difficult to breed and, to keep small, a diminutive bird such as the Gloster canary than to maintain size in larger breeds. To make it more difficult, one has to breed a small crested bird (Corona) with a small plainhead (Consort). The head consists of a neat little crest of feathers. Most important in this context is the composition of the feathers. They should resemble the petal of a flower with a dark black vein and green edging. It is most essential that the feathers of the corona

181

Gloster canary: Corona.

Gloster canary: Consort.

radiate from its centre, and that the corona is positioned centrally on top of the skull. It should be in line with both eyes and have a nice droop of feather, but should not obscure the eye. If the bird is held at eyelevel in a showcage, half of the eye should be discernible. The back of the corona should blend into the nape of the neck. The tip of the beak should just protrude through the front of the corona. A too-short crest is just as bad as an overlong one. In the normal corona, the feathers are dark regardless of the colour of the body of the bird. Clear coronas are, however, quite common and fully accepted, as is the black-flecked version known as 'grizzled'. Normally these birds are exhibited in classes along with clear examples. All versions of the Gloster appear with the intensive (yellow) and non-intensive (buff) feather. They can be found in the normal yellow ground colour and in the mutated dominant white form. The cinnamon mutation is also seen in the Gloster with some examples of the agate mutation also appearing in recent years.

Faults in the corona usually arise when the feathers radiate from a point which is not central. Noted faults include: a narrow-fronted skull with a broad back (or vice versa), a shield-shaped crest, a broad-fronted crest tapering to nothing at the neck, a tufted crest, splits in the crest, holes in the crest at the nape of the neck, and wispy hairy crests. The ultimate in crest perfection is an evenly rounded corona with a good centre and a lovely dark rib and green web, evenly distributed feathers radiating from a definite centre, and just-discernible eyes. This means a corona not too long or too short. When perfect, the bird is a truly pleasing sight and will attract 20 points in the standard of excellence.

The Consort, the partner to the Corona, is a very important factor in obtaining good Coronas because, if the head of the Consort is out of balance, it cannot be expected to place a corona of feathers in the right position. The head should be in context, nicely rounded, even all around with a slight rise over the top of the head from side to side, or from eye over to eye. The rise is not prominent as in a Border canary. Always remember side to side. When viewing a Consort, one should visualise placing the corona on the head of the bird. If the front skull is narrow, it will give a mean effect on the Consort and a shield effect on the Corona. The same applies if the back skull is narrow, as it will give a hole in the nape of the neck.

The length of feather on the heads of both the Corona and Consort is important if a perfect crest is to be produced. A tip given many years ago by Bert Widdowes is to hold a Consort in the hand, with the head protruding between thumb and forefinger, and, using a small coin and starting at the nape of the neck, to drag the feathers forward. By doing this, it will be possible to see if the frontal skull feathers extend to the end of the upper mandible. If so, the Consort can be considered suitable for the production of good Coronas.

A heavy eyebrow on the Consort is very desirable, going along above the eye and blending and tailing off into the side of the head, beyond the eye.

To complete the head, close attention must be paid to the beak. It must be a small beak. A coarse beak on such a small bird would spoil the head completely. A maximum of 5 points are awarded for the beak.

Being such a small bird, any defect will show up immediately. The Gloster is a short cobby bird. The back, from the neck to the rump is straight and the front of the bird is slightly rounded and well filled in, and curves from the under beak to the vent in a gentle flowing manner, without any prominence. That gentle roundness must not be heavy; the cut-away through the legs to the vent must be clean cut. Wings must be close fitting to the body, just meeting at the base of the rump. Shoulders should be well defined and not too heavy. Looking down at the bird, the shoulders should be defined, but not too fine, just matching in with the roundness of the body. Too-long flight feathers will spoil the effect of the short cobby bird that is being sought.

The neck is very important and it must mould into head and body without blemish. Long wry necks are out and too heavy a neck is also unacceptable. A cut-away under the beak is a very bad fault. The neck must be full so that the head, neck and body are in conformity and balance. Wings again should be short and well braced to the side of the body. If they are too long, the balance is spoiled. They should meet at the base of the rump, just touching each other. If they are too long they will overlap, which is a bad fault. If they are too short, however, a gap is left at the base of the rump. Do not get discouraged if these faults appear as it is a question of balancing your pairings.

The tail must be short and held well together. If too long, or fanshaped, the contour of the bird is spoiled. The legs must be small and delicate. If a bird has coarse legs or too big a beak, it will look like a hawk and such examples should be avoided at all costs. Only ½ inch (12.5 millimetres) should be visible between the perch and the underside of body. Anything at all which is big and coarse is undesirable as far as the dainty little Gloster is concerned.

It is the quality in feather which gives the lovely silky effect to the little Gloster and this is essential in such a small bird. It is a bird of contour; any defect in shape or feather quality will be highlighted. It must be emphasised that quality in the colour and feather is of major importance. It must be both rich and soft and must look alive and vibrant, not dull and lack-lustred. The breeder must control these factors. The author uses self green birds to acquire this asset, although it must be emphasised that the green sought is of a lovely bright green colour, with black lacing. Dull green birds with a brassy sheen are avoided. By being discriminate and not using this type of bird, the desired aims should be achieved.

When colour is discussed what is meant is the lovely rich ground colour that comes through in the body looking vibrant and alive. If green or variegated birds are used as the basic stock colours it is suggested that the desired beauty in your birds will be built up. Buff (non-intensive) to buff pairings have been employed over the years

as a means of building up size and shape but skill is also required
with the use of good-ground-coloured birds. Deviation from these
rules can lead to lumps appearing in your stock, a point that will
be covered later. Buff (non-intensive) to yellow (intensive) pairings are those most used by breeders today. In the past, yellow
(intensive) stock was brought into a breeding plan only once every
3 years. Of the resulting youngsters, the buff birds were of a good
colour and, if mated back to a well-coloured buff, the results were
generally acceptable. Care should be taken, however, to use only a
good short cobby yellow, not a long thin example. More yellow birds
are being bred now because with the extra classification for these
birds at exhibitions, there is more encouragement for breeders to use
these birds in their studs.

Youngsters bred from yellow pairings, especially good-coloured
buff birds, should be used in a stud wherever possible. These good-
coloured buff birds paired to a good-coloured buff mate will enhance
the overall quality of the stud and will avoid the production of dull,
lifeless, coarse-coloured examples. The use of variegated, self and
three-parts dark birds are recommended. A good example is a bird
with a grizzled crest paired to a three-parts dark, or a foul or a self
bird. This pairing will give all the different forms of variegation
needed from clear to self. There is one more point to mention whilst
on the subject of bird markings. Breeders in the last century were
preoccupied with producing evenly-marked birds and the Gloster
provides the perfect subject to resurrect these aims. Imagine a clear-
bodied Consort with two evenly-marked wings and small pear-
shaped markings above each eye. Another example is a Corona,
again, with evenly-marked wings, a clear body and a dark crest. This
is known as a '3 pointer'. To conclude this section it is again
recommended that stock should be closely and constantly studied
and evaluated for good ground colour and variegation.

The author's methods of stock management will now be
described. It must be stressed that these are the systems that have
proved successful for the author. Some ideas may be helpful to other
breeders who may be unsuccessful currently in breeding Glosters. It
must also be remembered that climatic conditions vary in different
parts of the world. The author has visited the USA and has seen
premises where fanciers are obliged to breed in basements, where
winter temperatures are often below 32°F (0°C) and summer temperatures are over 104°F (40°C). Another example is South Africa
where the temperature only ranges between 72°F (22°C) in winter

185

and 100°F (38°C) in summer. Successes in breeding are noted in both instances, which confirms that systems of management can vary tremendously and, if your existing system is successful, no changes should be made.

The birdroom used by the author is of timber construction and approximately 12 × 6 feet (365 × 182 centimetres) × 7 feet (213 centimetres) high with two large adjoining flights outside. Access holes allow entry to the birdroom from the flights. There is a full bank of cages running along the back of the birdroom. These are built on the shelf principle. Using slides, one can have single cages, double cages or other combinations. The cages are 36 × 15 inches (900 × 380 millimetres) × 12 inches (300 millimetres) high and the cage fronts are fitted with retaining clips which allow them to be removed completely for cleansing purposes. Care has been taken to ensure that the drinker and feeding holes are not over-large, thus preventing youngsters escaping. The usual seed hoppers, with either top-hat or jumbo drinkers, are used, together with fountain-type containers for grit, which keeps it from being soiled by excrement.

Perches are ½ × ⅜ inches (12 × 10 millimetres) in cross-section with a shoulder, and are of the twist-on design. The perch ends about ½ inch (12 millimetres) from the back of the cage as a small amount of movement prevents corns or hard pad forming on the toes. Fertilisation of eggs is not adversely affected, as has been proven by their use over a number of years.

With regard to floor covering, nothing else is used but good clean sterilised pine sawdust. A variety of nest pans are used and plastic, clay etc. have all been used to advantage. The nest pans are fixed to ½ inch (12 millimetre) metal strips, 6 inches (150 millimetres) in length, by means of cheesehead bolts with nuts and washers. The pans are placed between the perches so that the lip is just under the perch; thus, when the female leaves the nest, she rises and any eggs or babies will drop back into the nest and not onto the floor. An additional benefit is that, when youngsters void their excrement, it drops onto the floor. A small rake is then used to keep the floor clean.

It is recommended that best-quality seed mixtures are purchased, even though less expensive mixtures may be offered elsewhere. Greenfoods are always made available to the birds and the use of wild plants is traditionally preferred, particularly chickweed. Unfortunately, owing to the increase in the use of insecticides, this has been impossible. Aerial spraying carries on the wind for a great distance and it is better not to take the risk than to lose one's stock. Years of building up a stud can be lost overnight. The use of comfrey, lettuce, or spinach, which can all be grown in a garden, are recommended as substitutes.

Glosters are very free breeders and, as parents, are beyond compare. It is firmly believed that the best stock which can be afforded should always be purchased and the young should always be culled heavily, regardless of their origin. Birdrooms should never be overcrowded and stock should always be kept to manageable numbers. Overcrowding leads to troubles such as feather plucking, fighting and all the associated problems. Line-breeding is practised by the author, with three family lines running. These are inter-mixed when it suits the strain. One important factor is the strict keeping of records. These are essential references for keeping track of your stock. Even whilst breeding, a card-index system is used, with all details being transferred later into a stock book. It will be found that some pairs are more compatible than others but only the very best of these youngsters should be retained. These are then paired up in the line-breeding system.

Using these systems, a reasonable crop of average-to-good birds should be produced with the odd superlative examples appearing. These are the birds from which stock should be built up. It must be emphasised that ruthlessness in culling of stock is essential. Any birds with a tendency to revert from existing standards should be culled immediately. The aim should always be to progress in quality year by year; it is rare for rapid improvements to appear. As a further means of control, closed rings are fitted to all youngsters bred. This is invaluable in keeping track of all birds in a stud.

The most anxious time for many fanciers is spring, the start of the breeding season. To make things easier, good preparation is required and, with live stock, it is a full-time job all the year round. Immediately after the last show of the season, the cocks are placed into long double breeders, one per cage. If they are put together, they will fight. Females have indoor flight cages, with access through a pop-hole into outside flights 6 × 6 feet (182 × 182 centimetres) × 8 feet (244 centimetres) high. This has been found invaluable for bringing hens into tip-top condition. In particular the upward flight from ground to upper perch, a distance of 6 feet (182 centimetres) is most beneficial. At the end of February, the females are brought in and placed side by side with their selected mate in a double breeder, with the divider about ½ inch (12 millimetres) from the back of the cage. In this way, they get to know each other and breeding usually starts at the end of March.

During the period in which the females are in flights, they are offered staple mixed canary seed with greenfoods. Remember it is winter and the choice of greenfood is restricted; therefore, brussel sprouts or dark cabbage are used together with softfood which is offered twice weekly. Emphasis is placed on having the males a shade ahead of the females in condition. Before placing the birds in cages, the claws should always be cut. The vents should also be trimmed but the sensory feathers on the female should be left alone as they act as ticklers and bring the male into condition for a good mating. If you are not sure about cutting the claws, get an experienced fancier to show you. If you accidentally cut the claw a bit too high and it bleeds, get a bit of charcoal and apply this to the cut. If charcoal is not be readily available, light a match, blow it out, and there is your charcoal. The charcoal coagulates the blood, thereby stopping the bleeding. Always remember that, when claws are cut and vents trimmed, it will set birds back a week in condition.

Have all your nest pans, linings and pedestal stands ready before the season starts. Commercially-produced linings are not used by the author, preference being given to those made by a lady who does a lot of crocheting. Made out of wool, these linings wash well and will last for at least 10 years. For nesting material, a hessian sack is used cut down into 1 inch (25 millimetre) squares; this is teased out in odd moments while studying the birds. It makes a wonderful, neat compact little nest. If a female is given some pieces to play with, you will see that she runs the strand of hessian backwards and sideways in her beak. When she takes it right back in her beak, this is a sign that she is nearly ready for mating. It is recommended that the male should be a little ahead in condition compared with the female. His singing and dancing on the perch will encourage her to start calling to him. When she crouches on the perch and insistently calls him, withdraw the slide and mating will take place. If they agree and only slight bickering occurs, let them stay together; she will build her nest in a short time. It has been noticed that, after the act of mating has occurred, the male will throw his head backwards and from side to side and give a low song of pleasure. This is a sure sign of a good mating and the resulting eggs will be fertile.

Much water will be drunk at this time and quantities of grit will be devoured. For most of the year, a good mineralised grit is used and, at breeding time, oyster-shell grit with a sprinkling of charcoal. The female will lay her first egg about a week later. If the spring is a cold one, the eggs are left in the nest as she lays them. If not, as the eggs are laid, they are taken out and replaced with a china or clay egg. On the third evening, the eggs are put back in the nest. The 'T' card is marked with the date the eggs were laid and when they are due to hatch. Six days after the eggs are set, they are examined. If they are full, they are fertile; if clear they are discarded and the nest is taken away. Within a fortnight, the female will be ready again for mating. This saves time and it works well.

The evening prior to hatching, a little eggfood is offered because, for the 14 days of the incubation, no rich food is given, just seed and water. Next morning you should notice egg shells on the floor; do not be anxious to see how many chicks she has. The less disturbance the better, is the rule, and the female should be allowed to vacate her nest in her own good time. Do not worry if there are no egg shells, she may be a day late. Just be patient.

Only a small portion of eggfood is offered, morning and evening, and the amount is increased daily as the chicks grow. At lunchtime, milksop, just bread soaked in milk is offered, preferably hot, with a touch of glucose on the top of the cube of sop, and a small sprinkle of maw seed. Use dried full-cream milk as it is less likely to turn sour in the summer.

Inspect your nests every day, making sure there are no mites. The author sprinkles anti-mite powder into all nests; it will not hurt the babies. Keep your eyes open and, if any babies are pulled out of the nest, place them in the palm of one hand, cover them with your other hand in a cup shape, then gently breathe into the hollow. When you see the legs move, place the chick back with the others and it should be alright. If you close ring, which you should do at about 5 or 6 days after hatching, take the chick in your hand and, with your fingers, close the three front claws together. Slide the ring over to the back claw, pull it over the back claw and then, with a pointed match stick or finger, pull out the back claw; it will not hurt the chick. They feather up by 14 days. Up to 12 days after hatching, if the nest gets badly fouled, change it with a clean pan. Do not do this after 12 to 14 days as you will find the chicks will leave the nest and you will not get them to return.

From 18 to 20 days, the female will be showing signs of wanting to nest again. Put another pan in and be sure to make nesting material available, otherwise she will strip the babies of their downy feathers. Normally, babies are weaned from 22 to 24 days simply by separating them from the parents with a wire slide. Eggfood is offered to young and adults; the young will quickly learn to feed themselves, assisted by the male through the wires. The female by now will be sitting on eggs again, while the first round of youngsters will be weaned and should be placed in a double breeder on their own. Usually about six are placed in a double breeder and a Border show cage is hung on one door while access to food is provided by the other door. Keep this cage on for 2 weeks, then hang on a Gloster show cage; the birds never forget this early training. After a month they should be placed in longer flight cages, then eventually in the outside flights. Keep your youngsters busy; give them plenty of room in the flight to dodge each other and they will get stronger in flight day by day. Place a dish of water daily in the flight as all birds love bathing.

Moulting is a critical point in both unflighted and flighted birds. Our first round of unflighted youngsters start dropping their feathers at about 10 weeks of age. You will notice that the body, neck and head are the principal areas of the moult. When they go into the next yearly moult they also drop their primary and secondary wing feathers, plus their tail. Hence the term 'unflighted' for first-year birds and 'flighted' for birds in their second year and above.

In both flighted and unflighted birds, care through the moult is of paramount importance. This is a time of stress in their lives, so everything is needed to help them through the moult quickly. The author is a firm believer in giving birds sufficient room to fly and always provides long flight cages. When they are seen flying from perch to perch in strong flight, then is the time to turn the birds into outside flights. It is most important that they have access to inside flights, so that they can seek inside shelter in intemperate weather.

To help build up their strength, greenfoods are offered – homegrown spinach, lettuce and, most of all, comfrey. Comfrey is a wonderful herb and has many medicinal uses; as a greenfood it is way out on its own.

Throughout the moult, softfood is still offered but is gradually reduced. It is given fresh once a day, then on alternate days, finishing up with twice a week. It is then offered once a week throughout the winter months, until the approach of spring.

Keep a careful watch on your stock during the moult, especially on your Coronas; give them their spell in the flights to gain strength. Upward flight from the floor to the top perches, usually about 6 feet (182 centimetres) will build up their wings and shoulder muscles. As wing carriage is most important, this is most essential. Hazel wands in varying thicknesses are used for perches.

Watch your Coronas; any damage to the crest will usually prove disastrous. It is, therefore, better to remove them from the flight and put two in a double breeder then, when they have quietened down, put them into single cages. The same applies to good Consorts. Hang a training cage on the breeding cage door; this will steady them down ready for show training. When in stock cages, hang a bath on daily, particularly on sunny days, as the birds will dry more quickly. As an adjunct, the author removes birds from the stock cage and sprays them; all this is good for steadying up your birds.

Now comes the time for comparison of your stock. If line-breeding, place your first round in a row of cages, side by side. If your planning is right, you will see an improvement each year. Do not expect miracles. Building up a winning strain takes time and patience. Pick out the likely birds (birds not quite up to standard) and place them back in the flights, but please do not discard any birds until they are fully through the moult.

Coronas are never through the moult until October, and sometimes later in the case of the second round. Coronas should be regularly sprayed. Pin feathers in the head will be noticed and these are always the last to break. Pay care and attention to keeping your cages clean and use a good sawdust. Sterilised pine sawdust is probably the best as there is no dust in it. Change perches frequently as this stops the feet getting dirty and keeps them in good condition. Most important are your seed hoppers: empty the seed into a sieve, clean it and wash out the hopper regularly once a week. You cannot take enough care of your birds if you wish them to breed successfully.

You should have now reached the point where you have assessed your stock, and made up your pairs for next year's breeding. Now is the time to sort out your show teams, trying to cover both Corona and Consort classes. Shed yourself of all your surplus stock, always keeping a few spare females. Never overload your shed with Glosters. They will need plenty of room, light, good ventilation and good food. Give them all the care and attention you can and they will repay with countless hours of pleasure.

The only way to learn whether you are on the right course with your breeding plans is to put your birds on the showbench and compare them with birds of other Gloster fanciers. Imagine the thrill of your first red ticket and, better still, the quiet satisfaction of

191

knowing you are on the right track. Progress each year, little by little; this is where the enjoyment lies.

The show cages are standard. If in doubt, specifications can always be obtained from a Gloster specialist club. During the breeding season when the weather is fine, get the cases out, touch up the paintwork both inside and outside and attend to the cage front and black drinker. Make sure your perches are the right ones and that they are securely fastened. There is nothing worse for a judge than to try to assess a bird's good points with loose perches. A wise maxim is that a good bird needs a good setting, i.e. a sound, clean, well-painted and well-appointed cage. There is nothing worse than to see a tip-top bird in a dirty, dilapidated cage.

As the show season progresses, you will see that your birds take on a grubby appearance. This is where the true fanciers can score. One week before the show date, the birds should be given a good bath, followed by a gentle spraying in the next 2 days. The softer the water, the better. No further spraying should be given and the final treatment, known as 'silking', can be applied. The author uses a piece of silk (preferably Shantung), large enough to roll up into a ball. He holds the bird in his left hand and the ball of silk in his right hand, so that the edge of the silk shows between his clenched fingers and the palm of his hand. Starting at the base of the neck, he draws the silk down the bird, holding it about ⅛ inch (3 millimetres) away from the feather and using the little finger of the right hand as a guide just barely touching the bird. If you touch the feather with the silk, it will become scorched, but the action of drawing the silk over the feather creates a static which, in turn, draws out the oil in the feather and gives that lovely gloss on the feather. Please practise on birds of poor quality rather than show birds. You will soon become accustomed to the use of the silk.

Do not forget to dress the legs and beak. Make sure that they are clean and the beak and claws well-trimmed. Take some witch hazel in a small container, dab a small piece of cotton wool in it and gently rub the legs, claws and beak. The witch hazel will leave a faint shine, as well as being good for the feet, legs, claws and beak.

Ensure that your cage is well supplied with seed, in both floor hoppers and end hoppers and make sure that there is a black water-drinker. After judging, when you are allowed in the hall, ensure that your bird has water and seed. Show officials and stewards are good in this respect but nevertheless it is wise to make certain.

On return from a show, place the birds back in their stock cages with fresh water and seed. If a pick-me-up is needed, put two drops of whisky in the black drinker; it works wonders. Some people prefer to use small squares or cubes of sponge cake, with two drops of sherry on each cube of cake. Take a word of warning, do not overshow your birds because, if you do, they may not give you a good breeding season. You will have taken too much out of them. As in all things with birds, gently does it.

Enjoy your hobby.

Note
Although much of this chapter covers ground previously described in Chapter 1, because of Mr Wolfendales' long experience in the Fancy it has been printed verbatim so that an alternative point of view on various points could be expressed.

G.B.R. Walker

LANCASHIRE

The Lancashire canary was probably created in the first quarter of the nineteenth century from a cross between the Old Dutch canary and the original crested Norwich. The Old Dutch – long extinct – was a large, upright, heavily-feathered bird and the Crested Norwich of the period was a medium-sized smooth-feathered canary with a neat daisy-type crest.

From its inception, the Lancashire's popularity was confined entirely to fanciers living in the cotton towns of Lancashire and breeders jealously maintained a standard for show that allowed no variegation whatsoever, other than a grizzled (grey) crest. This exacting standard, and the need to maintain size, may have prevented the variety from gaining wider popularity but its influence on the Canary Fancy was immense and, in the early 1880s, Lancashires were used to transform the neat Norwich, in both its plainhead and crested forms, into a much larger and more substantial bird. Indeed, for a quarter of a century afterwards, the crested Norwich was to reign as the 'King of the Fancy', whilst the Lancashire, the 'Giant of the Fancy', continued to languish as a minority breed.

It appears from show reports and the Fancy press, that Lancashires were readily attainable up to World War 1 and the records of the old Lancashire and Lizard Canary Association, which promoted the variety's interests, reveal that, as late as 1938, a few birds of high quality were being exhibited. They were, however, in the hands of very few fanciers and no Lancashires survived when peace returned in 1945.

Today's Lancashires have, therefore, had to be recreated, a straightforward if time-consuming task, given our knowledge of the bird's history and the abundance of crested canaries and Yorkshires available. The aim is to produce a massive bird with a 'horseshoe'-shaped crest. Size and length are readily attainable from the modern Yorkshire, which unlike its small, thin ancestor of 100 years ago, has been developed to a size and substance that approximates to the standard of the old Lancashire Plainhead. The difficulty breeders have encountered, however, is that, when compared to a crested canary, the close short feather of the modern Yorkshire inevitably leads to a lack of length of feather in the crest. Although many good-sized Lancashires are now staged, the Coppies invariably tend to be difficult in crest properties, particularly in the length of the frontal feathers.

This is a challenge and fanciers wishing to take up Lancashires could do worse than start with an oversized rough Yorkshire mated to a Crest or Gloster canary with an abundance of frontal in the crest. Thereafter, by selective breeding from the progeny, they can play their part in recreating this fine old breed.

In the days when the Lancashire was most popular, it was referred to as the Lancashire Coppy rather than the Lancashire canary. At one time its name was almost superseded by 'Manchester' but breeders in other 'Lancashire' towns protested vehemently and the original name was retained. The original name, 'Coppy', was something of a misnomer in that it only referred to the crested version, the Lancashire obviously appearing in both crested and non-crested varieties. 'Coppy' is the term now adopted for the crested version with the expected 'Plainhead' for the non-crested version.

As with all crested breeds, in normal circumstances, a Coppy should be paired to a Plainhead which, following the accepted inheritance pattern, will give 50% Coppy and 50% Plainhead young, on average.

In the Lancashire, the largest variety now bred, size is most important with feather quality being of little significance; in consequence buff (non-intensive) to buff pairings are common. The use of yellow (intensive) birds should not be totally discounted however as these birds, with their finer feathers, although distracting from the general impression of size, can be most beneficial in

1 Buff Green Norwich

2 Clear Buff Norwich

3 Buff Cinnamon Norwich

4 Clear Buff Yorkshire

5 Variegated
Yellow Yorkshire

6 Clear Capped Gold Lizard

7 Clear Capped Silver Lizard

8 Broken Capped Gold Lizard

9 Broken Capped Silver Lizard

10 Clear Yellow Border

11 Cinnamon Variegated Yellow Border

12 Three-Parts Dark Cinnamon Border

13 Yellow Green Border

14 Variegated Yellow Fife Fancy

15 Clear Buff Fife Fancy

16 Clear Yellow Irish Fancy

17 Variegated Buff Irish Fancy

18 Munchener

19 Berner

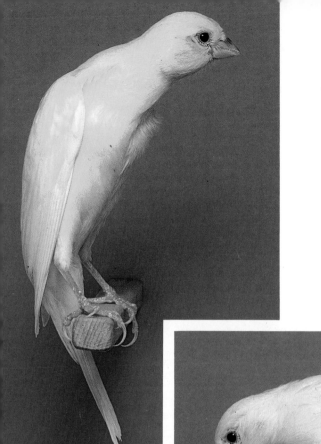

20 Scotch Fancy

21 Belgium Fancy

22 Raza Espanola

23 Japanese Hoso

24 German Crest

25 Lancashire Coppy

26 Lancashire Plainhead

27 Variegated Crestbred

28 Variegated Crest

29 Heavily Varie[
Buff Corona G

30 Blue Corona (

31 Heavily Varie[
Buff Consort (

32 Northern Dutch Frill

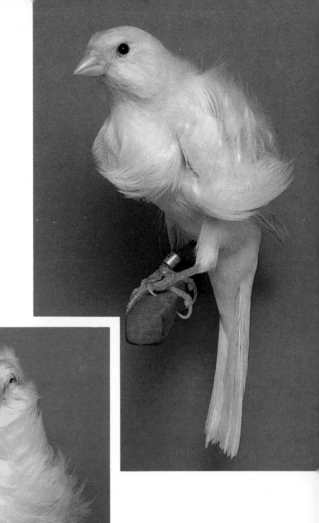

33 Parisian Frill

34 French Frill

35 Swiss Frill

36 Giboso Espanol

37 Gibber Italicus

38   Coloured Frill

39   Padovan Frill

Japanese Crest

Crested Columbus Fancy

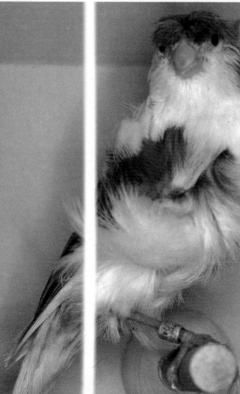

42   Florin

43 Black-Hooded Red Siskin Male

44 Black-Hooded Red Siskin Female

45 Wild Canaries

46 F$_1$ Hybrid

47 Intensive Red

48 Non-Intensive Red

49 Intensive Clear Gold

50 Non-Intensive Rose

51 Intensive Clear Gold Ivory Satinette

52 Clear Recessive White Satinette

53 Clear Red Dimorphic Male

54 Clear Gold Dimorphic Female

55 Intensive Bronze

56 Non-Intensive Bronze

57 Dimorphic Bronze Female

58　Intensive G

59
Non-Intensive
Blue

0   Intensive Red Brown

61   Silver Brown

Dimorphic Red Brown Female

63 Dimorp
 Agate

64 Dimor
 Agate

65   Silver Agate

66   Intensive Red Agate

67   Intensive Gold Agate

68   Intensive Rose Isabel

69   Non-Intensive Red Isabel

70 Dimorphic Red Agate Opal

71 Non-Intensive Rose Agate Opal

72 Recessive White Agate Opal

73 Non-Intensive Gold Agate Opal

74 Intensive Green Opal

75 Dimorphic Rose Bronze, Opal Paste

76 Recessive White Brown Opal

77 Dimorphic Rose Brown Opal Fem

78 Intensive Rose Isabel Pastel

79 Non-Intensive Gold Ivory Isabel Pastel

80 Dimorphic Red Agate Pastel Male

81 Silver Agate Pastel

82 Dimorphic Bronze Greywing M

83 Non-Intensive Gold Ivory
Green Greywing

84 Silver Brown Pastel

85 Recessive
    White Brown
    Ino Male

86 Recessive
    White Brown
    Ino Female

87 Dimorphic Gold Brown Ino Fe...

88 Dimorphic Red Brown Ino Fe...

89 Non-Intensive Rose Brown

90 Intensive Gold Isabel Satinette

91 Silver Isabel Satinette

Dimorphic Gold Isabel Satinette Female

93 Non-Intensive Rose Isabel Satinette

94 Silver Blue Topaz

95 Silver Agate Topaz

96 Non-Intensive Red Agate Top

improving certain aspects of the overall appearance of the bird. Until the newcomer to the species is totally conversant with the breed and the type of youngsters produced by his stud, the more usual buff (non-intensive) to yellow (intensive) pairing is recommended. This can be achieved by using either a buff or yellow cock with its opposite mate, i.e. the pair being a Coppy and a Plainhead.

Unlike other varieties of canary, variegation on the body, wings or tail is not permitted on the show bird, the only dark feathers allowed being a grey or grizzled crest.

Although the current-day show standard makes no mention of the colour of the plumage, commentators of yesteryear were insistent that the colour should be pure, with no doubt existing in a spectator's mind as to whether the bird on view was a yellow or a buff. Colour feeding is not permitted. Care must be taken when selecting breeding pairs to ensure, wherever possible, that over-buffed birds, whether yellow or buff, are not paired together, the probable expectation of such a pairing being even more overbuffed youngsters. It is an irrefutable, if inexplicable, fact that the constant pairing together of clear birds results in a loss of plumage colour. The use of ticked birds which, together with variegated to full self birds, is known to be beneficial in improving colour, is recommended but only as one of the pair.

The only peer of the Lancashire in respect of size is the Parisian Frill and standards call for the breed to be 8½–9 inches (220–230 millimetres) long, which, when combined with the overall substance of the bird, accounts for 25% of the points awarded at shows. In order to assist the bird in achieving this great size, length of tail, although it obviously must be in context with the body and neck, is important. In some countries, only young birds can be exhibited and, as the replacement tail feathers following the first full moult are longer than the originals, it is advantageous to remove the tail of the young bird soon after it is weaned, thus forcing the production of longer tail feathers.

The only aspect of the Lancashire to be considered of more importance than overall size is the coppy (crest) or, in the case of the Plainhead, the head. To carry a good crest, the head of the Lancashire needs to be long, very broad and with a tendency to flatness, although not actually flat; this applies equally to Coppy and Plainhead. In addition, the Plainhead should carry long feathers on its head which lead to heavy, overhanging eyebrows; the non-overhanging feathers should be long and droopy.

The coppy or crest of the Lancashire must be neat with a well-placed, well-defined centre. From the centre, the crest should flow to the front of the beak and radiate regularly from the tip of the beak to the sides in a good horseshoe-shaped pattern. The back of the skull should show no trace of crest radiating smoothly into the feathers of the neck. One of the problems confronting breeders of Lancashires is to get the front of the crest flowing properly over the beak. In some instances this fails to happen because the short bristly feathers, present in all canaries, are very dense and grow upwards rather than, as normal, lying down over the beak. Where present, these upward-growing feathers invariably divide the crest, causing it to be 'split fronted'. When purchasing stock, this fault should, wherever possible, be avoided, whether in Plainhead or Coppy birds, as its existence could cause resultant youngsters to be spoilt. It is always easy to introduce faults but it is very difficult to eradicate them.

As far as show standards are concerned, the shape of the Lancashire is judged on two areas: the neck and the body. Inevitably, however, they form an integral part of the whole and, unless in proportion to each other, will render the bird of no use for exhibition, although there may be a case for its retention for breeding purposes. The neck needs to be long, thick and straight although, if too thick, it will lose some of its apparent length. The head should blend into the neck and at no time should it appear to be suspended on a stalk. The shoulders should be broad and well filled but should not show any of the prominence of the Yorkshire. The back should be long, broad, well filled in and as straight as possible. This will enable the bird to adopt the required erect stance. With all long birds, the tendency is for the back to curve and, whilst a slight curvature is accepted, this must be minimal. The breast should be very full and prominent with the body tapering, albeit not too finely, and it should show plenty of side.

The wings should be long and, ideally, should lie neatly down the back onto the tail with no crossing at the tips. With large examples, particularly buff ones, this is difficult to achieve but should be looked on as the ideal. As previously mentioned, the tail should be long.

The stance of the Lancashire is important in order for it to demonstrate its overall vastness and, when in a show cage, it should stand tall, erect and bold. Its legs should be stout, in accordance with the rest of the bird.

196

As with many of the larger breeds, the Lancashire is not the best of feeders and it is advisable to have pairs of the smaller, more prolific species available as foster parents. Being larger and, therefore, needing more nourishment in order to grow to the required size, it is recommended that smaller breeds are asked to rear no more than two Lancashire youngsters. Apart from this necessary precaution, up to weaning no special management techniques need to be adopted other than the precautionary trimming of the heavy feathers around the vent with a small pair of scissors, taking care to avoid the bristly 'feeler' feathers.

Once the birds have been weaned, however, it is essential that the diet offered is rich in protein to encourage growth to the vastness required. Also, to avoid damage to the crest in the Coppy youngsters, it is recommended that food and drink holes in cage fronts be made larger than normal.

The show standard for the Lancashire canary is given on p. 202. This can be compared with the standard required in 1908 by the Lancashire and Lizard Association which is given below:

Head: coppy	25 points
Neck (for fullness and thickness)	10 points
Back (round full and long)	10 points
Wings (meeting at tips)	5 points
Length of bird	20 points
Length of feather	5 points
Position (upstanding)	10 points
Condition and cleanliness	10 points
Colour	5 points
Total	100 points

Show Standards

COLUMBUS FANCY

Colour	15 points
Feather quality	10 points
General condition	10 points
Body	20 points
Head	20 points
Wings	5 points
Tail	5 points
Legs	5 points
Size	10 points
Total	100 points

CREST

Crest (or head in crestbred)	45 points
Beak	5 points
Base of skull	5 points
Shape	10 points
Feet and legs	5 points
Feather quality	10 points
Presentation	10 points
General condition	10 points
Total	100 points

GERMAN CREST

Crest	20 points
Shape	15 points
Colour	20 points
Feather quality	15 points
Size	10 points
Presentation	10 points
General condition	10 points
Total	100 points

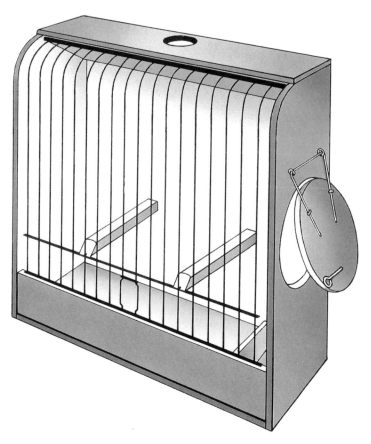

GLOSTER

Crest (or head in Consort)	15 points
Central point (or eyebrows in Consort)	5 points
Shape	20 points
Tail	5 points
Feather quality	15 points
Presentation	10 points
Feet and legs	5 points
Size	15 points
General condition	10 points
Total	100 points

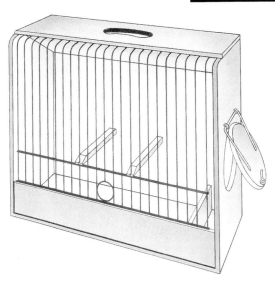

LANCASHIRE

Crest (or head in Plainhead)	30 points
Neck	10 points
Back	10 points
Size	25 points
Position and shape	15 points
Condition and presentation	10 points
Total	100 points

FRILLED VARIETIES

COLOURED (MILANESE) FRILL

Opinions seem to differ considerably on the origin and subsequent evolution of the Coloured, or Milanese, Frill. Today, few examples are exhibited outside Italy and correspondents report that those that are exhibited in that country inevitably are the white version, better known as the Milanbianco.

Original attempts, it would seem, were directed towards the production of a white frilled canary very similar in appearance to the Parisian Frill. The experiments appear to date back to the 1920s, when Parisian Frills were extensively imported into Lombardy. Fanciers from Milan and Monza, in particular, set about the task of producing non-variegated white, yellow and red examples of a new breed, combining the characteristics of the newly-imported Parisian Frill and the established variety of Northern Dutch Frill.

Although contemporary reports are somewhat hazy, crossbreds from these pairings would seem to have been further outcrossed to common white canaries. The white offspring from these pairings were, in turn, bred with the crossbreds which were produced from Yorkshire and Lancashire canaries by crossing with common white canaries, probably German Hartz or Roller canaries.

Understandably, the resultant offspring varied in size and extent of visual frilling and they were subdivided into three varieties:

1) Milanbianco Gobbuto (a hunchback);
2) Milanbianco Leggero (small);
3) Milanbianco Gigante (large).

It is probable that the birds kept today are descendants of the Gigante and, whilst it has proved impossible to keep the size consistent with that of the Parisian Frill, large birds have been bred, notably during the 1950s, when the breed reached the peak of its popularity.

At the same time, experiments were carried out to introduce to the breed the various ground colours and mutations of the coloured canaries. (Those available at the time were notably the red ground colour and the agate, isabel and ivory mutations.) This was attempted by outcrossing the Northern Dutch Frill to coloured canaries and gradually improving both colour and frills until a bird roughly resembling a coloured Parisian Frill was produced. All colours, with the exception of yellow, green and variegated, were accepted. Unfortunately, the best Frills, by virtue of their voluminous feathering, could not present the various colours at their best and records show that the most acceptable were found in the gold ivory and orange versions. Colour feeding was not accepted, nor is it accepted today, although it remains an academic point as there would appear to be no true Coloured Frills still in existence.

Some birds, which are said to be Coloured Frills but are, in fact, colour-fed Parisian Frills, appear occasionally at World Shows but are exhibited in the Any Other Variety classes.

All Milanbianco examples exhibited must be totally lipochrome to be considered perfect but allowances are made for a maximum of three tick marks each of up to 100 square millimetres in size.

In all other respects, the show standard required of the Coloured Frill is almost word for word that of the Parisian Frill and, rather than be repetitive, it is suggested that would-be breeders of this variety should refer to the section on the Parisian Frill (p. 214) to determine the standards and methods of management.

FRENCH FRILL

The exact date of the creation of the French Frill, or the breeds used to produce it, does not seem to be well documented. Contemporary writers describe it as an ancient breed but its existence is not documented in avicultural books published at the end of the last century. The centre where it gained popularity, and the area where, no doubt, its standards evolved, is the Mauges area in the west of France. Other types of frilled canaries were also bred in Picardy, Flanders, northern France and Belgium, but these are described as being heavier and they, like so many other breeds, have become extinct. Through the years the bird has been given several different names, i.e. 'Bossu Frisé' (Frilled Hunchback), 'Frisé du Sud' (Southern Frill) and 'Hollandais du Sud' (Southern Dutch – a name still used today in some circles). Although it can be neither proved or disproved, given the bird's shape and its frill pattern, it is not unreasonable to suppose that the Belgium Fancy and Northern Dutch Frill figured to a great degree in the bird's family tree. It is also known that, in turn, the bird has been used in the creation of the Swiss Frill (p. 218) and the Gibber Italicus (p. 206).

The French Frill is a bird of posture and position and, in consequence, great care must be taken to ensure that young birds become used to the confines of a show cage and will, almost on request, adopt the show position. Obviously, access to show cages attached to flight cages is the first step; the bird should gradually be accustomed to spending more and more time within the show cage so that it does not take fright and damage itself when handled by strangers at a show.

The position of the bird on its perch is all important when judging is taking place. Although the ideal position is described as following a figure seven, in fact a slight crescent effect, with the tail touching or just passing under, the perch is preferred. By necessity, however, the neck and head must protrude from the body horizontally, a position which is difficult to attain. The head, which should be small and easily distinguished from the neck, should, when viewed from the front, give an appearance of the two eyes and head of a snake. It should be held forward on the neck, which itself should be long, thin and horizontal and well detached from the shoulders, which should appear to protrude. The back is slightly curved with the tail continuing this curve up to or just under the perch.

The ideal length of the bird is 6½–7 inches (160–170 millimetres); lack of size is considered a greater fault than an oversize example.

The frilled feathers are restricted in each instance; whilst well defined, they should not be over-long. Firstly, the feathers of the shoulder should develop from a central parting. These frilled feathers should continue evenly down the entire length of the back but should not extend beyond it. It is extremely important that, when viewed from above or from the front, the frills are equal in length, shape and position. The second area of frilled feathers is on the flanks, where perfectly-shaped outward frills should curl upwards towards the flight feathers. The third area of frilled feathers is on the chest, where shell-shaped feathers should form a well-developed but not an overdeveloped rose formation, giving the illusion of a flower in bloom. The feathers of the neck and head, together with those of the thighs, should be short and neat. The wing feathers should lay neatly down the back and should not droop onto the flanks. The tail should be narrow and straight with a slightly V-shaped end.

In order for the bird to achieve the correct position, it should grip the perch firmly with both sets of claws, with the knee joint obviously being held rigid.

The French Frill appears in both intensive (yellow) and non-intensive (buff) forms and the pairing of one to the other, in order to keep the balance of feathering at a correct level, is recommended. Birds from clear through to self are accepted as exhibition specimens and the use of variegated stock to maintain size, feather quality and evenness of colour is recommended. Undersize birds tend to prove less reliable breeders than their larger-sized counterparts and thus care must be taken to ensure that overall size does not diminish within a stud.

Frills of all descriptions tend to be less ready and prolific breeders than a good many non-frilled varieties but the French Frill is one of the easier types and is recommended to the breeder wishing to start a stud of frilled breeds.

GIBBER ITALICUS

Beauty, it is said, is in the eyes of the beholder. In the author's opinion this must be so to explain the fact that the Gibber Italicus and its new Spanish equivalent, the Giboso Espanol, were first of all created and then subsequently persevered with. The word beauty, as generally accepted, appears to be a misnomer in the case of both these varieties.

Attempts to breed the Gibber Italicus started in the 1920s and it seems probable that its ancestors were primarily the French Frill with some introduction of the Belgium Fancy (Bossu Belge). As with other breeds, two types of the variety existed for many years. Initially, experiments took place in the Mediterranean areas of southern Italy, the aim being to produce an Italian version of the French Frill. Slowly, experimental breeders in central Italy, then Milan, Monza and Como, took up the challenge so that finally two versions of the bird existed: the Hunchback Frill of northern Italy and the Cerlino of southern Italy. These birds differed little in shape but the influence of the northern climate resulted in birds being produced with longer feathers. The more southerly based breeders decided to 'improve' their Cerlino by crossing only intensive (yellow) birds together, using line-breeding and inbreeding techniques. Ultimately, they achieved smaller birds with thin short feathers and breasts, stomachs and thighs devoid of plumage. This gave rise to the bird's nickname – the 'striptease' canary.

French and Belgian breeders called the new canary the Bossu Frisé Italian (Italian Frilled Hunchback) and managed to delay its official recognition by the COM until 1951. A Mrs Giamminola of Como is credited with persevering with the variety and, at the time of recognition, the Italian breeders chose the name we use today –

the Gibber Italicus. The Frilled Hunchback of northern Italy seems to have disappeared completely.

With the continued appearance of the Gibber Italicus we must reconsider previously-held opinions that the homozygous intensive (yellow) bird is non-viable. Certainly, no non-intensive (buff) specimens appear on the showbench. Apart from one breeder out of the several with which the author has communicated, no one claims to have viewed a non-intensive example. All breeders of the variety confirm that it is a difficult bird to breed, with small numbers of offspring being produced each year. The birds are also noted for their nervousness. The latter characteristic could be attributed to the policy of intensive inbreeding, which could also account for the poor breeding results. If as previously thought, the homozygous intensive (yellow) bird is non-viable, this could also explain the low number of youngsters that are reared to maturity. This conjecture, however, does not explain why no non-intensive (buff) birds appear. The outcrossing of the Gibber Italicus to non-intensive examples of any other breed should confirm whether or not this breed is in fact a homozygous intensive (yellow). All youngsters from such pairings would be heterozygous intensive (yellow) examples should the case be proved. Alternatively, the presence of *just one* non-intensive (buff) bird in the progeny would disprove the theory. Should the latter occur, Gibber Italicus breeders might well need to study their birds further in order to determine whether the difference in the structure of the feathers of intensive and non-intensive examples is identifiable. If so, this would allow them to make scientifically-based pairings with the associated benefit of not producing non-viable homozygous intensive (yellow) birds. Alternatively, should the presence of the homozygous intensive (yellow) be confirmed, breeders of other varieties might well have to reconsider whether such a bird could be useful to them either to eliminate certain faults or to enhance any particular characteristic. Surprisingly the author is unable to find anyone who has carried out this extremely easy experiment.

On then to a description of the bird itself. The ideal size is 5½–6 inches (140–150 millimetres) and, as with most of the 'hunchback' species, the Gibber Italicus has working and resting positions. The working position, i.e. the one by which it is judged, is one in which the bird firmly grips the perch, stands very erect and extends its neck and head horizontally with the beak held forward. To persuade it to attain this position, it is normally necessary for the judge to

207

scratch gently on the bottom of the cage; if the bird has been properly trained, then the required figure seven position will be produced, albeit only for a few seconds. It is not unreasonable to assume that, because of its lack of plumage, the bird finds it difficult to balance in this 'unnatural' position and is thus incapable of holding it for long periods. It is obvious that the bird finds difficulty in balancing because, when it is in the resting position, the tail is often used as a third leg (in the manner of a tripod in photography) to support it against any available object while the legs are held wide apart to maintain balance.

The plumage is short, crisp and scanty and, with the exception of the three frilled areas, is required to be held closely and smoothly to the body.

As with most other frilled varieties, three areas of frill are sought. The mantle is formed by the feathers of the back which are divided by a central, longitudinal parting, giving a symmetrical frill between the two wings. The jabot or craw consists of frilled feathers on each side of the breast curling forwards and inwards forming a frilly 'shirt front'. Again, these frills must be symmetrical. The third area of frills – the fins – are composed of two bunches of feathers, starting from the region of the thighs on each side of the bird and rising upwards.

Of equal importance to the frills are the featherless areas of the bird. These are the legs and thighs and an area of 100 square millimetres on the chest. The legs of the Gibber Italicus are long in relation to its overall size and this characteristic is given even more emphasis by the naked legs and thighs.

The neck of the Gibber Italicus should be long, carrying smooth feathering, and should stretch forward horizontally when in the show position. The head should be small and shaped like the head of a snake. Large eyes, surrounded by a ring of bare skin, and the flat skull, give the impression of the bird having a large beak.

The shoulders need to be narrow but high, with a symmetrical mantle and long wings held close to the body and a long narrow tail, carried vertically, touching the perch when the bird is in the show position.

Because of its lack of feathers, the Gibber Italicus, although hardy, is susceptible to changes in temperature. In warm surroundings, the frills are normally profuse and distinct. When it is cold, however, the feathers fold smooth and tight against the body, as they do when the bird is tired or not in prime condition. This fact must be taken into consideration when thought is being given to exhibiting this variety.

The general management of the Gibber Italicus is as for other breeds with two minor additions. Firstly, because the birds find balancing difficult, they often roost with one foot gripping the cage front (this in fact, seems to be the characteristic position). In consequence, sufficient perches need to be installed to allow each bird in a cage to have the opportunity to roost in this manner. It is also suggested that birds of this variety appear to consume double the amount of seed than birds of comparable size in other breeds. This could be explained by the bird's need to produce more energy to keep warm than those with normal plumage, and care must obviously be given to ensure that seed hoppers are constantly full.

GIBOSO ESPANOL

The most recent variety to be accepted by the COM is the Spanish version of the Gibber Italicus – the Giboso Espanol. The author's attempts to determine the exact parentage of the variety have proved fruitless but, given its shape and stance, it is reasonable to assume that the French Frill and the Belgium Fancy figured prominently. As with the Gibber Italicus, the bird is seen only in an intensive (yellow) form but, being relatively new, it would appear that, as yet, it does not suffer too greatly from the breeding and nervousness problems of its Italian equivalent.

Whilst there are many similarities between the Giboso Espanol and the Gibber Italicus there are also several fundamental differences.

To start with the Giboso Espanol is a larger bird, the ideal size being 6¾–7 inches (170–180 millimetres) and, for the bird to properly display its posture characteristics, it is necessary for it not to be undersized.

The working, or show, position is the most important feature and, in consequence, it is here that most points can be won or lost on the showbench. The total silhouette is, in general terms, that of the continental figure one, i.e. almost an inverted V, and it is this position that a judge will need to coax from a bird when evaluating it. As is normal with birds of posture and type, this is done by gently scratching the bottom of the cage.

By examining each of the specific areas, it can be determined how this position can be achieved. Because of its importance in the over-

209

all shape, the neck is considered a good starting point. From the top of the shoulder to the end of the beak (when pointed downwards) the distance should be 2½ inches (65 millimetres). The neck should be thin and, although scantily feathered, should show no baldness nor frilling. The head should be small in proportion to the neck and body and should be in show position with its beak pointing forward. Although the feathers of the head will be very small and thin, no trace of baldness is allowed, even around the eyes – a basic difference from the Gibber Italicus – nor are any frills permitted. The head will be reminiscent of a snake's head, oval in shape with a flat skull giving an impression of very large eyes and a large beak.

The chest is judged on a combination of two quite different qualities. Firstly there should be an area devoid of feathering from the base of the neck extending as far as possible down the chest. Secondly, the frilled feathers of the jabot (craw) should start from the extremes of the rib cage and curl outwards and inwards to meet symmetrically in the centre, covering the sternum. Whilst it is considered important for the sternum to be covered, the frills should not attain too much exaggerated prominence.

The wings and back are judged as a single entity. The frills of the mantle should be symmetrical, well formed but not too large, and should not extend above the shoulders, the other feathers of the back being small and held closely to the body. The long wings, given the thinness of the feather quality, are generally well placed to lie properly along the back. Contrarily, also because of the thinness of the feather, they often tend to cross over at the ends, which is considered as great a fault as if they are 'dropped'. The length of the back is considered ideal at 2¼ inches (60 millimetres).

With a length of 2⅛ inches (55 millimetres), the tail is an important feature of the Giboso Espanol, not least because, with the stiff-legged stance of the bird, it is used as a balancing aid, particularly as the variety tends to spend more time than other breeds crawling around the floor. This, in consequence, leads to the feathers of the tail being either fanned out or broken which, in turn, leads to problems of posture when the bird is on its perch in the working position. Ideally, the tail needs to be tightly held, as close as possible, and dropping at an angle of 170° with the line of the wings.

The fin frills should be small but well defined, starting at the top of the femur and growing vigorously out and upward over the wings.

One of the most important features of the Giboso Espanol is the form of the legs. They need to be very long (2⅛ inches or 53 millimetres) and rigid up to the second joint where the 'elbows' are required to bend forward. With the feet firmly gripping the perch, pushing the bird upright, the position of the shoulder should be immediately above the erect legs. The front of the thighs should be devoid of feather and the muscles should protrude from the femur, giving an impression of having no bones. Those feathers on the back of the thighs should be thin and straight but should be evident.

The Giboso Espanol would not win any beauty contest judged by the author but is, nevertheless, an interesting and challenging addition to the range of canaries available. Because of the peculiarities of the breed it is certainly a challenge to present it in a clean and perfectly feathered form on the showbench. Whilst normal management techniques should prove adequate to breed the bird successfully, additional baths and more regular cleansing of cages will be required because of the length of time that the bird will spend on the floor.

JAPANESE FRILL (MAKIGE)

The most recent breed to reach Europe is the Japanese Crested canary, known in Germany, where it was first imported, as the Makige. Although presented at the 1984 World Show it was absent at the 1985 exhibition and cannot therefore be accepted by the COM as a recognised breed until 1987 at the earliest.

As with many breeds in existence today, the Japanese Frill was created by originally pairing together two different established species. In this instance, the breeds involved were the Belgium Fancy and the Northern Dutch Frill. From this pairing two breeds were created: the Kanto Frill and the Kansai Frill. Details of these birds are not readily traceable but, either as a result of a further selective breeding programme of one or the other type, or as a combination of the two types, the Japanese Frill was created. Following this, further outcrosses must have taken place as the bird now exists in the full spectrum of the coloured canary variables, i.e. with red, yellow or white ground colour and in intensive, non-intensive and dimorphic feather types. Clear and variegated examples exist and are considered suitable for exhibition. The author has not been able to ascertain whether the various melanistic mutations have been introduced but, as no points are awarded for colour of variegation, there would appear to be little merit in developing different phenotypes except for their intrinsic beauty.

As with the Japanese Hoso, the Frill is a bird of position and posture, with the position being of paramount importance.

The description of the ideal bird has been prepared by the Japan Frill Canary Club and, whilst the English translation from the original Japanese is somewhat confusing, in the absence of any further information, an attempt will now made to give details of what is required.

The bird can be said to be one of the least elegant on the showbench in that it is required to be square shaped when viewed from either the front or the back. The bird achieves this by carrying its legs widely set apart and by adopting a figure-seven stance when in the show position. It is required to stand at a 90° angle to the perch and, very importantly, to hold its head so that it looks forwards at all times.

The head, as with the Belgian Fancy, is required to be small, oval, narrow and sleek. The neck should be slim and long and should have a clear distinction from the shoulders. The shoulders themselves need to be square, very wide and proud.

In order for the legs to be wide set, the body of the bird needs to be round, thick and long, extending well back behind the legs. The legs are required to be very thick at the top of the thighs and to join the body in a central position. The thighs, when the bird is in show position, need to be fully exposed, with the whole leg held at an angle of 90°. The bird needs to grip the perch strongly in order to hold this position. The tail should be long and drop naturally when not in the show position.

As a frilled species, the extent and direction of the different frills are obviously important, as, in fact, are the non-frilled areas of the plumage.

Starting at the neck, the standard calls for feathers to be clearly parted from under the beak to the throat.

The first of the frills is found in the area of the breast, where a round shape of widely formed, large feathers, starting at the extremities of the breast blend inwards and join at the centre of the breast.

The remaining feathers of the body should be thick and intertwine like folded hands at the centre of the abdomen.

Large feathers from the upper part of the legs, where they join the body should flow upwards over the back of the bird to the centre, whilst long, but not excessively long, feathers from the inside of the thigh should flow upwards and outwards around the back of the thighs.

This leaves the main frilled feathers on the back of the bird. Here a well-defined centre from the top of the shoulder to the centre of the back should be evident. From this central parting, long thick feathers should curve upwards and outwards.

The wings should be held tightly to the body with the tips lightly crossed.

As yet no points standard has been approved and no mention is made of either the ideal size or the type of show cage to be used.

With little accurate information on which to work, no real comment can be made on specialist breeding techniques but it is reasonable to assume that the techniques observed with other frilled varieties should be followed. Obviously also, where red birds are being bred, colour feeding will need to take place (see p. 56).

NORTHERN DUTCH FRILL

It is generally accepted that the Northern Dutch Frill is a direct descendant of the 'Old Dutch' canary. The 'Old Dutch' is described as a massive bird and many of today's varieties are said to be its descendants. Type, as such, did not seem to have been a prime consideration and much greater value was placed on the length and massiveness of the bird. A good bird was said to have been over 8 inches (200 millimetres) long with a large shapely head, a neck of good length and thickness, broad shoulders which were not elevated, a broad full chest and a stout body with long wings and tail. The feathering was said to have been somewhat coarse – although the feathers were of a fine silky texture, they were a little open and rough.

The Northern Dutch Frill has been in existence for at least 100 years and it seems likely that it originated by selection from 'Old Dutch' birds displaying some form of frilling until features were fixed. The only apparent differences between today's standards of excellence and those published at the turn of the century relate to the bird's stance and the presence of frilling on the rear of the neck.

Nowadays, to be considered perfect, the bird should carry three areas of frilling, greater importance being placed on symmetry than the actual volume of frill. The frills of the back (the mantle) should curl out from a central parting, those of the chest (the craw) should curl inwards to a central parting, giving a shell-like appearance, and those of the flank area (the fins) should be well formed, bulky and rising towards the shoulders. The frilling should be profuse but crisp in appearance, with each particular area of frilling separate and different from the other. Whereas, in the past, the presence of a small shell-like frill on the back of the neck was accepted, if not considered ideal, today's standard of excellence requires that all feathering, except in the three frilled areas, should be perfectly smooth. Past standards also required the bird to be massive in length, today's bird should not be small but a limit of 6¾ inches (170 millimetres) is considered ideal. The Northern Dutch Frill is similar to the Belgium Fancy in shape except that it carries its head higher and the frilling of the mantle masks the prominent shoulders. The legs are long, inclined to be stilty, and are only slightly bent, allowing the bird to stand almost erect; an angle of 85° from the horizontal is the ideal. The tail is long and narrow and continues in a straight line from the back. The standards of 100 years ago allowed the bird to stand in a slightly curved position with its tail touching the perch. The head is small and neat with a fine beak and sits on a neck rather long and thin for a bird of such size.

The bird appears in intensive (yellow) and non-intensive (buff) forms and no consideration is taken of whether the bird is clear, ticked, or variegated; thus normal rules of pairing together opposites (i.e. intensive (yellow) to non-intensive (buff)) apply.

As with all frilled varieties, in the weeks leading up to a show, the birds should be accustomed to being handled in their show cages by a variety of people. As a means of keeping the plumage clean and in good condition, spraying is preferable to offering the bird a bath.

PARISIAN FRILL

As with many breeds, the creation of the Parisian Frill is the result of the work of a number of breeders in a small geographical area. In this instance, as the bird's name suggests, breeders in the Paris area of France met, in about 1867, and decided to form a club to improve upon the extent of curling in the feathers of the partially-curled or frilled Dutch canaries, which were available at the time, and also to increase their size and popularity. It took 53 years for the full transformation to succeed and, in 1904, when the club changed its name to La Societé Serinophile 'La Nationale', a standard was raised and a new breed created. This standard was updated in 1978 to give the one used today.

The Parisian Frill is one of the largest breeds of canary existing today; with a size of around 8 inches (200 millimetres) and a wingspan of 12 inches (300 millimetres), it is an imposing sight on the showbench.

The frills of the Parisian Frill are set in two sections: the principal frills and the secondary frills.

Looking at the principal frills, we start with:

1) The chest area (the jabot or craw), where the frills curl forwards and inwards from each side towards the centre to give a shirt front or closed-shell appearance.
2) The fins – large paired frills starting on the thighs and rising upwards around the wings. These obviously need to be long and well curved.
3) The feathers of the back – the mantle. These large frills, starting from a central parting at the base of the neak and continuing almost to the rump, should fall outwards across the secondary flight feathers.
4) At the base of the mantle, a fan-shaped frill area falling between the wings exists in good examples. This is known as the bouquet.

The secondary frills are found on the head, neck and rump. The head should carry three distinct types of frill:

1) Curled upwards rolling over each other to form a cap;
2) Curled downwards on both sides of the head;
3) Sweeping each side of the face to give 'full' cheeks.

There should also be a number of 'whiskery' feathers coming from directly around the area of the beak. The neck should carry a collar of curled feathers in the form of a ruff to act as a break between the frills of the head and those on the back.

Rump feathering should commence at the start of the femur, where the tail starts to take form, and must be long and bushy. The feathers should separate where the tail commences and fall down each side, covering as much of the leg as possible, similar to the sickle feathers of a cockerel.

On the legs, short silky feathers are to be found but, in the preferred type, these are covered by the feathers of the rump.

The wings are required to be carried close to the body and must not overlap. The long secondary flight feathers must not extend over the large flight feathers.

The tail must be long, straight and closely folded. The end should be square, a large fork being a fault, as also is a raised tail.

A major characteristic of the Parisian Frill, and one that is unique to the breed, is its claws. In all other breeds, claws are required to be short and straight. With the Parisian Frill, they should be long and bent and, ideally, of a corkscrew pattern. They should also be thick.

This breed is said to exist in three feather types:

1) Fine silky feathers, i.e. buff (non-intensive). These are the most sought after and make the bird ideal for exhibition.
2) Medium soft feathers, which are intermediate between yellow (intensive) and buff (non-intensive).
3) The genuine yellow (intensive).

Invariably the buff birds are those which win major prizes at shows and it is therefore human nature to pair buff to buff in order to increase the number of showable youngsters. To a limited degree this is acceptable but care must be taken not to overdo these pairings for, if care is not taken, the feathers will become limp, the curly frills will become indistinct and the fins will slope excessively and mingle with the breast curls.

In an attempt to encourage greater use of yellow birds, the Societé Serinophile la Nationale de France (La Nationale) – National Posture Canary Club of France (The National) – in 1977, introduced a rule whereby a yellow Parisian Frill could be declared a champion if it scored 88 points at a show rather than the normal 90 points. Unfortunately this rule only applies to French shows and so the breed is still likely to be lost in other countries.

It is also a mistake to pair clear bird to clear bird indefinitely as the youngsters from these pairings, as with many other breeds, will lose size, feather quality and colour. Variegated and self birds are accepted totally as show birds and the use of these birds in a stud is highly recommended.

The Parisian Frill, although a large bird, is robust and proves to be a ready breeder. It can be kept and reared successfully using the management system detailed in Chapter 1. Care must be taken when pairing frills. Any breeder not knowing the precise origin of his birds must study them closely before pairing to ensure that the same fault is not present in both members of a pair. It is regrettable that we still have no precise knowledge of the inheritance details that standardise specific frills but, if we apply basic genetic principles, we may be able to prevent certain faults from multiplying. By applying the basic Mendelian ratio (i.e. 1:2:1) to the fins, for example, and assuming the pairing of a male with good fins to a female with one good fin and the other one pointing downwards, we can expect, on average, 50% of the young to have good fins, 25% to have good fins but to carry the factor for bad fins, and 25% to have bad fins. The problem is that it is impossible to differentiate between the 50% incapable of producing bad fins and the 25% visually good but capable of producing bad fins. It is therefore possible to perpetuate the problem for many years. Unacceptable as it may seem the only way to overcome the problem totally is to cull all birds displaying the fault so that, in theory at least, the fault will disappear totally in 3 or 4 years. This principle applies, of course, to every other facet of the bird and, with so many different frills involved, one can begin to realise the challenge involved in consistently breeding good examples.

Once bred, great care must be taken with the youngsters to ensure that no damage occurs to their feathers. Ideally they need moulting out in twos or threes in cages of approximately 24 × 32 inches (620 × 320 millimetres) × 15 inches (380 millimetres) high. Food and water should be placed as high as practicable as the chicks must be encouraged, wherever possible, to keep off the floor. This is for two reasons:

1) To avoid feather damage.
2) To encourage the bird to present itself properly.

One of the major assets of a winning Parisian Frill is the elegant way in which it stands up and presents itself. To ensure that the bird exercises its feet, perches of different shape and size are recommended.

As with most breeds, show training is essential and the best way to encourage birds to accept and become familiar with a show cage is to attach one to the front of a normal cage with the doors open to allow easy access. Putting titbits into the show cage will encourage the bird to enter and, after a period of time, it will prove easy to get the bird to enter the show cage when required. This is particularly important for two reasons:

1) Handling of Parisian Frills is to be discouraged because of fear of feather damage.
2) The show cage can be used as a spray cage.

Parisian Frills need access to a bath or to be sprayed once a week.

They should be only lightly sprayed; if made too wet, the feathers may stick together and spoil the overall image.

To summarise, the Parisian Frill is a magnificently elegant bird that presents a major challenge to would-be breeders. Its many different frills need to be full and positioned as described but, above all, these frills must, where applicable, be even and symmetrical in appearance.

SWISS FRILL

At first sight the Swiss Frill resembles the French Frill almost totally and it seems probable that it shares the same ancestors, although this cannot be proved. The major difference between the two is their show position. The French Frill is required to stand in a continental figure seven position whereas the Swiss Frill stands in a curved form not dissimilar to the Scotch Fancy.

It was about 100 years ago that frilled canaries were first exhibited by a French breeder, at an exhibition organised by the Ornithological Society of Basel in Switzerland, and they aroused great interest. The birds were referred to as Parisian Frills although it seems improbable that they resembled the birds which are known by that name today. All the birds on display were purchased by Swiss breeders and great interest was shown in reproducing them. By 1899, it is reported that frilled canaries were very numerous throughout the Basel region. Little by little, the desire grew to breed frills, but of a smaller size than the birds normally seen. At this time, the Dutch Frill made an appearance in Switzerland and thoughts were given to judicious cross-pairings to arrive at the preconceived phenotype. Breeders then visited all the main areas in France where various types of frilled canaries were being bred, and purchased stock for their experiments. The towns of Roubaix, Lyon, St Etienne, Gard and Strasbourg were high on the visiting list. As one might imagine, the indiscriminate crossing of the various breeds created an incredible mixture of birds of different types and standards. From these experiments, however, a bird somewhat resembling the sought-after phenotype evolved and a standard of excellence was drawn up. Although purchases of birds from other areas continued, it was on a much more discriminate basis, with breeders only buying stock that would enhance the quality of the birds in their breeding rooms. Evidently the judging of the new race was carried out in a severe manner, causing vast numbers of breeders to abandon the cause. However, a small number of idealists remained and formed a club to encourage further participation. The standard of excellence that had been drawn up was officially adopted and remains unchanged to this day.

The shape of the bird in show position is that of the new moon, its overall length being 6¾ inches (170 millimetres) with ⅕-inch (5 millimetres) tolerance. The head should be long and fine, ending in a delicate beak, and should blend into a long thin neck. The frills are, of course, of major importance and are in three forms. The back frills should be full, spreading up and out from a central parting on the back and fully symmetrical in appearance; they should rest on the shoulders. The frills of the chest should not be too voluminous but, from a central area on the outer chest, should again spread inwards symmetrically in a basket shape. The third set of frills, those of the flanks, should spread out and up over the wings. All other areas of plumage should be short and neat. The tail should be long, tightly held together and curved inwards so as to touch the perch. To attain the show position, it is necessary for the bird to grip the perch strongly and hold its legs rigid. For a bird to do this almost on command, extensive show training is required.

The Swiss Frill has a reputation, as have most frills, for being difficult to breed. The likelihood of producing several youngsters from a pair in one season is certainly acknowledged as improbable – three or four from two nests is considered satisfactory. The breed is, therefore, recommended rather as a secondary stud for more experienced breeders who enjoy a challenge than one suitable for beginners.

As with most type varieties, the Swiss Frill appears in intensive (yellow) and non-intensive (buff) forms and to have a balanced stud one needs to be paired to the other. Variegated birds are not penalised and their value in a stud for retaining vigour, size and colour is not to be underestimated.

Show Standards

COLOURED FRILL

Colour	15 points
Size	10 points
Feather quality	15 points
Presentation	10 points
Craw	10 points
Flanks	15 points
Head	5 points
Wings	5 points
Tail	5 points
Mantle	5 points
General condition	5 points
Total	100 points

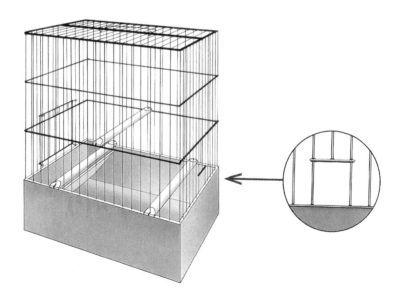

FRENCH FRILL

Presentation and shape	10 points
Size	10 points
Feather quality	10 points
Shoulders/mantle	10 points
Craw	10 points
Fins	10 points
Legs and thighs	15 points
Tail	5 points
Wings	5 points
Head	10 points
General condition	5 points
Total	100 points

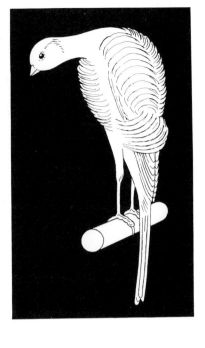

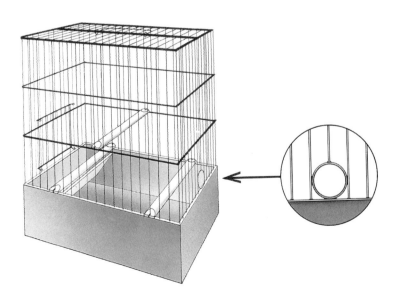

GIBBER ITALICUS

Position and shape	20 points
Head	6 points
Neck	15 points
Feet	15 points
Wings	6 points
Shoulders and mantle	10 points
Tail	6 points
Craw	10 points
Flanks	6 points
Size	6 points
Total	100 points

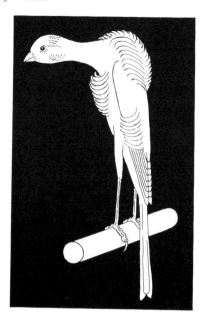

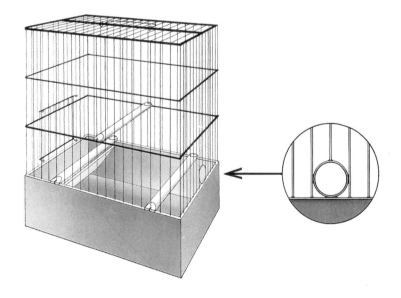

GIBOSO ESPANOL

Position	20 points
Neck	20 points
Legs	10 points
Craw	10 points
Wings/mantle	10 points
Size	10 points
Head	5 points
Tail	5 points
Fins	5 points
General impression	5 points
Total	100 points

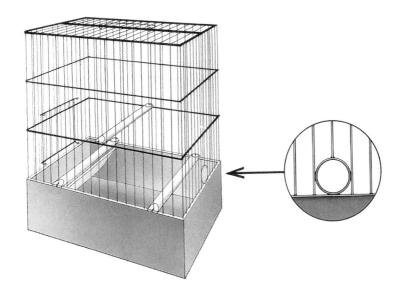

JAPANESE FRILL

Stand	40 points
Head and neck	10 points
Mantle	10 points
Frills of the chest	10 points
Frills of the lower stomach and thighs	5 points
Throat	5 points
Shape	5 points
Tail	5 points
Size	5 points
General impression	5 points
Total	100 points

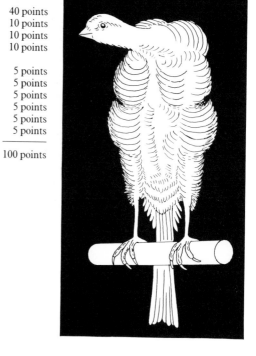

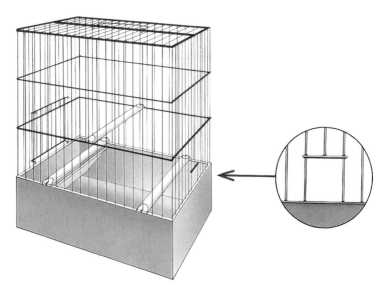

NORTHERN DUTCH FRILL

Position	15 points
Size	15 points
Mantle	15 points
Fins	15 points
Craw	15 points
Stomach	5 points
Head and neck	10 points
Tail	5 points
General condition	5 points
Total	100 points

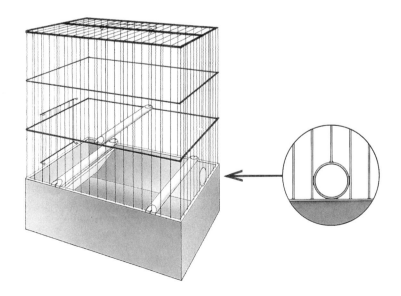

PARISIAN FRILL

Size	10 points
Feather quality	10 points
Presentation	10 points
Mantle	10 points
Craw	10 points
Fins	15 points
Head	7 points
Neck	3 points
Cock's feathers	5 points
Wings	5 points
Legs/feet	5 points
Tail	5 points
General condition	5 points
Total	100 points

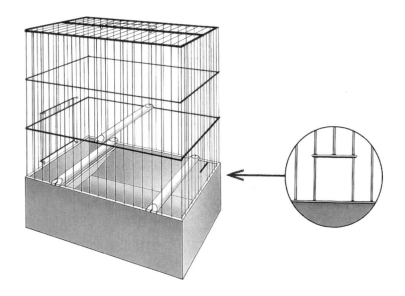

SWISS FRILL

Shape and size	30 points
Head and neck	10 points
Back and length of feather	20 points
Craw	10 points
Feet and legs	10 points
Tail	10 points
General condition	10 points
Total	100 points

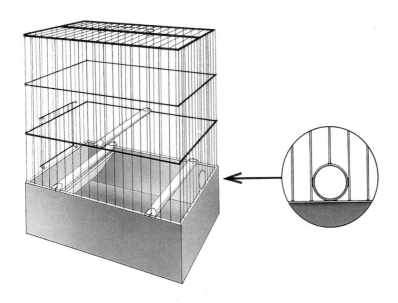

FRILLED CRESTED VARIETIES

FLORIN (FIORINO)

It is not until one has the opportunity to either meet or correspond with a true pioneer of a specific breed that one is able to contemplate realistically the problems inherent in creating a new breed. The author is fortunate in having had the first-hand experience of Del. Prete Michèle related to him in the creation of the Florin canary. At the time of writing, the Florin has still to be accepted by the COM as a new breed. By the time this book is published, it is hoped that this will have happened.

It was in the early 1950s that the idea of producing the Florin was originally conceived. Dr Livio Susmel, a native of Florence, Italy, sought to produce a small frilled canary, white in colour with a black crest. The frilling was perceived as imitating that of the Parisian Frill but the size and crest was to resemble the Gloster canary. Thus there was envisaged a small, vivacious, frilled canary, easy to breed unlike so many of its larger counterparts. To produce such a bird, small Parisian Frills were outcrossed to Glosters and the resultant off-spring interbred. Unfortunately, the experiments failed. It is easy to be wise in hindsight but perhaps this was inevitable. It must be extremely difficult, if not impossible, to produce a perfect Gloster crest on a frilled breed which not only normally has a tufted crest at the back of the head but also produces large 'cock' feathers. Add these problems to those of producing white-only birds with black crests and, without doubt, the enterprise, without quite exceptional luck, was doomed to failure.

In the late 1960s, other breeders revived the experiment but this time with the aim of producing a bird with a new type of frill, small in size with the Gloster crest and no restriction on colour.

Again, the breeders chose the Gloster as the outcross to introduce the crest. This is reasonably easy, as has been discussed on p. 97. The crest 'factor' is created as a result of a heterozygous dominant mutation; thus a Corona Gloster paired to any other type of bird will, on average, produce 50% crested and 50% non-crested offspring. The birds chosen for pairing with the Gloster were simply defined as 'frills' but it seems probable that they were of the Northern Dutch variety. The offspring of a frilled to non-frilled pairing do not seem to follow any specific definable pattern but, in the second year, frills do seem to return and, with selective breeding, it is relatively easy to return them to their original form.

228

After 10 years, birds that regularly produced offspring resembling their parents had started to evolve, the five main characteristics being the size, the crest and three main frills.

It was not until 1980 that the first birds were presented for exhibition; this was in the Bologna area and, by then, the breed had extended into Venice, Lombardy, Piedmont and Tuscany. Although now accepted as a new breed by the Italian authorities, it still, as mentioned earlier, awaits official COM recognition.

The size of the ideal Florin should be 5 inches (130 millimetres) at most, with all parts of the bird being in proportion. The bird should be alert and lively, presenting itself at an angle of 55°. The head of the bird should be round and wide, thus allowing the crest, when present, to be fully expressed. The beak should be short and thick. Unlike the Gloster, the neck of the Florin, whilst being robust, needs to stand out from the body. In order that the three frills can be properly presented, the body of the bird should be rounded and sturdy, showing neither hunched shoulders nor excessive fatness in the chest. The wings need to be held close to the body and should be neither parted nor crossing. The tail should be short, narrow and straight.

The three main frills are those of the back (mantle), craw and flanks (fins). In each instance they should be full and symmetrical. Wide shoulders will allow big, well-developed frills to rise up and fall over the sides of the bird. The craw should be full and well developed without showing any opening, particularly at the top. The flank frills should be particularly voluminous, extending over the top of the shoulders.

With the exception of the frilled areas, the other parts of the plumage, i.e. the lower abdomen, the neck and, when a crest is not present, the head, should be smooth-feathered showing no hint of frilling.

The crest is similar to that of the Gloster, i.e. full and round, blending into the back of the neck rather than being separated. The crest should extend over the beak but should not cover the eyes. A small but distinct central point should be present from which the crest radiates. The Consort, as the plainhead is known, should have a smooth rounded head showing no sign of a crest and with well-defined eyebrows.

The major problems experienced by breeders of frilled canaries are that the birds are indifferent parents; this is not so with the Florin. Being a small active bird, the breed is proving to be free breeding and the general principles of breeding contained in Chapter 1 can be adopted. The Florin is a small bird, diminutiveness being a major characteristic. Care should, therefore, be taken to ensure that the tail feathers are not picked or pulled in its first year. Replacement tail feathers always grow longer and, if present in a young bird, will not only destroy its proportions but will possibly make it longer than 5 inches (130 millimetres) and, therefore, subject to penalisation at an exhibition.

PADOVAN

As with so many of the now recognised breeds, many years and much confusion passed between the concept being originally discussed and an acceptable variety being produced and exhibited. Such is the case with the Padovan. Although not so named at the time, the Padovan was originated in 1932. It was not, however, until the mid 1970s that it was presented as a new variety by the FOI to the COM.

The breeders of Padua, who were responsible for the origination of the Milanbianco Gigante, decided to introduce a crest to their frills and chose initially, as an outcross, the Lancashire Coppy, stocks of which were being bred in Piedmont and Lombardy. The best of the crested white youngsters produced were, understandably, found to have incomplete crests and frills. This was the result of using the Lancashire which, itself, had no frills and also an incomplete crest at the back of the skull. Those with black crests were, therefore, outcrossed to Crests to improve this feature and then the serious work of reintroducing the frills began in earnest. In 1940, white birds showing a dark crest and black flight feathers were considered the ideal and, in Italy, they were officially recognised as a new breed.

It was, however, at around this time that 'red colour fever' was at its height. Many of the Italian breeders were feeding their birds colouring agents and work on really establishing the Padovan slowed considerably. With the introduction of the real red factor, by means of the black-hooded red siskin, outcrosses were made to red coloured canaries with the understandably disastrous results. A large, frilled, elegant bird was, at a stroke, turned into a small, less than elegant, badly-frilled example. Some breeders seem to have persevered in their experiments but, as is noted in the section on the Coloured Frill (p. 203), any successes they may have had have now disappeared.

At this time, much crossbreeding was taking place with all of the frills, particularly the Padovan and the Milanbianco. It was some years before sanity prevailed and the FOI decided to specify the Padovan as a separate breed and to encourage the production of elegant, frilled canaries less robust and showing less voluminous frills than the Milanbianco.

The Padovan, up to recent times, was not allowed to be a variegated bird, the only melanistic pigment present was that in the crest. This characteristic, as with the Lancashire, was and still is much sought after, but totally clear crested birds are accepted. On the showbench, the dark crested bird is preferred in the event of equal points being awarded. The crest itself, until recently, was similar to that of the Lancashire, i.e. more of a 'toupee' than a 'hat'. Recent modifications to the standard of elegance, however, call for the bird to have a complete but not too flowery crest. At no times should the feathers of the crest mask the eye or extend across the beak. The back should blend into the feathering at the base of the skull.

The three frilled areas are similar to those in the vast majority of the frilled breeds, i.e. the mantle, the craw and the fins, and in each instance, they are required to be totally symmetrical. The mantle runs down the back from the base of the neck to an area just above where the wings join. From a central 'parting', the frills are required to radiate upwards and outwards. The crest of the craw radiates outwards and inwards to form a neat parting running down the centre of the chest. The fins need to radiate outwards and upwards from the flanks. As previously mentioned, it is a fault for these frills to be too voluminous as this detracts from the required overall presentation of a proud and elegant bird.

As with the Parisian Frill, the Padovan is required to carry a large robust tail and to display even length 'cock' feathers on both sides of the tail. The thighs should be heavily feathered, giving an impression of the bird wearing shorts.

The Padovan is encouraged to display 'corkscrew' nails which probably indicates, somewhere in its ancestry, that the Parisian Frill has been used as an outcross, but, as with the Parisian Frill, it is difficult for the bird to demonstrate this feature in its first year – the only year it can be exhibited throughout mainland Europe.

In order for the Padovan to exhibit an elegant pose, it must attain the minimum acceptable length of 6½ inches (170 millimetres).

As with all crested varieties, it is strongly recommended that crest is bred to non-crest, thus avoiding the allegedly non-viable state of the homozygous crest. The recommendations made for breeding Lancashires (see p. 193), particularly in relation to the choice of non-crested examples for use in the production of crested birds nearing the standards of excellence sought, are equally relevant to breeding quality Padovans and need not be repeated. Equally the management principles mentioned in Chapter 1 apply.

Show Standards

FLORIN (FIORINO)

Size and shape	15 points
Presentation	10 points
Feather quality	10 points
Shoulders/mantle	10 points
Fins	10 points
Craw	10 points
Head and neck	15 points
Wings	5 points
Legs/feet	5 points
Tail	5 points
General condition	5 points
Total	100 points

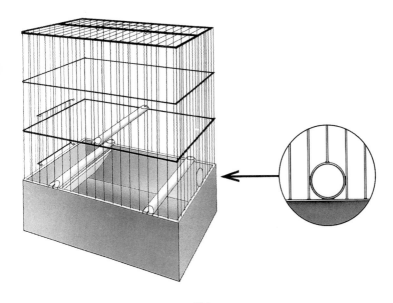

PADOVAN

Crest (or head in plainhead)	15 points
Colour	15 points
Feather quality	10 points
Size	10 points
Mantle	10 points
Craw	10 points
Fins	10 points
Wings	5 points
Tail	5 points
Presentation	5 points
General condition	5 points
Total	100 points

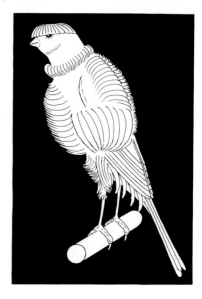

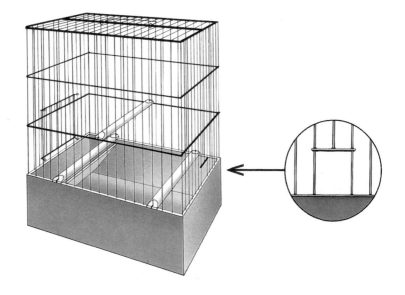

· CHAPTER 5 ·
COLOURED CANARIES

LIPOCHROME VARIETIES

To the breeder of type canaries the ground colour is generally of secondary importance, although its purity is normally of prime consideration. With coloured-canary breeders this is not so; in fact, the production of a non-normal colour by hybridisation rather than mutation has been a major driving force in their ranks. Thus, we now have at our disposal for experimental purposes, not only the original ground colour – yellow, but also the two white mutations (dominant white and recessive white) and the unnatural red. Add to these the modifying ivory mutation and it is easy to work out that the coloured-canary breeder has eight possibilities with which to work.

In the UK, as far as coloured canaries are concerned, few yellow- or white-ground birds in a clear form (i.e. totally avoiding melanin pigment) are seen on the showbench. The majority of breeders prefer to concentrate on red-ground birds, although the mutated red- and yellow-ground ivories, known as rose ivory and gold ivory, do receive some support. In mainland Europe, however, this is not the case and it is unusual not to meet large numbers of clear gold and recessive white examples at most shows, although the dominant white clear bird attracts little support.

In the UK, lipochrome varieties carrying varying degrees of melanistic pigment (known as variegation) are accepted as show specimens, albeit in classes designated for this purpose. The majority of other countries, however, adhere firmly to the rule that a clear bird should be just that and any trace of dark pigmentation, be it within the plumage or on the horny areas, will result in the bird's disqualification from the showbench. This does not automatically disqualify it from a place in a breeding stud. In fact, most serious breeders would not consider keeping a lipochrome stud without some variegated birds to interbreed with their clear examples.

A brief summary of the terms used may be helpful at this point:

1) *Clear* is used to denote a bird totally devoid of melanin pigment.
2) A *ticked* bird is one with a single area of melanin pigment that can be covered by an object one square centimetre in area.
3) A *variegated* bird is one that has more melanistic pigment than a ticked specimen, but has some areas of lipochrome feathering visible.
4) The term *foul* is given to a self bird with feathers in wings or tail that are devoid of dark pigment.
5) A *self* bird is one that has melanin pigmentation in all its feathers.

The normal domesticated version of the canary is that known as a green, i.e. a yellow-ground bird on which black and brown pigmentation is deposited, giving an optical illusion of green. This pigmentation, which is derived from protein in the diet, has no known direct effect on the ground colour, unlike the lipochrome colouring which is fat-based. The actual manifestation of the melanin pattern is determined by a set of genes called *variegation factors*. The areas of the body most receptive to the deposit of melanin are the crown of the head, the eyes and cheek, breast, flanks, wings, outer tail feathers, back, beak and toes. This is confirmed not only by viewing the birds that are bred today but by historic reports that record the first *sports*, dark birds showing light areas. The pattern of melanin deposition is controlled by this factor and a secondary variegation factor is responsible for the depth of colouration of the melanin. It, therefore, follows that the closer one gets to producing a clear bird, the further one departs from the normal.

Non-pigmented (clear) canaries can be produced because of the strength of these variegation factors and because of the presence of a mutation which suppresses the formation of melanin. Thus the use of the Mendelian ratio (see p. 99) to determine the theoretical production of clear and/or variegated birds is only limited, although, with the absence of anything more positive, it is perhaps useful as a guide. To illustrate the possibilities, a capital letter V is used to represent the normal variegation-forming factor and a small v to represent its mutant allelomorph. Thus VV is a self or foul bird, Vv or vV a variegated bird, and vv a ticked, or clear bird. If birds with a double factor for the production of melanin, i.e. birds that do not carry the mutant allelomorph, are paired together, the only possible offspring must also be self or foul birds. Using the representative letters, *VV* to *VV* can only produce *VV* progeny. Pairing *Vv* birds together will theoretically produce 25% *VV* self or foul birds, 50% *Vv* variegated birds and 25% *vv* clear or ticked birds. It follows that the pairing of *vv* parents can theoretically produce only *vv* clear or ticked offspring.

As the number of variegation factors formed varies considerably, neither the mutated nor the normal genes are fully dominant over the other and, therefore, other factors that have never been fully explained, nor properly investigated, must be involved. Whilst an explanation has never been put forward as to how these factors work, there can be little doubt of their existence.

The amount of variegation that exists from one bird to another in a *Vv* bird varies considerably, from one carrying two tick marks to an almost foul-marked bird. By observing any mutation, we can see that, if birds possessing similarly-mutated genes are paired together over a number of years, the offspring will become progressively inferior, weaker, smaller, poorly coloured, more poorly marked or a combination of these traits. Exactly why this happens is not known but it is a common occurrence in all types of livestock.

If a clear canary is paired to a clear canary over a number of years, this phenomenon becomes apparent as size diminishes and depth of colour is reduced. Thus breeders of clear varieties are well advised to introduce self, foul or variegated stock to the stud in alternate years. Birds of the green series, i.e. green, bronze or blue, depending upon the ground colour involved, are the ones recommended for this purpose but not birds of the brown series.

By studying the following tables, which are based on the Mendelian ratio, it can be seen that a number of clear birds will be produced from two of the three featured pairings and it is often that these are superior to clear young produced from a clear to clear pairing.

Pair 1 SELF × CLEAR

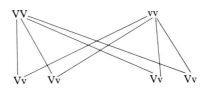

all variegated young

Pair 2   VARIEGATED × VARIEGATED

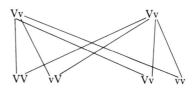

25% foul or self (VV)   50% variegated (vV or Vv)
25% clear or ticked (vv)

Pair 3   VARIEGATED × CLEAR

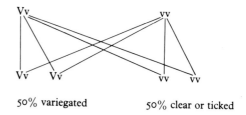

50% variegated   50% clear or ticked

Colour

Having discussed the lipochrome varieties generally, let us now study the various ground colours available.

YELLOW (GOLD) GROUND

The original colour of the wild canary is yellow and, in the earliest domesticated forms, until the early part of the current century when experiments took place to annex the red lipochrome of the Black-hooded red siskin (*Spinus cucullatus*), it formed the major colour not only in all forms of type canary but also in coloured canaries. Whilst its influence, although remaining important, has decreased in coloured canaries, it continues to this day as the main colour variety of type canaries.

Despite yellow being the original ground colour, it remains difficult to produce specimens showing the required shade in appreciable quantities for the showbench. The colour most sought after is a bright luminous green-yellow, occasionally referred to as citron-yellow. This colour can only be achieved when the bird possesses the optical blue/reduction of brown factor. As we have discussed, the clear varieties of canary are in fact green birds in which the melanistic pigment has, for one reason or another, been prevented from appearing. Notwithstanding this, the genes for the production of both eumelanin black and phaeomelanin brown exist within the bird's genotype and, although when attempting to describe inheritance patterns etc., we speak of the mutation of a single gene, in practice there are many genes for the production of these melanin pigments. A bird possessing the optical-blue factor has a much greater proportion of black-producing genes than brown-producing ones. When this occurs, the luminous ground colour – in all ground colours – appears. The biggest problem is that no guarantees are possible covering the inheritance pattern of this desirable characteristic, which seems to be random in its distribution. However, certain strains of birds do seem to produce greater percentages of the desired characteristic and, in consequence, the keeping of extremely detailed notes on the progeny of all pairings is recommended so that the strain is not lost.

Now the ideal has been described, it is perhaps opportune to mention the major faults. These are: a very pale colour, patchy colouring, a dull yellow colour and an orangy tint in the plumage.

Patchy colouring is rarely found in yellow-ground birds, as no colour feeding is necessary and it rarely occurs in naturally-coloured, naturally-fed birds.

Pale colouration more often than not indicates a low level of the carotenoid lutein, the natural substance in the diet which produces the yellow in yellow birds. If the bird gets a well-balanced diet, the colour should appear quite automatically but, if it does not, the balance of the seed mixture offered should be adjusted. Ensure that a sufficient percentage of the seed is plain canary and black rape and increase the amount of greenfoods – particularly brassicas.

Dull colouration normally indicates the opposite effect on the lipochrome of a bird not possessing the optical blue factor, i.e. a predominance of brown-producing genes over black-producing genes. Whilst, logically, birds displaying this undesirable characteristic should be culled from a strain, ironically some of the finest birds bred have been produced from such examples and it is, therefore, difficult to be dogmatic on the subject. Again, the keeping of records should indicate traits and, by studying these, the breeder should be better able to determine his approach.

Orange tints in a bird are to be avoided and, whilst in some self varieties it is necessary to retain the birds within a stud, in clear varieties, culling is recommended. There are two possible reasons why a yellow-ground bird displays an orange tint: the first is accidental, i.e. where it has accidentally had access to food or water containing the colouring agent fed to red-ground birds. Should this be the case, the recommendation to cull the stock should obviously be ignored. The other reason is that the bird is not a homozygous yellow and contains some genes for the production of red. With new mutations invariably now occurring in self varieties, the task for experimental breeders is not only to transfer the mutation to the four classic colours, i.e. green, brown, agate and isabel, but also to transfer it to all ground colours. Should the mutation have occurred in a red-ground strain, the normally undesirable process of pairing red to either of the white mutations (each of which as we will discuss later are masking yellow) or directly to yellow-ground birds is necessary. Only by adopting careful breeding techniques will the change-over from red to yellow come to fruition, and it will take up to 5 years with, even then, the occasional throwback to red ancestry. Thus, wherever possible, this pairing is to be avoided.

With ample stock available everywhere, no necessity exists for pairing yellow-ground birds to red-ground, hence the recommend-ation not to use this pairing and, in the event of orange-tinted birds appearing in a stud, to dispose of them.

RED GROUND

By far the most popular of the ground colours in coloured canaries is the red ground. Unlike the two white-ground colours, which occurred through mutation, the red ground was achieved by hybri-disation. Experimental breeders, aiming to produce a red lipo-chrome in their canaries, started by crossing a black-hooded red siskin male (*Spinus cucullatus*) with a yellow canary female. The females from this pairing were found to be infertile and consequently of no use. Limited fertility was, however, found in the F_1 hybrid male and these then had to be paired back to yellow females, giving a further reduction of the sought-after siskin genes, in the F_2 hybrid. Females from this pairing to yellow-ground females reduced even further the pool of genes derived from the siskin ancestor. Limited fertility was found in a small proportion of the F_3 females and thus began the complex business of selective breeding for colour.

It will be studied later how relatively easy it is now to produce the 'red factor' when, in our example, we outcross to recessive white. Even so, with unlimited red canaries at our disposal, it may still take 5 or 6 years to achieve our aims. Imagine then the time and patience required of our predecessors in the attempt to achieve their aims. As World War 2 slowed down, and even halted, experiment-ation, it is difficult to determine at which precise time canaries which were being freely bred together could be claimed to be red in colour. Certainly, the quest was still continuing until the mid-1960s, when the feeding of synthetic colouring agents was first allowed. Until that time, ruling bodies were adamant that no colour feeding, other than natural products which could be grown in a garden, was permissible. The ground colour of the canary is dictated by genes responsible for giving the signal for the production of colour. This colouration is derived from food that the bird has eaten. The normal yellow-ground canary gets its colour from carotenoids contained in its food, the yellow being derived from a pigment called xanthophyll while the red results from one called carotene. Whether the gene for red is capable of utilising both pigments is unknown but it has been confirmed that the gene for yellow does use carotene as a source of colour. Any canary deprived of carotenoids in its diet will go white regardless of its ground colour.

It is known that the siskin male will lose colour if not given a diet containing carotene, which suggests that, in part at least, the red-ground colour is dependent as much on food supply as on genetical make-up. The problem facing early breeders of red canaries was to find naturally-grown products containing high quantities of caro-tene. Analysis has shown that only six of the many vegetable products analysed contained a carotene content in excess of 100 parts per million and, of these six, only three were readily accepted by birds. Of these three, carrots, with a carotene content of 120 parts per million, were found to be the most readily available but, in spite of feeding this vegetable in every conceivable form, including liquid, a visually red canary was never bred. The other two high-percentage carotene products – dried grass with 160–250 parts per million and grasses with 117 parts per million – were also fed but with little results. With the introduction of an artificial colouring agent, with a carotene content of 10%, the dream of producing true red canaries became a reality. When first introduced, these agents were viewed with some mistrust, the feeling being that such artificial methods of feeding would prevent accurate assessments being made of a bird's ability of produce red. Tests on yellow- and white-ground birds have, however, proved conclusively that, unless a canary possesses genes for the production of red, regardless of the amount or type of colouring agent offered, it will not moult out red. What then remains unknown is whether the ultimate colour had in fact been achieved many years earlier but was not appreciated by breeders. Certainly, over the last 20 years, little improvement seems to have been made and it must, therefore, be assumed that the achievement of the ultimate possible colour is very close, if, indeed, it has not already been realised.

Certain birds, when fed on artificial colouring agents during the moult, will subsequently assume a dull red, purple or brown appearance, these colours being predominant around the head. That this is due to overfeeding of the colouring agent is still hypothetical, although the author continues to be sceptical. Experiments, carried out by the author in conjunction with other breeders, in which the colouring agent has been fed to excess, have substantially proved that the appearance of dull red or the alternative colours is due not to the feeding of a colouring agent, but to the genetical make-up of the bird, i.e. birds appearing bright red possess the optical blue factor whilst those appearing dull have a large percentage of brown-producing genes within their make-up. It is a sad fact, that few genuine experimental breeders remain and, in consequence, this theory is unlikely to be proved conclusively without further research. It is a fact, however, that no bird can show colour deeper than its assimilation peak; only the actual inheritance of genes controlling colour can affect the amount of colour which can be maximised in a canary and a poorly-bred bird can never achieve the colour of a better-bred bird.

When discussing colour, two further points need to be examined. Firstly, the effect of diet. It must be remembered that the bulk of the diet of a canary consists of a seed mixture and, whilst of less importance to red-canary breeders now than before the introduction of artificial colouring agents, it is an aspect that must be taken into consideration. The minus factors for the red-canary breeders do, however, often become plus factors for the breeder of yellow-ground birds. Rape, thistle and hemp seeds all contain relatively large percentages of the yellow-producing carotenoid lutein whilst oats (and, therefore, groats and pinhead oatmeal), maw and niger seeds contain none. The second consideration is the question of environment. It has long been thought, although it is difficult to determine whether this is legend or based on fact, that birds moulted in strong sunlight will be partially bleached and so will not display the same depth of colour as those moulted out in an environment that excludes direct sunlight. With no evidence to contradict this theory, it is perhaps advisable to take it into consideration. It would be interesting, however, to know how the feather, once formed and therefore dead, can be so affected.

DOMINANT WHITE

Although as far back as the seventeenth century, records show that white-ground canaries existed, little attempt seems to have been made to study the inheritance patterns and to establish strains. Whether these birds, or those recorded as having appeared in German stock later, were birds we now call dominant white or recessive white is not known.

The dominant white appeared on the showbench in the 1920s but records do not show whether this bird was a new, spontaneous mutation or whether it was an offspring of a long-standing strain. As its name implies, this version of white canary is a dominant heterozygous version and, therefore, in single dose, is dominant to all other forms of lipochrome colouring. Consequently, a bird is either a dominant white or not; it cannot carry the factor. The inheritance pattern is exactly the same as for the intensive feather i.e.:

Pair 1 DOMINANT WHITE × DOMINANT WHITE

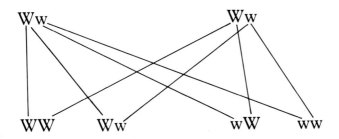

N.B. *W* denotes the unchanged normal gene and *w* its mutant allelomorph.

Thus, from this pairing of dominant white to dominant white, the expectation is 25% *WW* normal coloured, 50% *Ww* heterozygous dominant whites and 25% *ww* homozygous dominant whites.

Pair 2   DOMINANT WHITE × NORMAL

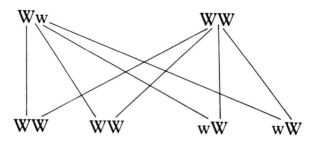

From the pairing dominant white to normal (the word normal indicates a non-dominant white example – its actual colour is irrelevant), the expectation is 50% *WW* normal coloured and 50% *wW* heterozygous whites.

The males and females in the above examples can, of course, be interchanged to give identical results.

Obviously, if we pair together two normal coloured birds, no dominant white offspring will appear.

Although the pairing of dominant white to dominant white has been illustrated, this pairing is not recommended as it is recorded that, when the mutation is present in double dose, i.e. when it is a homozygous dominant white, the chick becomes 'non-viable' and, whilst it is suggested that the chick can be hatched, it cannot grow to maturity. The use of the words 'it is recorded' is deliberate as no scientific evidence has been put forward to confirm this suggestion. The limited records of dominant white to dominant white pairings carried out by the author are unable to either substantiate the statement or contradict it. As no significant indication of losses, either through dead-in-shell eggs or chicks failing to mature, have been noted, one is left to conject whether there is any truth in the statement or whether it is another example of the folklore that persists throughout the Fancy and which has no scientific basis.

As with all heterozygous dominant mutations, there are degrees of dominance. Intensive birds carry frosting (see p. 255) in varying degrees and similar traits can be seen with the dominant white mutation. The effect of the mutation is to mask the true colouration of the subject. Normally, this is yellow. It is, however, usual to see isolated areas of lipochrome colouring deposited throughout the plumage. These normally appear in the flights, wing butts and neck areas, their intensity and distribution differing from bird to bird,

244

and becoming more apparent on intensive specimens. Having stated that, normally, the dominant white mutation masks yellow, it should be said that this is due to historical rather than scientific reasons. There is absolutely no reason why it should not mask red, and, should this be the case, care must be taken to mention this to prospective purchasers so that they do not inadvertently pair such a bird to a clear yellow example and, thereby, at a stroke, probably destroy many years' work in establishing a well-coloured yellow strain. When fed Carophyll Red® or another synthetic colouring agent, the lipochrome not masked by the dominant white factor will change colour, as with any other bird, to orange or red, depending upon whether the bird is in fact, a yellow or red example. This has in the past confused people who thought they had rose ivory birds in their birdroom. The confusion is caused by the overlap of the white feathers on the red, which gives an optical illusion of pink. Thankfully, now that the ivory mutation is more established, the confusion seems to exist less.

The exhibition standard of the clear dominant white calls for a bright luminous white plumage with traces of normal lipochrome non-evident. The brightness of the white, as with all other lipochrome varieties, is produced by the bird possessing the optical blue factor, but, in the case of the dominant white, this can sometimes be an added complication. When trying to eradicate the obvious yellow lipochrome, the factor will act on this lipochrome colouring as well as the white, making it more obvious. Although not a complete answer, the introduction of the ivory factor – which will be covered in more detail on p. 249 – will assist. The action of the ivory factor is to modify the normal lipochrome colour: when added to yellow, it changes the colour from bright yellow to a pale lemon colour, whilst as to be expected it will have no effect on the white. For reasons as yet unexplained, the addition of the ivory factor also eradicates any trace of lipochrome from the flight feathers – the area where deposition of lipochrome is most often present.

It has been a long-held fallacy, particularly within the ranks of type-canary breeders, that dominant white birds should only be paired to non-intensive (buff) partners. The reasons seem lost in folklore but one can only assume that it was felt that the dominant white factor in some way caused a deterioration of feather quality. This, of course, cannot be true as the factor is responsible for the restriction of lipochrome colouring in the feather, not the structure of the feather. Although more difficult to distinguish, both intensive and non-intensive feathers are quite common and, by studying them, we can ensure that the normal intensive to non-intensive pairings are effected. In coloured-canary terminology, the dominant white bird is referred to as a 'silver' and, where this term is used, it can be assumed that a dominant rather than a recessive white bird is being described.

RECESSIVE WHITE

The recessive white mutation is a homozygous recessive version, i.e. for the factor to be observed, both of the pair of genes responsible need to have mutated. Thus, unlike its dominant white counterpart, the recessive white factor may be carried by a bird which is thereby capable of producing a white bird if paired with a partner that is either a carrier of the factor or displays it. This can be seen by examining the tables below:

Pair 1   RECESSIVE WHITE × RECESSIVE WHITE

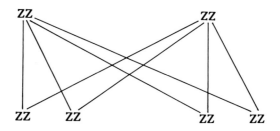

N.B. *Z* denotes the normal gene and *z* its mutant allelomorph.

Thus, a recessive white paired with a recessive white will give all recessive white young.

Pair 2   RECESSIVE WHITE × NORMAL carrying (or split for) RECESSIVE WHITE

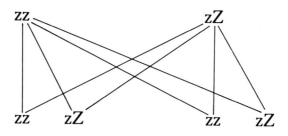

The pairing above shows that a theoretical 50% recessive white and 50% normal carrying recessive white youngsters will be obtained from full recessive white to normal carrying recessive white parents.

Pair 3   NORMAL carrying RECESSIVE WHITE × NORMAL carrying RECESSIVE WHITE

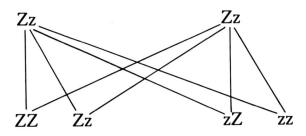

A normal carrying recessive white to normal carrying recessive white will give 25% homozygous normals, 50% heterozygous normals and 25% homozygous recessive whites. The only problem with effecting such a pairing is that the phenotype of the homozygous and heterozygous normal youngsters will be identical and all of them will need to be test mated to determine their genotype.

Pair 4   RECESSIVE WHITE × NORMAL

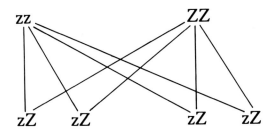

The fourth possible pairing is of a full (or homozygous) recessive white paired to a homozygous (or non-carrier) normal bird. With this pairing only visually normal birds can be produced, but all of them will carry, and, therefore, be capable of producing, the recessive white factor.

The males and females of the above examples can, of course, be interchanged and will give identical results.

The first recorded example of the recessive white is a ticked bird

247

bred by a Miss Lee of New Zealand in 1908 and it is from this that all existing strains are thought to have originated. The action of the mutation is to prevent totally the expression of lipochrome colouring in the plumage. The skin colour of the bird also changes from the normal pink to a lilac colour, although this is only normally visible during the first few days of the chick's life. Unlike its dominant white counterpart, the recessive white will always remain pure white, regardless of what is added to its diet. A problem sometimes exists in differentiating between extremely good examples of the dominant white and the recessive white. This can quite easily be overcome by examining the fat of the bird – normally visible immediately above and below the rib cage. In the recessive white, the fat is white – and remains so regardless of diet, whereas in the dominant white, the fat is yellow and, in this case, the colour will change depending upon diet, even turning red when the bird is fed on a synthetic colouring agent. The great benefit of the recessive white is that it can be intermated with clear-red varieties without the breeder needing to concern him- or herself about the segregation of youngsters when colouring agents are offered during the moult. Although it is very difficult to remove all traces of red from a yellow-ground strain, it is not too difficult to breed good-quality red birds after 4 or 5 years when outcrossing to yellow-ground or white-ground birds either dominant or recessive varieties which are masking yellow. The recommended system is to start with a deep-red bird and pair it to a recessive white. The youngsters from such a pairing will, when colour fed, usually achieve a medium-orange colour. If only one experimental pair is being used, brother should be mated to sister in the second year and any recessive white birds produced (by our inheritance tables it can be seen that 25% of the offspring should be recessive white) should be retained for the third season. These birds should then be outcrossed to a totally unrelated deeply-coloured red bird with a brother to sister pairing of the deepest-coloured birds taking place in the fourth year. Again, any recessive white youngsters should be outcrossed to a deep-coloured red bird to breed carriers of the recessive white factor, a large percentage of which should themselves be close to the accepted shade of red required. After this, it is relatively easy to establish a strain of recessive white birds masking red. As with dominant white birds masking red, care should be taken to advise purchasers of their genetical make up so as not to spoil an established yellow-ground strain.

It is widely accepted that the recessive white mutation is unable to convert the Vitamin A in its food into an assimilable form and therefore care must be taken to ensure that the bird does not suffer from deficiencies of this vitamin and subsequent ill health. This is easily done by adding vitamin supplements to the seed or water and by giving the birds Carophyll Red® – itself high in Vitamin A, during the moult. A more traditional method is to offer the birds constant supplies of beef suet. The statement that the recessive white is unable to use Vitamin A is made purely on information handed down over generations of birdkeepers and, through lack of evidence to the contrary, it would be inadmissible to disagree with it. The author, however, can state that recessive white breeding stock within his own birdroom receive exactly the same management as other varieties, no additives whatsoever being offered and, over a period of years, success in breeding and rearing the recessive white mutation has been equal to any other.

At one time, recessive white birds were thought to be more delicate than other varieties and, in consequence, it was strongly recommended never to pair recessive white to recessive white in clear examples as the offspring would be extremely delicate and difficult to rear to maturity. With self varieties, the problem seemed less apparent. Over the last 10 years, the author, because of his own breeding results, must question this statement. By using common-sense, and pairing together only strong, fit and healthy examples, no adverse results have been noted in recessive white to recessive white pairings, it should be pointed out, however, that youngsters bred from such a pairing are themselves paired to normals carrying recessive white.

THE IVORY FACTOR

Around 1950, a Dutchman, the late P.J. Helder, breeding with a normal intensive red to non-intensive red pairing, produced a pale-coloured chick which, on moulting, turned a pink colour rather than the expected red; the chick was a female.

By test mating, it was proved possible to produce this phenotype with the inheritance pattern following the sex-linked recessive format.

Another mutation was, therefore, established and the expectation table is as follows:

Pair 1   NORMAL MALE × IVORY FEMALE

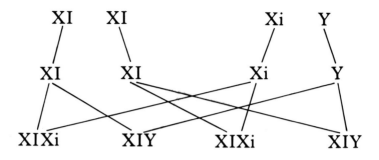

N.B. *I* denotes the normal gene and *i* its mutant allelomorph. As is now known, with sex-linked recessive mutations, a male needs to possess both mutated lipochrome-producing genes, which are sited on the X chromosome, to reproduce the mutated phenotype. A female however, having only one X chromosome, must either be a normal or a mutated specimen. Male offspring of the pairing shown above, although having the same phenotype as a homozygous normal, will be capable of producing the mutated version regardless of the genotype of its mate, as we will see from the succeeding tables.

Pair 2   NORMAL MALE carrying IVORY × IVORY FEMALE

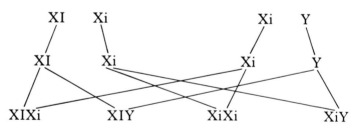

Pair 3   IVORY MALE × NORMAL FEMALE

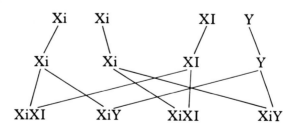

Pair 4   NORMAL MALE carrying IVORY × NORMAL FEMALE

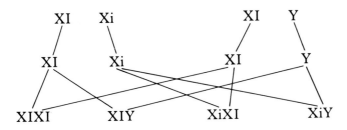

The expectations from our four pairings are therefore:

Pair 1: normal male × ivory female will produce 50% visually normal males carrying ivory and 50% normal females.

Pair 2: normal male carrying ivory × ivory female will produce 25% ivory males, 25% visually normal males carrying ivory, 25% normal females and 25% ivory females.

Pair 3: ivory male × normal female will produce 50% visually normal males carrying ivory and 50% ivory females.

Pair 4: normal male carrying ivory × normal female will produce 25% normal males, 25% visually normal males carrying ivory, 25% normal females and 25% ivory females.

Obviously, if we pair an ivory male with an ivory female, all of the offspring will be ivories, i.e.:

IVORY MALE × IVORY FEMALE

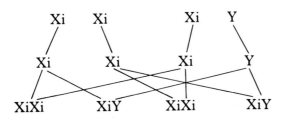

Although the mutation is called ivory on each of the ground colours, this term is preceded by a descriptive word and hence a red ground becomes a rose ivory (in the UK the word ivory is dropped,

251

the bird simply being referred to as rose), a yellow ground becomes a gold ivory and the white counterpart a silver ivory. When first imported, the mutation was referred to as the ivory pastel but, because of the confusion caused by the presence of the self mutation (at that time called the melanin pastel), this word was dropped from the name.

As stated, the modifying effect of the ivory mutation results in a red bird becoming pink; similarly, a yellow bird becomes a pale lemon colour with the white version showing little change. The most evident change in the phenotype of the silver ivory is usually the disappearance of the yellow lipochrome deposit commonly seen in the flight feathers of a dominant white. If examined closely, a faint suffusion of pale lemon colouring can be seen throughout the whole plumage of the bird. This is not normally visible unless the bird is colour fed, when the greater concentration of the lipochrome allows the colour to be more readily seen.

When early specimens of the mutation were imported into the UK, a bird appeared which was described as being 'the colour of old piano keys' and was reputed to be a different version of the mutation in that it had a lower red gene content than the rose. We know now that the expected phenotypes of the rose, gold and silver ivories in no way resemble this description and thus we can be reasonably sure that the birds in question were of a colour intermediate to red and yellow. They appeared as a result of pairings being made in an attempt to transfer the mutation from the original red to yellow ground. Except for experimental work, this pairing is not recommended and beginners are certainly advised to concentrate on the pure ground colours.

Although the ivory factor modifies the ground colour of a bird, it does not influence the stength of the lipochrome-producing genes in normal birds and thus depth of colour is as important in ivory birds as in their normal counterparts. When first introduced to the UK, the ambiguous description of 'coloured like a wild rose' was given to the red version. This had the effect of causing controversy between breeders, each attempting to produce birds that resembled their ideal. It should here be stated that the wild rose in the UK is of a pale pink pastel shade. That this colour was a pale pink gave credence to the fallacial thought that the introduction of the rose to an established stud of intensive and non-intensive reds resulted in a reduction of colour in the normal birds.

With all ground colours, depth of colouration is a prime requisite and, eventually, preference was correctly given to ivory birds showing as deep a shade of pink or lemon as possible, and this is accepted today as the ideal standard. Once this objective had been clarified, it was discovered that, compared with the time when paler versions were being bred, no adverse effect was evident in the birds used to produce ivories. Thus more options were open to breeders who wished to keep only clear varieties.

An interesting side effect of the mutation is that an evenness of colour is automatically achieved, compared with the normal red or yellow, where the shoulder butts and rump usually appear slightly deeper in colour.

All the normal rules for breeding clears apply to the ivory mutation, i.e. ground colours should not be mixed, intensive birds should be paired to non-intensive and, as with all mutations, the ivory should be paired back to a normal at least in alternate years. It is just as difficult to retain depth of colour in ivory birds as it is with normal coloured birds and thought must be given not only to back crossing but also to introducing variegated stock. This, in addition to assisting with quality of colour, will also help to prevent loss of shape and size.

In all types of ground colour, the ultimate depth of colouration cannot be determined by the colour of the nest plumage. Quite often, the deepest-coloured youngsters in the nest may become less colourful following the first moult and vice versa. This applies not only to the ivory birds but also to normal examples.

It has already been mentioned that clear birds originate from self greens but, because of factors inhibiting the production of melanistic pigment, no variegation is evident. It, therefore, follows that the mutations that alter the phenotype of self varieties can be present in clear varieties, although usually there is no visual evidence of their existence. The exceptions to this are the mutations which alter the eye colour, in addition to the melanistic striations. The brown (cinnamon) mutation has been accepted for many years and has been useful as a guide to the sex of youngsters immediately after hatching. As with self browns, however, the eye colour darkens as the bird grows and it is usually quite difficult, if not impossible, to differentiate between a lipochrome bird of the green series and one of the brown series once they are both weaned. The other mutations affecting eye colour are the ino and satinette mutations, where a bright red eye is a characteristic.

In mainland Europe, these birds are totally accepted and classes are added at the larger shows to cater for them. Where these classes do not exist, the birds are exhibited alongside their dark-eyed counterparts. In the UK, they are something of a rarity and, in consequence, suspicion and confusion surrounds their presence in lipochrome classes. This is because, in experimental pairings, self birds have been produced with red eyes which are apparently totally devoid of melanistic pigment, e.g. the combination of satinette or ino with opal will give this phenotype. Notwithstanding this, close examination of such a bird will reveal traces of dark pigmentation in the underfeather whereas a true lipochrome example will always carry a pure white underflue and must be exhibited in classes provided for lipochrome examples.

The colour of the eye will in no way affect the ground colour of the bird and many breeders find red-eyed clears a desirable addition to their stud. It is obvious that the eye will be more apparent with gold- or silver-ground birds, as there is a greater contrast, but red-eyed red-ground birds are being bred. Back crossing a mutated bird to a normal in alternate years is still recommended in order to retain body size and shape. The inheritance pattern of the satinette mutation – the one most frequently used in red-eyed lipochrome pairings – is exactly the same as for the ivory mutation. If the ino mutation is being used, and it should be pointed out here that it is impossible to differentiate visually between the two mutations in clear varieties, then the inheritance table used to describe the Recessive White (p. 246) should be used.

Feather Type

It is important to study the make-up of the feather because the type of feather can influence the overall phenotype of a bird, although it does not affect the lipochrome deposit.

All feathers break through the skin as dermal papillae. The outer layer of the papilla is the feather sheath, or quill and the inner layer is the actual feather. The case of the feather is embedded in a feather follicle from which a new feather will grow. During the growing process, the soft central cavity of the feather is fed by blood vessels. The lipochrome colouring, which provides the background or ground colour, is transmitted by the fatty constituent of the blood and the melanistic pigment by the protein constituent. Once the feather is fully grown, it loses its sheath, expands fully and hardens. Once this happens, the blood supply ceases, growth is completed and the feather is effectively dead. Nothing will then affect the colour of the feather other than staining applied externally.

INTENSIVE AND NON-INTENSIVE

The normal feather of the canary is the frosted, now called non-intensive in coloured canaries or buff in type canaries. This feather is relatively wide and, near the body on the lower third, shows the primary colour involved – black in the green series, mid-grey in the brown series and white in all clear versions, whether genetically green or brown. This is known as the underfeather or *underflue*. The remainder of the feather in clear varieties assumes the dominant colour of the bird, i.e. red, yellow or white, except for the tip of the feather which is white. The lipochrome is thus partially masked by the effect of the white tip. This is known as *frosting*. The best illustration of this point is to imagine the feathers as tiles or slates on a roof where at least half of each tile is covered by another laid over it. Similarly, a frosted feather lying over the lipochrome colouring masks the true density of colour resulting in a frosting effect.

At some time, possibly during its domestication, the normal non-intensive feather mutated to give another form of feather, longer and thinner than the non-intensive type with the lipochrome colour extending right through to the feather tip. It has been recently renamed as the intensive feather in coloured-canary circles, previously having been called the non-frosted. In type canaries, it is called the yellow. Although all show standards call for intensive examples to display no frosting whatsoever, some birds, particularly females, still show a slight frosting.

The mutation that produces the intensive feather is a heterozygous dominant version and whether the presence of frosting results from the mutation not being totally dominant in all instances or from secondary sex characteristics is not yet known.

As can be seen from the tables below, an intensive bird paired to a non-intensive bird will theoretically produce 50% intensive and 50% non-intensive offspring. A pairing of non-intensive can only produce non-intensive youngsters whereas a pairing of intensive to intensive will give theoretical average results in the Mendelian ratio, i.e. 25% homozygous intensives, 50% heterozygous intensives and 25% homozygous non-intensives.

255

Pair 1   INTENSIVE × NON-INTENSIVE

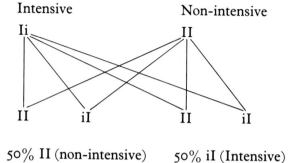

50% II (non-intensive)   50% iI (Intensive)

Pair 2   NON-INTENSIVE × NON-INTENSIVE

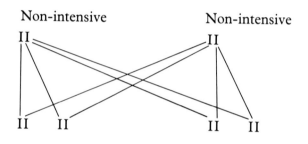

100% II (non-intensive)

Pair 3   INTENSIVE × INTENSIVE

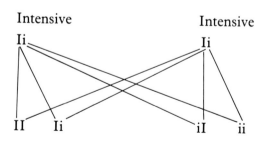

25% ii (homozygous intensive)
50% Ii (or iI) (heterozygous intensive)
25% II (homozygous non-intensive)

256

N.B. *I* denotes the normal gene for feather type and *i* its mutant allelomorph. In the above examples, of course, it makes no difference which bird is male and which is female; identical results will be obtained.

It has been thought for many years that the homozygous intensive is not viable (i.e. it is not able to grow to maturity) but this argument must now be questioned as the Gibber Italicus type canary only seems to be an intensive. With this in mind, past hypotheses suggesting that the homozygous intensive, if viable, will appear as a very thinly and sparsely feathered bird, would seem to be borne out.

With the ultimate intent of producing the deepest but brightest colour available in each ground colour, together with an even light frosting in non-intensive examples, the use of intensive to intensive, and non-intensive to non-intensive, pairings continues to provoke more controversy than any other aspect. It should, however, be pointed out at this stage that the pairing of non-intensive to intensive should form the basis of all matings as it is known that the majority of the progeny will approach the accepted standards of feather quality in both intensive and non-intensive birds. Other pairings, i.e. intensive to intensive or non-intensive to non-intensive, should only be contemplated for a specific purpose, usually for experiment, and the results will have to be very carefully documented in order that they may be usefully analysed if the intention is to establish or improve a characteristic or to disprove the above advice.

The use of non-intensive male to non-intensive female produces a flurry of scientifically-unsupported theories, the major one being that the amount of frosting will increase so that the ultimate result will be a bird whose frosting totally masks all form of lipochrome pigment. This theory, whilst fairly widespread, can, in the author's opinion, be safely discounted. It follows that the majority of wild canaries (*Serinus canaria*) would be of the non-intensive feather type and, were there any truth in this hypothesis, it should automatically follow that they would be apparently devoid of lipochrome pigment, which clearly is not the case. Further to this, there is experience of breeding the ino mutation non-intensive to non-intensive over several years because wider feathers are necessary to allow the phenomenon created by this mutation to be fully expressed. From the results, there is no evidence to substantiate the above theory.

Thus, in all pairings one would normally recommend intensive to non-intensive pairings but, having said that, consideration should be given to the degree of frosting in both the non-intensive and intensive examples so as to produce offspring of both types as close to perfection as possible. It is unlikely that a heavily-frosted intensive will produce either a true intensive or a finely-frosted non-intensive. Equally the pairing of a true intensive with very narrow feathers to a very finely-frosted non-intensive will not give the desired results. Having made this statement, there is experience to suggest that, more often than not, a particular line will produce only good intensive birds or good non-intensive birds. Therefore, not only must care be taken in selecting mates of different feather types but, occasionally, the pairing of birds with a similar feather type may be the correct mating to make.

Probably the most exciting factor is that, however clever we may seem, and however careful we are in pairing our birds, nothing is guaranteed. Only by observing the offspring of our pairings, and carefully recording these results for consideration in the following breeding season, can we increase the chances of producing that which we seek.

It is, however, not unreasonable to make one or two assumptions which, in theory at least, will lead us down the path to achieving our aims, and, before considering these, it is perhaps worthwhile re-stating these aims. A non-intensive bird should carry a bright deep colour, evenly distributed throughout its plumage and covered by equally evenly distributed fine frosting. Care should be taken to ensure that there is no excess of frosting anywhere, particularly on the back of the neck.

Conversely, areas devoid of frosting (usually the chest) should not be present. An intensive bird should carry a bright deep colour evenly distributed throughout the plumage with no trace of frosting whatsoever being present.

To correct a fault in a bird, therefore, a mate should be selected which shows the opposite extreme of the fault in question. Thus, if a female is a very heavily frosted non-intensive (and it should perhaps be mentioned here that, as with the female intensive, frosting seems to be more prevalent in females, probably due to the secondary sex characteristics), its partner should be a true intensive male showing not only no frosting whatsoever, but also carrying particularly thin plumage. The theory is that a balance of the two extremes will result in young of the centre path, i.e. much closer to the ideal.

To summarise as a generality, a non-intensive example should be paired to an intensive and, in every second year, one of the pair should be a variegated specimen.

DIMORPHIC

To conclude this section, we must consider the third feather type prevalent in coloured canaries – the dimorphic. As with the intensive and non-intensive feather types, the dimorphic is equally important in the self varieties but, until fairly recently, its presence has been more frequently found in clear examples. In the early pairings, made by experimental breeders attempting to produce a red lipochrome, a very pale type of female occasionally appeared and often these were discarded as inferior examples. Eventually, however, German breeders succeeded in developing a strain of red canaries that were called 'Carmines'. These birds were much more strongly coloured than others previously bred and this was attributed to the use of these pale-coloured females, although with present-day knowledge, the validity of the statement must be queried. These pale females were referred to as being 'dimorphic' and, upon inspection, it was noted that the feather was much broader than that in the normal non-intensive.

There are two main forms of feather:

1) Completely non-coloured feathers which are usually found around the vent and flank areas.
2) Frosted feathers, which are of two types. Firstly, there are extended-frosted feathers, i.e. white (in the case of a clear bird) on the lower third to half and on the tip with the lipochrome colouring showing between. The frosting on the tip is greatly extended when compared with the normal non-intensive feather so that the colour is limited to a small area in the centre. So wide is the frosting that the overlapping of these feathers gives a visually white appearance. Secondly, there are feathers which, although frosted at the tip, have a greatly reduced amount of frosting and thus show a solid colour effect. These are found in the area of the colour points.

It is thought that the distinctive pattern of the dimorphic was a throwback to the black-hooded red siskin from which red canaries are derived. The male is a highly-coloured bird of carmine red with a black hood whereas the female is mostly grey with some colour points. The colour points are situated on the rump, wing butts, upper breast and around the eyes. This difference is known as *sexual dimorphism* and is attributable not to the genes for colour but to separate characteristics which are associated with sex because the genes responsible for them are situated on the sex chromosome. Other characteristics, which are visible in individuals of one sex only, are known as *sex-limited* factors; these do not function on a sex-linked basis because the genes responsible for their appearance are not situated on the sex chromosome but are on the somatic chromosomes. In spite of this, the normal hereditary patterns do not emerge and the characteristics involved appear in one sex but not in the other. It has been suggested that this is due to either testicular or ovarian hormones playing a part in restricting these characteristics to one sex only.

It is evident, in the case of dimorphism related to the black-hooded red siskin, that the factor is partially sexual, which gives rise to the theory that the male black-hooded red siskin carries the factor involved. This theory is based on the fact that, regardless of the type of canary female paired to such a male, the female F_1 hybrids almost always appear very similar to the female siskin.

So far as is known, no thesis has been published on the exact inheritance pattern of the dimorphic. It would seem to be partially sex linked, partially dominant and partially recessive, indicating that more than one gene, coupled with one or more different factors in the canary, are operating either independently or in conjunction with the genes from the siskin.

At the time when dimorphic females were beginning to appear, the real driving force of experimental breeders was the production of a red lipochrome. Therefore, little, if any, work was done to establish the dimorphic as a distinct breed to be kept and enjoyed for itself. As a consequence, the existence of a male dimorphic was considered to be impossible. Some years later, however, a few experimental breeders worked with the dimorphic and produced a theory that the male dimorphic did, in fact, exist. This was considered somewhat startling and was greeted with scepticism by the majority of breeders. The bird described as a male dimorphic resembled a non-intensive red, except that it carried more frosting, particularly around the neck and along the back; it also had deeper colour points. Also especially noticeable were the areas of white feathers which extended backwards and forwards around the vent. It is a matter of speculation whether these birds were true dimorphic males or merely poor non-intensive red specimens that were partly influenced by the gene(s) responsible for the production of the dimorphic female. It is, however, known that, when paired to dimorphic females, the resulting female offspring more closely resembled the ideal for which breeders were striving.

Little experimentation is conducted nowadays on the production of dimorphics from the black-hooded red siskin source. These hybrid birds, however colourful they may be, in no way approach the standards of excellence now found in the new dimorphics which will be studied below. In earlier breedings of the original dimorphics (known as classic dimorphics), a non-intensive red male showing as heavy a frosting as possible was paired with a female showing as much white as possible. A young male showing the largest amount of frosting in the region of the vent was then paired back to its mother. Future generations were similarly paired, with vigorous selection, until a true breeding strain was achieved.

Mention has been briefly made to the new-type dimorphics and these are the birds that almost universally appear on the showbench with only a very rare example of the classic dimorphic being seen today. Their growth in popularity, particularly in the self series, has been dramatic. This is probably due in part to the non-arrival of any new mutations for several years.

The new dimorphics appeared during the late 1960s in Italy. Unlike their classic counterparts, this new variety, particularly in the females, appeared perfect, being snow white with the lipochrome-coloured points both distinct and limited to the designated areas. With the classics, however good, the colour tends to extend into the wings and around the face instead of being restricted to a red extension of the eyes and to the wing butts. The male version also caused remarkable excitement in that, at the time, it had a light pink background colour, white areas on the vent, flank and inner chest and bright red colour points. It also carried a bright red mask resembling that of the goldfinch (*Carduelis carduelis*). Today, further improvements have been made and birds almost totally white with bright red colour points are being produced.

Although the genetical behaviour is different from that of the classic, it is still impossible to be precise about the expected progeny from a pairing of anything other than new type to new type, from which all new type youngsters can be expected. Certainly, the new type dimorphic seems to have greater dominance than the classic type with 'dimorphic type' youngsters being bred from a new type dimorphic paired to a heavily-frosted non-intensive. It must also be asked whether there are intensive and non-intensive versions of the new dimorphic and, if so, in what way do they differ in appearance. This is relevant in an attempt to determine how very white examples can be bred with colour points showing no hint of frosting, whereas, historically, one is used to viewing birds with only frosted colour points. Another question that appears to be without answer at this time, is whether 'carriers' of the new dimorphic factor can exist and, if so, is the inheritance pattern determined by sex linkage or by recessive factors. This is posed because of the appearance of near-perfect examples from dimorphic-type birds being paired either together or to new type mates. As there is no scientific evidence at present on which to base a theory, only the recording and comparison of results by a large number of breeders over a long period will, by establishing a consistent pattern, solve these mysteries.

It should be made clear here that not all new-type dimorphics are perfect examples and breeding skills are just as important for these birds as for all other varieties. In fact, it is the author's opinion that the perfect dimorphic is by far the most difficult of all feather types to create.

Possibly as a result of poor breeding results during the first few years of the bird's introduction into the UK, or possibly because of the problem of feather lump inheritance, much to many peoples' amazement, the popularity of new-type dimorphics in their clear form has not been established.

Certainly, the breed does not seem to be as robust and free breeding as most other clear varieties and feather lumps, so common with all wide- and soft-feathered breeds, can cause problems if the prevention of this fault is not properly considered when selecting breeding pairs. The aim is always to produce as many near-perfect examples as possible of whatever species is being bred. It must be remembered, however, that this is the *ultimate* aim and matings should be chosen to produce offspring which will assist in its achievement in the second generation.

By pairing together the whitest examples year after year, the percentage of high-quality examples will certainly increase, but so will the percentage of chicks with lumps. As the reason for the appearance of lumps is not fully understood, it is not possible to eradicate the problem by selection. The only way to avoid making the problem worse is not to breed from any bird carrying lumps. With care, however, the number of offspring showing this feather fault can be reduced but, unfortunately, the number of perfect examples bred will be reduced at the same time. By pairing together a new type male with a classic dimorphic female, extremely white females are normally produced, together with very poor-quality males, resembling overfrosted non-intensive examples. If those males are paired to genuine new type females, and the young females are paired to new type males, a high percentage of youngsters can be bred in the second year which will resemble the standard sought. The width of feather, thought to be a major consideration in birds with lumps, is reduced in both generations and, if records are kept of such pairings and proper thought given to suitable mates, there is even hope that a large percentage of all birds bred in successive years will be of high quality.

Dimorphics of either type should display lipochrome pigment only in defined and restricted areas. In the female, the pigment should appear:

1) As an 'eyebrow' with the colour running neither from eye to eye, nor down to the cheeks.
2) As a small distinct area on the wing butts which does not extend to the flights.
3) On the rump limited to that area and not extending to the back or underbody. Ideally, the chest should be devoid of lipochrome pigment. This, however, is extremely hard to achieve without a corresponding loss of colour from one or more of the colour points and a slightly-coloured chest is accepted on the showbench. The colour points of the male are the same except for the face, where the goldfinch-type mask, distinct, bright and restricted to the front face, should be present. Elsewhere the bird should be as white as possible, although it is unrealistic to think that the whiteness of a male can ever match that of the female.

Dimorphics should be colour fed in exactly the same way as other varieties because the distribution of colour is effected not by the amount of carotene consumed but by the genes responsible for colour distribution. As it is important for the wings to be as near white as possible, thought should be given to the diet offered to the parent birds prior to and during the breeding season. As has been discussed earlier (p. 242), certain natural foods contain varying amounts of carotenoids, all of which, to a lesser or greater degree, will affect the nest feathers of the chicks. As the chick will not moult its flight feathers in the first year, any deposition of colour will remain and an otherwise perfect bird could be spoiled.

Although the remarks made in this section have been directed towards the breeder of red-ground varieties, dimorphics can and do exist in all ground colours. In recent years, there has been a large increase in the number and quality of yellow-ground examples in both clear and self varieties. It is to be hoped that breeders will expand their imaginations and experiment in order that perfect examples in all ground colours may be presented in the near future.

Similarly, this section has been mainly concerned with the breeding of clear varieties but the rules and suggestions put forward apply equally to self varieties. Although less points are awarded for ground colour and feather type in self breeds, these areas are, nevertheless, of paramount importance and require as much thought as the creation of birds displaying perfection in the pattern of melanistic striations.

SELF (MELANIN) VARIETIES

In the section on clear varieties (p. 235), ground colour and feather type was discussed, these being the only areas on which adjudication is possible. Although fewer points are allocated to these attributes in self varieties, the production of birds possessing the standard of excellence called for in clear or lipochrome varieties is of equal importance.

A self bird is one in which the normal melanistic pigment is evident i.e. the variegation factors previously described (p. 236) are not inhibited and this allows the dark pigment to be present.

Classic Colours

GREEN (BRONZE OR BLUE)

In all essential characteristics, the original domesticated canary resembles the wild canary (*Serinus canaria*) in that it has a green phenotype on which black and brown striations are superimposed. The green appearance is, in fact, an optical illusion. The canary, in fact, possesses no green pigment, but the superimposition of the black and brown pigment on a yellow ground colour gives the appearance of green.

Although not conclusively proved, it is now generally accepted that there are three forms of melanistic pigment. Firstly, there is the brown edging to the feather known as *phaeomelanin brown*.

Secondly, there is the black pigment located on each side of the centre shaft of the feather and throughout the lower third of the feather – i.e. the underfeather or underflue – and also throughout the horny areas, which is known as *eumelanin black*. Thirdly, there is another brown pigment, either intermingled or separately deposited but masked by the black in the same areas, which is known as *eumelanin brown*.

When these pigments are present on a yellow ground the bird is known as a green, on a silver ground as a blue, and on a red ground as a bronze. When the ivory factor is visible, the prefix 'ivory' is added to the green and the blue and the term 'rose bronze' is used to describe the red-ground version.

Within the UK, few examples of green birds are seen on the show bench, as breeders prefer to keep these birds as outcrosses for the production of other mutations. Certainly, their stamina and clearly-defined variegation patterns make them invaluable for this purpose. This is not the case in many other countries, however, and large numbers of green birds can be viewed at most exhibitions. A full description of the ideal show bird can be found for the green and all other mutations in the section on judging coloured canaries (p. 307). It is sufficient to state here that the ideal bird should be of an even, grass-green colour with dark black legs, feet and beak. Its striations should be broad and well defined and should not only extend from the head down the back but also be very evident on the flanks and extend around the chest. The latter point will always be more evident in females than in males. The distribution of striations, as described briefly here applies to all mutations in which striations are required. Variations, particularly the width of the striations, will be evident, depending upon the mutation involved, and these are commented upon in the relevant section.

The greatest problem facing breeders of green varieties for exhibition purposes is the excessive presence of phaeomelanin brown. This not only breaks up the definition of the desired black striations but also visually dulls the brightness of the lipochrome colouring.

This fault can be caused by two things:

1) The bird in question carrying too much frosting – a fault that can be eradicated by pairing the bird back to an extremely intensive example.
2) An imbalance in the genes responsible for producing both

265

phaeomelanin brown and eumelanin black. This fault is not easily corrected and will require careful monitoring if it is not to become prevalent in the stud.

For breeders of green birds the ideal pairing is self green to self green, both birds ideally being homozygous but generally, as long as a heterozygote example is carrying only a factor which is itself non-diluted, there is no reason why good youngsters cannot be produced.

When seeking to produce exhibition green birds, three factors should, at all costs, be avoided:

1) The dilute factor – expressed as an agate in the green series and an isabel in the brown series (see pp. 270).
2) The ino factor in which the presence of phaeomelanin brown is sought.
3) The satinette factor because the mutation can be produced only in the dilute form.

There are, however, two further points to be noted:

1) We have discussed producing an ideal exhibition-quality green, but a green bird can be used as a useful outcross to accentuate certain characteristics sought in the newer mutations. It is an indispensible outcross for the ino mutation but rather than an exhibition-quality green, one exhibiting an excess of phaeo-melanin brown should be used. (The reasons for this are explained in the section on the ino mutation p. 274.) Thus any birds presenting this phenotype should not be automatically culled.
2) A fancier with limited means, cages etc. may sometimes have to use stock which, in an ideal situation, would not be used. This applies particularly to breeders attempting to introduce a new mutation. In this situation, a bird referred to universally as a *passe partout* (or more correctly as a green carrying isabel) is the obvious answer. The passe partout must, of course, also be carrying the nominated new mutation. The usefulness of such a bird lies in its ability to produce green, brown, agate and isabel female offspring regardless of the female used. When using such a bird, however, great care must be taken to ensure that the rules for producing exhibition examples of the four classic varieties are implemented as soon as possible.

To summarise, if exhibition stock is required, a green can normally be paired successfully to brown, green pastel, brown pastel, green opal or brown opal but should not be paired to isabel, agate, isabel pastel, agate pastel, isabel ino, agate ino, isabel satinette or agate satinette.

Although the correct genetical make-up is necessary to produce a green bird with the jet-black horny areas required, the author has noted improvements in this quality when birds are moulted in direct sunlight. It is again emphasised that this practice can only improve the depth of black, it cannot create it. Only proper pairings can achieve this result.

Until the late 1970s, green series birds appeared only occasionally with genuine jet-black horny areas. More recently birds, particularly bronze examples, have started to appear in which this characteristic is more fully defined. They are advertised as 'super-oxidised' and their source seems to be Italy but there are few records of this, or of their subsequent distribution. Two interesting points arise. Firstly the inheritance pattern seems to be totally unpredictable with no clear pattern emerging. Even the pairing together of two super-oxidised birds fails to guarantee that all the offspring will be similarly dark. Secondly, when the factor is present, it is accompanied by a duller lipochrome colour – particularly in the rose series. This latter feature is particularly difficult to comprehend because the super-expression of black is usually to the detriment of brown and normally assists in the production of a luminous lipochrome. No explanation has been forthcoming from the author's most knowledgeable acquaintance's and his own experiments have produced no conclusions on which to base a theory. It will be interesting to see what emerges in the near future.

The green bird has been used as the basis for these notes but the comments apply equally to blue and bronze examples. The comments made on the pairings of birds of different ground colours in the lipochrome section apply equally to all self birds

BROWN (CINNAMON)

The brown canary, known in type-canary circles as the cinnamon, appeared as the result of a spontaneous change (mutation) in the gene responsible for the production of eumelanin black. We know that it was being cultivated in the early eighteenth century but it is not known whether the mutation occurred in wild or domesticated stock. Its appearance is of no great surprise as there are cinnamon versions of a great many types of bird.

The effect of the brown mutation is to change the colour of the black striations to a deep chocolate brown. With the underfeather being a mid-grey colour, the eumelanin black, as expressed in the horny areas, is changed to a flesh colour. Also, the eye colour becomes a ruby red although this is normally only evident during the first week of the chick's life. Canary breeders universally refer to it as pink, which is somewhat misleading. The changed colour of the eumelanin pigmentation is called eumelanin brown but whether it is of the same composition as the assumed third melanistic pigment carrying the same name is still undetermined.

With green series birds, great emphasis is made on excluding, wherever possible, the presence of phaeomelanin brown but the presence of the optical-blue factor is a major plus. With brown series birds, the reverse is true to a certain degree. The width and distribution of deep-chocolate-brown striations is a major requirement, as is the presence of a bright luminous ground colour. However, the presence of an overall chocolate-brown phaeomelanin suffusion is also a prime requisite in an exhibition bird, which is one of the enigmas that continues to puzzle the author. Thus, whilst the brown is accepted as a suitable partner in a pairing selected to produce exhibition-quality greens, it must be emphasised that the brown should not itself be of exhibition quality. By now it should be evident that not every bird produced can be exhibited and separate studs need to be kept, particularly in the classic varieties (green, brown, agate and isabel), in order to produce exhibition-quality birds in the different mutations. To produce good greens, a brown bird should present the qualities sought after in a top-quality green, i.e. broad well-defined striations and an absence of phaeomelanin brown; such an example is also used for the production of quality opals and, arguably, satinettes. The exhibition-quality brown, whilst unsuitable for producing first-class examples of these mutations, is ideal for producing quality pastels and inos. Great thought must be given, therefore, to the practicalities of the size of the stud kept and the mutations that are to be bred.

The brown mutation is a sex-linked recessive and, therefore, the passage of the gene producing brown is determined by the sex (X) chromosome. Thus a male bird can be one of three types:

1) A non-brown (green).

2) A brown carrier (green with one normal allelomorph and the other mutated).
3) A brown.

The phenotype of examples 1 and 2 is the same whilst the third example, having inherited one brown gene from the father and one from the mother, is different.

A female, which possesses only one X chromosome, must be either a brown or a green, i.e. it cannot carry the factor.

There are five possible pairings that can be considered when studying the inheritance of the brown factor and these follow precisely the pattern studied in the ivory factor i.e.:

Parents		Young	
Father	Mother	Sons	Daughters
Pair 1: green	brown	green/brown	green
Pair 2: brown	green	green/brown	brown
Pair 3: green/brown	brown	green/brown brown	green brown
Pair 4: green/brown	green	green/brown green	green brown
Pair 5: brown	brown	brown	brown

Where two possibilities exist, the theoretical expectation is always quoted as 50% of each.

Using information featured in the section on the ivory (p. 249), and using the letter B to denote the brown factor, the pairings appear as follows:

	PARENTS		YOUNG	
	FATHER	MOTHER	SONS	DAUGHTERS
PAIR 1	XX	XBY	XBX (or XXB)	XY
PAIR 2	XBXB	XY	XBX (or XXB)	XBY
PAIR 3	XBX (or XXB)	XBY	XBX (or XXB) XBXB	XY XBY
PAIR 4	XBX (or XXB)	XY	XBX (or XXB) XX	XY XBY
PAIR 5	XBXB	XBY	XBXB	XBY

Subject to the rules previously explained, it is usually possible and, in many instances, desirable to pair brown to brown. By studying recognisable mutations, however, it can be observed that, by pairing together any mutated specimen to its like over a period of 2 or 3 years, size, colour and, when applicable, deposition of melanin, starts to diminish. This can easily be rectified by outcrossing to a green bird, say every 2 or 3 years. Care must be taken, however, to ensure that the correct type of green is used in order to preserve the particular characteristics that are already present within the brown birds in the stud.

The brown, unlike its green counterpart, retains its name regardless of ground colour, the actual colour involved being used to prefix the term brown. Thus a yellow-ground bird becomes a gold brown, a red a red brown and a white-ground a silver brown. The term ivory is also used where applicable.

AGATE AND ISABEL

The ino, pastel, opal and topaz mutations all appear in four possible forms: green, brown, agate or isabel. The satinette appears as either an agate or an isabel. Thus, although the brown and agate/isabel forms are themselves mutations, they, along with the green, are referred to as the 'classic' colours.

Long before the start of the attempt to produce a red canary – most peoples' idea of a coloured canary – there had been mutations of melanistic pigment, the brown being the mutation studied to date. Another mutation was recognised as having occurred in the Netherlands in about 1900, although a bird of similar phenotype was recorded in France in 1709. This bird, an offspring of a pair of greens, was referred to as an agate. The agate factor acts as a modifier of all forms of melanin pigment, causing the black eumelanin striations and the phaeomelanin in tips to the feather to become paler and less broad, the underfeather to change to a charcoal-grey colour and the horny areas to revert to a flesh colour. With the reduction in width of the melanin striations, more lipochrome colouring can be viewed and so the bird appears to have a deeper colour, e.g. yellow with black stripes. Selective breeding over the years has resulted in birds being bred to the set exhibition standards so that a top-class example has striations very distinctively sited over the head, down the back, along the flanks and around the chest. This, as previously stated, is a prime requirement in all mutations where striations are required but the width of the striations is very restricted. This absolute ideal is easier to achieve in an intensive feather as, in the wider non-intensive and dimorphic feathers, there is a corresponding increase in the width of the striations. The final requirement of an exhibition agate, and this applies equally to cases where the bird has some of the newer mutations annexed to it, is the presence of a moustache – Mexican variety – i.e. descending vertically from the point at which the upper mandible joins the head. Although the agate has had its periods of popularity interspersed with periods of neglect, particularly when the later mutations were appearing, until recently examples were only viewed in the intensive or non-intensive form, with the emphasis being on red-ground birds. Since the new type dimorphic factor was introduced and perfected in self birds, the agate has received a well-deserved boost in popularity, breeders having found that the combination of the agate and dimorphic factors gives an extremely pleasing effect.

With the introduction of the satinette mutation, breeders found that, unlike any other mutation, agates carrying this factor displayed a different phenotype from their homozygous counterparts; the black striations and the black colouration in the wing and tail feathers took on a most pleasing silver overlay. For a few seasons, such examples, particularly in the dimorphic feather type, acquired major prizes at exhibitions until judges of strong character insisted on either judging birds to the written standard or rewriting the standards. As a result of this, the written standard has now been more or less universally accepted and agates representing the original phenotype are now predominant on the showbench. As with any type of canary, the rules regarding the pairing together of feather types apply equally and the advice given on lipochrome varieties (pp. 235–264) should be implemented here. This will ensure that birds well endorsed with good ground colour and distribution of melanins are not spoiled, for example, by overfrosting.

When breeding agates or isabels, which we will study further in due course, all other things being equal, like should be paired with like; agate to agate is ideal, with agate to isabel the next best alternative. Only in the most exceptional cases, such as when attempting to stabilise or extend a new mutation, or in the event of suitable stock being unpurchasable, should an agate or isabel be paired to a green or brown. The resultant offspring from such a pairing are invariably either overmarked agates and isabels or poorly-marked greens and browns. Only selective breeding over a number of years will eradicate these faults. Although it is generally accepted that the pairing of agate to isabel will improve the distribution of striations in the isabel stock, rarely, for reasons the author is unable to explain, is the opposite pairing of benefit. It must also be remembered that, as one of the four classic types, the agate can have other mutations 'attached' to it and it is equally unwise to pair, say, agate to green pastel as it is to pair agate to green. The rule must obviously be to discount all other considerations when pairings are being made and to concentrate solely on the classic colour involved.

The agate mutation is a sex-linked recessive – as is the brown – and consequently five possible pairings are possible:

Pair 1: agate male × normal female which produces normal males carrying agate and agate females.

Pair 2: normal male × agate female which produces all normal stock with males carrying agate.

Pair 3: normal male carrying agate × agate female which produces normal males and females – the males carrying agate – and agate males and females.

Pair 4: normal male carrying agate × normal female which produces normal males and females and agate females. 50% of the males will carry the agate factor but their phenotype will be the same as normal non-carriers.

Part 5: agate male × agate female which will produce all agate young.

Already we have referred to an agate and an isabel and this is the only instance in which we use different terms for one mutation; agate is a diluted green and the isabel a diluted brown. Originally, the factor was known as dilute, this term being used to prefix the words green and brown.

The isabel mutation occurred in green stock but, by following the inheritance tables used so far in the section on coloured canaries, it is difficult to determine how the isabel was ever produced. If we pair an agate male to a brown female (using the letter D to indicate the agate (or dilute) gene and B to indicate the brown gene), we have as our parent birds XDXD for the male and XBY for the female. The chart demonstrating the separation of genes and the recoupling in the young is as follows:

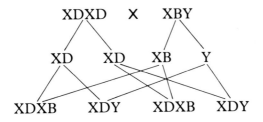

Thus, we have produced green males carrying dilute and brown (XDXB), which should enable us to produce isabel females regardless of the female used.

For the purpose of this next illustration we will use an agate female. Thus our parent stock is XDXB × XDY and the table follows the predictable pattern:

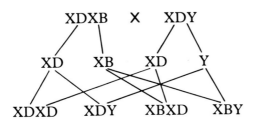

Remembering that D equals dilute and B equals brown, and also remembering that, with sex-linked recessive characters, both sex chromosomes of the pair in the male and the sole sex chromosome of the female need to have mutated before the new phenotype is present, it can be clearly seen that the females produced from such a pairing will be either agates (XDY) or browns (XBY).

Practical experience tells us that this is not so. In fact all four of the classic colours can be produced and other factors must, therefore, be at work. The answer is to be found in the crossover of genes (p. 100).

So far as the author is able to determine, it has never been proved how frequently the crossover occurs. In consequence, it is difficult to determine how soon the isabel appeared after the arrival of the agate and also whether it appeared as a result of a planned pairing or by accident. The beauty of the isabel has now been appreciated for many years, particularly in the intensive red versions.

In the exhibition-quality isabel, as in its agate equivalent, the striations are well distributed and narrow in size, but the colour is

273

chocolate brown rather than charcoal-grey/black. The underfeather is a paler version of the brown, with more of a beige tint, and the eyes are appreciably brighter red in nestlings, although they also darken as the chicks mature.

An ideal mating is to pair isabel to isabel, although an outcross to an agate every third year is recommended, particularly to preserve the flank markings. Unlike its brown counterpart, the isabel should not carry an overall suffusion of phaeomelanin brown, which adds to the enigma that the brown should be required to show this characteristic. The ideal isabel presents itself as a bird devoid of phaeomelanin pigment with the optical blue factor fully expressed.

As with most other self birds, the words red, rose, gold and silver precede the words agate or isabel to denote the appropriate ground colour.

New Colours

INO

It is now several years since the ino mutation appeared and, whilst general agreement has been reached on what constitutes the ideal phenotype, little explanation has been given for the large variation in the phenotypes which exist. The mutation, which has a homozygous recessive inheritance pattern, occurred originally from a pair of classic red isabels. It was different in that little if any melanistic pigment was visible, the underfeather was a pale beige and the eyes bright red. This eye colour, unlike normal brown/isabel series birds, did not darken as the chick grew older. Conjecture at the time was that the new factor inhibited the appearance of both eumelanim and phaeomelanin, but this has been proved incorrect. Early pairings to stabilise the factor concentrated on transferring it to green and brown, thus producing, as was correctly guessed, a more interesting and different phenotype.

This early departure from the attempt to produce the ultimate in isabel and agate versions has unfortunately persisted so that few top-class examples of these variations have bred. In consequence, many fanciers, having never seen a good example, and relying on hearsay descriptions of these variations, have never attempted to breed what, in its perfect form, is a delicately-marked but nevertheless beautiful bird. It is true to say that the isabel ino and the agate equivalent (which incidentally carries a similar visual phenotype but a pale grey underfeather), if of medium quality, are a disappointment as they closely resemble the original mutated bird. Top-quality examples following the pattern now accepted in the ideal brown are, however, a different matter. To be considered excellent, a brown or green ino must carry brown sides and tips to the feathers, with white in the area normally taken up by the eumelanin pigmentation. The isabel factor has the effect of reducing the width of this pigment and the ino factor, strangely, reduces it further. The word 'strangely' is apposite as no such dilution appears in green or brown examples. As the phaeomelanin pigmentation still exists, split by white centres to the feathers, a pale twisted-rope effect results which is most pleasing to the eye. Ironically, whilst it is possible to achieve such a phenotype, given proper dedication, the lack of effort in the establishment of the agate and isabel inos, is probably the reason for International judging standards stating that the bird should be examined as a lipochrome. In this way, what one would normally strive to achieve in a melanistic mutation, is reversed and can only continue to undermine the popularity of what could and should be a beautiful addition to the birds kept by true coloured-canary breeders.

Throughout the years, three or more different phenotypes have appeared in both brown and green inos. The mutation, however, has attained universal acclaim and has not followed the fate of most of the other mutations by coming into vogue for a few years then disappearing from the scene for a time. The benefit of this continuous support is that many more breeders have made pairings resulting in the production of more top-class examples. Also clearer directives have evolved on how to breed a greater percentage of exhibition-quality birds.

The version of the green or brown ino which has been accepted as the ideal is the one where a broad chocolate-brown spangle edges the feather, the centre being white with lipochrome colouring filling the gap between the two. The spangled effect should be present from the top of the head to the tail, the undertail and upper tail coverts being similarly marked. The secondary and primary flight feathers, together with the tail feathers, should carry a brown edge. Striations should be very evident through the flanks and around the chest. The ideal will, of course, be found most often in the wider feathered non-intensive and dimorphic versions, but this does not preclude first-class intensive examples being produced.

Whilst many more birds approaching this standard are being

bred, it is not clear whether this is due to a genuine study of the various versions and their breeding traits or to the development of more selective breeding.

Certainly, in the author's experience, no safe and sure methods of breeding have been evolved. The two other most usual phenotypes to exist are ones which show:

1) A brown spangle as in the ideal but with no central white area and lipochrome colouring spreading throughout.
2) A reversal of these trends where the brown pigment is situated down the centre of the feather leaving white tips.

In every instance, the underfeather colouring – dark beige in the brown and dark grey in the green – is identical. Eye colouring varies greatly from pale to dark red.

Questions regarding the composition of the brown pigment are still unanswered. Rarely is phaeomelanin a chocolate-brown colour when viewed on a normal bird showing both eumelanin black or brown and phaeomelanin, although this colour is predominant in the eumelanin stripe found in good examples of brown series birds. Also, a recent discovery has shown that more than one gene has mutated to produce the ino phenotype. Thus, assuming the possibility of crossovers and considering the strength of all mutated genes relative to their unmutated allelomorphs, it must be asked whether the birds which show a different phenotype, and are now more widely seen, are of a type intermediate to the normal and the full ino.

Many questions are still unanswered and possibly never will be, but this fact alone should ensure continued support for this stunning mutation.

As the ino female shows a form of sexual dimorphism which entails a greater presence of phaeomelanin, it is not unreasonable to assume that it will usually illustrate the mutation better than the male. This is recognised and so a separate judging standard is applied to male examples. Up to recent years, the male ino was instantly recognisable as it carried only a limited amount of pigmentation – on the saddle and, in supposedly excellent examples, on the top of the head. Progress over the past few years has enabled the production of male birds well marked across the head, down the back and throughout the flanks, although they rarely possess, in any clarity, the sought-after spangled effect seen in the female. More often than not, there is a positive split in the pigmentation of the head and the back, with superior examples possessing pigmentation that flows from the eye area right through to the tail. These are obviously the birds most sought after.

In the early days of the mutation, possibly as a result of too much inbreeding, the ino was invariably difficult to rear and even when this difficulty was successfully overcome, problems were still experienced in weaning and development to maturity because of the bird's weak eyesight. In fact, many examples often seemed completely blind until they were 5 to 6 weeks old. Fortunately, this trait seems, in general, to have resolved itself, but care must still be taken when selecting breeding pairs. Although no guarantees can ever be given as to the quality and strengths of the progeny of specific pairings, it is believed that a greater chance of success will result if the following recommendations are followed:

1) Pair together ino to ino only when each of the pair have themselves been bred from the most recommended pairing of ino to normal carrying ino.
2) Ensure that one of the pair is a brown and the other a green. It is irrelevant whether the green or brown is male or female.
3) Ensure that the normal bird carrying ino is of the non-exhibition type, i.e. that it carries an excess of phaeomelanin, giving a sombre dirty look.
4) Cull from your stock any ino or normal carrying ino that shows or produces inos with gingery brown markings. Such birds are not suitable for exhibition purposes and are unlikely to assist in producing them.

The ino, being a homozygous recessive mutation, can be produced as follows:

Pair 1: ino male × ino female will produce all ino young.
Pair 2: ino male × normal female (or the reverse pairing) will produce all normal young carrying ino.
Pair 3: ino male × normal female carrying ino (or the reverse pairing) will produce 50% inos and 50% normals carrying ino.
Pair 4: normal male carrying ino × normal female carrying ino will produce 50% normals carrying ino, 25% homozygous normals and 25% inos.

Pair 5: normal male carrying ino × normal female will produce all normal young of which 50% will carry the ino factor.

N.B.

1) The word normal is used to denote any bird that is a non-visual ino.
2) The expectations are theoretical.
3) In pairs 4 and 5, all of the visually normal young will have to be test mated to determine which carry the ino factor.

OPAL

It was probably because the opal was a homozygous recessive mutation, not attached to the sex chromosome, that it took 10 or more years after its first appearance in 1949 for the mutation to gain deserved popularity.

From a pair of green Roller canaries in Germany in 1949, a lime-green bird with a different striation effect was observed amongst the offspring. The bird at the time was called a recessive agate but, on reaching the Netherlands several years later, its name was changed to that which we recognise today – the opal. Close examination of this bird showed that the black eumelanin striations had changed from black to a dark silvery grey with the underflue partly diluted to a dark silver charcoal colour. The dark black colour present in the horny areas of a normal green was not affected. In a normal green, the tops of the flight and wing feathers are black and the undersides a dark silvery grey. In this, and in subsequent opal progeny, the exact reverse is the case, suggesting a change in the structural make-up of the feather rather than a change in the make-up of the melanistic pigment. Phaeomelanin brown, present in a normal green, appears to be prevented from appearing. The overall result of these changes, which incidentally cause no dilution in either the width or distribution of the melanistic striations, is most pleasing. The combination of silvery grey with the various ground colours gives the bird a striking visual effect. The problem with the opal factor, fortunately associated only with the green variety, is that changes appear to take place in the composition of the feather. This often causes the secondary flight feathers to lie incorrectly and the body feathers, especially around the flanks and thighs, to curl in a manner not unlike that of a frilled canary. These irritating faults have caused all but the most devoted of fanciers to desert the ranks of opal breeders and, because of this, few exhibition-quality birds have been bred. These faults, although seemingly impossible to eradicate totally, can be controlled to a limited degree by careful selection of breeding pairs. Although it is not possible to give precise advice on pairings to guarantee progeny that will not display the undesirable characteristics, it is possible to give advice on the pairings to avoid. Because of the likelihood of the problems being accentuated, the following should *never* be paired together:

Pair 1: green opal to green opal.
Pair 2: two intensive birds, whether they are both opals, both normals carrying the opal factor or one of each.
Pair 3: an opal displaying frilled feathers with a mate – carrier or otherwise – which has less than perfect feather quality.

Pairings that do assist in preventing bad feather quality are:

Pair 1: green opal to normal green carrying opal.
Pair 2: green opal to brown carrying opal.
Pair 3: green opal to brown opal.

It is also known that agate and isabel opals, and their classic counterparts carrying the factor, can assist with feather quality. However, the damage done to the quality and density of the melanistic pigment by such pairings is far greater than the benefit gained in feather quality and is, therefore, not recommended.

For reasons which the author is unable to explain, the combination of the opal and pastel factors in green series birds also seems to assist in feather quality. Whilst the combination of two of the newer mutations has not been pursued generally because the end result is not thought to offer a pleasing phenotype, little difference exists between the green opal and the green opal pastel and, therefore, if the benefit of improved feather quality is evident, there is no reason why the combination of the two factors should not occur. The major difference in the phenotype of the opal pastel compared with that of the opal is the dilution of the depth of colouration on the underside of the flight and tail feathers and in the underflue. The striations appear marginally narrower and slightly more silver.

Breeding any mutation that is recessive and not situated on the sex chromosome requires both parents to have at least one of the genes of the appropriate pair in the mutated state. Thus, when the original opal was bred, it should ideally have been paired back to its parent.

Records do not indicate whether this happened or whether the bird had to be paired back to a bird having both genes of the pair in an unmutated state. From the latter mating, all of the youngsters would be visually normal but all of them would carry the factor. Thus, if one of these was then paired back to the opal parent, further opal offspring could be produced in the second year. The four possible pairings to produce opals are as follows:

Pair 1: opal male × opal female will produce all opal young.

Pair 2: opal male × normal female will produce all normal young carrying the opal factor. (The reverse pairing of normal male to opal female will give identical results.)

Pair 3: normal male carrying opal × opal female will produce 50% normals carrying opal and 50% opal.(Again the reverse pairing will give identical results.)

Pair 4: normal male carrying opal × normal female carrying opal will produce youngsters in the Mendelian ratio 1:2:1 i.e. 25% opals, 50% normal carrying opal and 25% normals.

N.B.
1) All percentages are theoretical.
2) The word normal denotes any bird that is not an opal.
3) In the case of Pair 4, all non-opal youngsters will need to be test mated to determine which are the carriers.

The agate opal is probably the most widely-kept version of this mutation. This may well be due to the fact that there are none of the feather problems that so bedevil its non-diluted counterpart, the green opal. Also, with the expected reduction in width and colouration of the melanistic striations leaving fine silver stripes, neatly arranged throughout the plumage, and with no phaeomelanin brown feather tips, the overall appearance is stunning. By virtue of the fact that the more pastel shades of the rose, gold ivory and silver ground colours allow a more definite contrast, these varieties are more widely kept than their red and gold counterparts. It is true to say, however, that all agate opals, when presented at or near perfection are a joy to behold and are well worthy of a place in any fancier's stud.

The rules regarding pairings, as explained in the section on the classic varieties, apply equally to the agate opal and it is recommended that no non-diluted stock is introduced.

The brown and isabel opals tend to be disappointing in that the presence of melanistic pigment, surely a prime requirement in a self breeder's stud, is at a minimum. In fact, in both instances, they can frequently be mistaken for lipochrome birds.

An ideal brown opal will carry very fine pale brown striations throughout the plumage and have a deposition of brown in the wings and tail. The underfeather is a pale beige. The isabel will invariably appear as a clear, with just a faint trace of pearly brown pigmentation distributed throughout the wing and tail feathers. The underfeather is so pale a beige that it appears white unless studied extremely closely.

PASTEL

Although it has now been with us for 25 years, the first pastel having appeared in the Netherlands in around 1960, the mutation still continues to surprise, particularly in the green version, and no one, as far as the author is able to ascertain, is able to guarantee set expectations from nominated pairs.

The first pastel was an isabel example appearing in the progeny of a pair of classic red isabels. Some experimental breeders had been attempting to breed an isabel totally devoid of pigmentation for several years and first impressions of the original pastel were that this dream had been realised. Closer examination, however, showed that the phenotype of the bird was so different from that expected in a normal isabel that a spontaneous change must have occurred on the melanin-producing gene. When moulted, the bird showed a pale suffusion of brown throughout the plumage instead of the expected fine striations. Test mating showed the factor to be a sex-linked recessive. Thus, as with all mutations having this form of inheritance, a male with its two X chromosomes can carry the factor, although presenting a normal phenotype, whereas a female, having only one X chromosome, is either a normal or a mutant.

With selective breeding over the years, the isabel pastel is now a well-established breed with many fine examples appearing each time the mutation passes into vogue. An ideal example will display no trace of eumelanin striations but will show a pale brown suffusion throughout the plumage. The underfeather is a pale beige colour.

The brown pastel is a darker version of the isabel, but showing fine brown striations, the underfeather is also darker. It was thought for many years that the pairing of brown pastel to isabel pastel caused no detriment to either. More enlightened commonsense now prevails, however, and to avoid either isabel pastels with faint melanin striations or, conversely, brown pastels devoid of melanin striations, it is recommended that brown pastels be paired only to other non-dilute birds and isabel pastels only to other dilutes. When discussing the classic brown (p. 267), mention was made of the two types of brown. The exhibition-model brown, which carries a deep and heavy suffusion, is an ideal outcross for a brown pastel in that the areas most sought after in both birds is present in this one bird. A brown bred for outcrossing to bronze does not make a suitable partner.

The agate pastel continues to be a centre of debate because its phenotype is so varied. In a perfect form, the bird is a joy to behold, all traces of phaeomelanin disappear and striations appear as a silver charcoal grey, as do the edges of flight and tail feathers. The striations are distinct and well distributed, the horny areas are clear and the moustache is clear and distinct. In contrast, the bird can display a suffusion of phaeomelanin brown – desirable in the isabel pastel, but unwanted in the agate pastel. The striations can appear in almost any colour, from that of a normal agate right through the intermediate colours to the one most sought. In some instances, the striations appear broken, in others they are distinct, although this is not usually the case. The colour of the underflue varies from almost black to a dark silvery grey. Interestingly, the underflue colour is invariably darker, even in a top-class example, than its non-diluted equivalent, the bronze pastel. This is the only instance, to the author's knowledge, where this occurs. It has been noted by many commentators, but never explained, that, when the ivory mutation is present – in whatever form – the bird carries a greater amount of phaeomelanin brown. This makes the ground colour appear dull. Certainly, this would seem to be the case with agate pastels. Rarely does a bird of exhibition quality appear with an ivory ground colour. This applies to all three ground colours.

Whilst normally one can recommend pairing together isabel and agate examples of the same mutation, with the pastel this does not apply. This is because, whilst the presence of phaeomelanin brown is sought in the isabel version, the reverse applies with the agate. This alone could be the reason why fewer than expected top-class examples of the agate pastel have been seen over the years. The introduction of the dimorphic factor in recent years has resulted in teams of birds appearing that represent birds which approach the written standard. Keeping in mind the presence and popularity of the classic agate in the dimorphic form, part of the answer to the problems of breeding good examples of the agate pastel may have emerged, i.e. the use of classic agate stock as an outcross rather than the more usual isabel pastel. Certainly, in whatever feather form involved, this would be the recommended pairing.

The phenotype of the agate pastel can vary enormously but that of the green pastel is even more varied. Birds appear that vary from almost the classic green to the ultimate and most sought after 'greywing'. The only real 'fact' to appear when breeding this version of the mutation is that a greywing showing maximum effect is invariably homozygous for the factor. Notwithstanding this, not all homozygous green pastels are greywings. A heterozygous version can appear in colours varying from almost that of a classic green right through to a partial greywing – known as a lacewing. In all versions, however, the underfeather is always a silvery grey, much paler in degree than any versions of the agate pastel.

The only acceptable version of the green pastel on the showbench in countries using COM regulations is one exhibiting the full greywing effect which, ironically, can only be viewed to full effect when the bird is held and the wing extended manually. In some countries, however, separate classes exist for greywings and bronze pastels which clearly is a nonsense. The exhibition-quality greywing will carry distinct iron-grey striations which extend throughout the plumage and wings and tail from which the dark plumage has been 'pushed back' into an area of about 3 millimetres on the tip of the feather in one direction and to the edge of the wing coverts in the other direction. In between these areas will be a wide patch of silvery grey plumage. The horny areas will be as black as a classic bronze. The male, carrying two X chromosomes, will be the only bird to express fully the greywing effect. The female, having only one X chromosome, although being able to present a phenotype that is unmistakenly 'greywing', can never achieve the degree of excellence evident in the male. The heterozygous versions vary in all degrees. Striations can vary in colour from black to silvery grey and they can appear broken or distinct. The pattern in the wings can vary from a solid colour to the lacewing effect where a series of bars extend across the wings and tail. The blackness necessary in the horny areas is invariably never as well defined in a heterozygous version as in a homozygous bird. Following conventional rules, it would seem advisable to recommend pairing bronze pastel to brown pastel, as with the agate pastel, but this is not the case because:

1) The presence of phaeomelamin is desirable in the brown pastel but not in the bronze version.
2) To achieve the full greywing effect a homozygous version is required.

Instead, an outcross to a homozygous bronze, showing an absence of brown and with jet-black horny areas, is recommended.

Once the flight feathers have been moulted or accidentally damaged, the replacements are inevitably less well marked in the greywing. This reduction in definition multiplies as each year passes. It is therefore critically important that young birds are caged separately during their first moult so as to avoid damage caused by feather picking.

SATINETTE

From its appearance in 1960 until well into the late 1970s, it was assumed that the satinette factor in all four classic colours carried the same colour underfeathers. The agate and green varieties were invariably identical and only in one instance could the isabel and brown versions be positively identified, causing queries in the minds of serious coloured-canary breeders. Add to this fact that non-dilutes, i.e. brown and green classic offspring from part-satinette parents, more often than not failed to display the depth and distribution of melanistic pigment expected in exhibition examples, and the mystery deepened. The answer was discovered by French breeders and, once their theories were tested and then published, the mysteries disappeared.

The satinette factor is, in fact, a secondary mutation of the mutated gene that produces the dilute factor (i.e. the agate or isabel) and, as such, is inseparable from this earlier mutation. To put this in its simplest form, the satinette can appear only as an isabel or an agate. It is impossible to breed a brown or green example. This phenomenon is known as multiple allelomorphism. Once it had been determined why these 'mysteries' were occurring, it was relatively easy to select breeding pairs more likely to produce exhibition-quality stock and, even more importantly, to select non-satinette outcrosses that would assist in producing good examples of satinette but could be kept separate from other mutations in which the intermediate phenotype of non-dilute classic stock would be extremely detrimental to the production of exhibition examples.

The effect of the satinette mutation, which has a recessive sex-linked inheritance pattern, is to inhibit totally the presence of eumelanin black and phaeomelanin brown pigment but to leave undisturbed the eumelanin brown. It also, like the ino, gives a bright red eye. As previously mentioned, the underfeather of both the isabel and agate satinette is similar, i.e. a dark beige.

The isabel satinette in an ideal form has neat, distinct broad brown striations which extend from the top of the beak to the base of the tail, complemented by identical stripes along the flanks and around the chest. The agate, more often than not, appears as a lipochrome, i.e. devoid of melanistic pigment but occasionally displaying pale and narrow striations.

Whilst not disagreeing with the sentiments involved, the author does find it somewhat confusing that all conventional rules related to breeding almost any other type of coloured canary have to be forgotten when seeking to produce exhibition-quality satinettes.

Firstly, any other isabel mutation is judged on the fineness of the striations. With the satinette, this is reversed and broad striations are sought. Secondly, two separate judging standards have been introduced for the agate version: the first is for a bird carrying no pigmentation, which is judged as a lipochrome, and the second is for a bird in which striations are apparent. Neither are preferred as the ideal. To achieve the preferred broad striations, the breeder should ignore the rules repeated often in preceding sections that under only the most extreme circumstances should non-dilutes (i.e. green or brown) be paired to dilutes (i.e. isabel or agate). Experiments have shown that the best examples are produced from particularly brown classic stock. The brown birds for this pairing should not be of exhibition quality in that, whilst broad, distinct chocolate striations are sought, phaeomelanin suffusion is not. This applies equally to green stock, although the situation is reversed in that exhibition stock is required as an outcross. It is worth reiterating, however, that non-satinette stock, produced from such a bird paired to a satinette, should not be used for outcrossing with other mutations.

With some agate versions showing striations, and with the knowledge that both eumelanin black and phaeomelanin brown are inhibited, thought has been given to the composition of the visible pigment. Not unnaturally, the hypothesis that the canary carried three rather than two forms of melanistic pigment carried most weight. This theory was that, within the black eumelanin stripe, there was deposited, either separately but hidden by the black, or intermingled with the black, a second brown pigment. This pigment has been called eumelanin brown but, up to this day, no fact has been presented suggesting that its composition is the same as that found in the classic brown. Of its existence, however, there can be little doubt.

In the confusion arising from early attempts to differentiate between 'brown' and isabel satinettes, various opinions were expressed on correct breeding pairs and the versions most pleasing to the eye and the vast majority of these can now be discounted.

Time has shown that the most beautiful and, therefore, most readily sought-after versions of the satinette are those with a pale background where the contrast of the pale brown melanin markings is more apparent. Thus only the dimorphic version of the red varieties has found lasting popularity, although the mutated rose-ground birds are still relatively popular in all three feather types. Most popular, however, are gold and silver versions with, surprisingly the intensive gold proving the most successful as an exhibition variety. In recent years, the introduction of the dimorphic feather type to gold examples has opened further possibilities which are still being exploited.

One advantage that the satinette mutation has over all others is that agate carriers of the factor do not have the same phenotype as their homozygous, classic counterparts. The change can be viewed in the primary wing feathers, where the colouration is subtly altered to dark grey. This is the only obvious change in intensive and non-intensive examples but, in dimorphic birds, the grey suffusion present seems to be more silvery. This change of phenotype is, of course, most beneficial in pairings where the classic offspring are possible carriers, making test mating and the consequent waste of a breeding season unnecessary.

The expected offspring from the five possible pairings which produce satinettes are as follows:

Pair 1: satinette male × satinette female will produce all satinette young.

Pair 2: satinette male × normal female will produce normal males carrying satinette and satinette females.

Pair 3: normal male × satinette female will produce all normal young with males carrying satinette.

Pair 4: normal male carrying satinette × satinette female will produce 25% satinette males, 25% normal males carrying satinette, 25% satinette females and 25% normal females.

Pair 5: normal male carrying satinette × normal female will produce 25% satinette females, 25% normal females, 25% normal males carrying satinette and 25% normal males.

TOPAZ

The topaz mutation, whilst still generally unknown to the great majority of coloured-canary breeders, has been in existence for a number of years although it may have escaped notice for some time before Mario Ascheri, the foremost coloured-canary breeder in the world, located the bird in Italy and started his experiments. His early work was consequently expanded by other experimental breeders in France and a thesis was presented in 1983. The mutation still has to be ratified by the COM and, in consequence, no judging standard is yet in existence, although it is not difficult to imagine the form it will take.

The original thesis showed that the presence of the topaz mutation was due to a 'deficiency'. Usually this is taken to mean that a *single* gene has mutated to give a different phenotype. In most instances, this is correct but, occasionally, a *group* of genes mutates to give a different phenotype and this is also known as 'deficiency'. It has been suggested that the topaz is a multiple allelomorphism of the ino gene. Whatever the reason, inheritance patterns can now be determined and the principal unanswered question is whether the intermediate birds, which will be discussed later (p. 289), are just that or 'semi-topaz'. Within this section we will assume that the original thesis is correct and will base our viewpoints on this premise.

Originally the topaz was recognised in the progeny of an ino pairing and it is therefore assumed that it carries some part of the group of mutated genes which are responsible for the ino phenotype. The difference in appearance occurs because some part of the group of ino genes is absent whilst another group, on the same chromosome, has changed. This can be illustrated as follows:

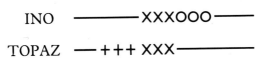

If we assume that the illustration shows an actual pair of chromosomes, it can be seen that the part of the mutated group of genes responsible for the change in phenotype from the normal to both ino and topaz is present – xxx.

The symbols xxx denote the normal genes. The area marked 000 denotes mutated genes which give the ino phenotype when present in double dose and the area marked $+++$ denotes mutated genes which give the topaz phenotype when present in double dose.

Thus we get an intermediate bird carrying part-ino and part-topaz phenotype which in itself, as far as we are aware, is unique. (The agate male carrying satinette is a possible exception and could give credence to the multiple allelomorphism theory.)

The phenotype of the four classic varieties of ino is covered on pp. 274–278. The topaz has certain known phenotypes but variations frequently exist at this stage of the development of the mutation. One reason is the unavoidable use of 'passe partout' males to produce all four variations, which results in progeny of differing degrees of intermediate phenotype, for example, between bronze and agate. It is difficult at this time to be dogmatic about the appearance of the ideal bird.

The bronze topaz, at first glance, resembles a classic brown as it carries a dark brown eumelanin stripe evenly positioned down the centre of the feather. Phaeomelanin is also a dark brown. As with all varieties this is more noticeable in the female. The flight and tail feathers, like the body feathers, show the same dark chocolate-brown colour, clearly positioned down the centre of the feather. This colouration is very dark on the short side of the main shaft but lighter on the longer side. The extremities of both the tail and flight feathers, together with the wing coverts, i.e. the area normally pigmented with phaeomelanin brown, are devoid of pigment. This is more evident in the male than the female. It is thought that this characteristic will be the most sought after when a show standard is written and thus the presence of the optical blue factor is desired. Time will tell if the clear feather tip can be extended to the body feathers. Unlike the ino, the narrower feather of the intensive is desirable, as it allows the clear-edge characteristic to be even more evident. The underfeather of the bronze topaz is a dark charcoal to black colour, the horny areas are flesh-coloured and the eyes are black. As previously mentioned, large variations do still exist, however, and birds resembling normal bronze but showing no clear tip to the feather have been produced. These birds must be bronze topaz because of the pairing used.

The brown topaz, in many ways, resembles a poor-quality brown ino. The pigmentation, which is distributed in the same pattern as the brown ino, is ginger brown rather than chocolate in colour and, in consequence, the clear edges to the feather are not so pronounced. In common with the isabel topaz, few brown topaz have been bred and it is therefore difficult to contemplate what the perfect example would look like. The eye colour is the plum red of the classic brown but it does not darken as the bird matures. The underfeather is very similar to brown ino, i.e. dark beige.

Having had the opportunity to examine only a handful of isabel examples, the author is loathe to be precise on the accepted phenotype of this version of the topaz and can only describe what he has seen at first hand. The melanistic pigment present is of a similar colour to the brown version, and has a similar distribution, but clarity and definition in all instances has been poor. The underfeather is a very pale beige with the eyes coloured bright red as in the isabel ino.

The version most likely to attract the highest number of admirers is the agate. It is truly distinctive and of a phenotype sufficiently different from all other mutations to warrant the attentions of the experimental breeders. In many ways it resembles the bronze topaz but with finer markings, as might be expected. With the finer markings and an automatic dilution in phaeomelanin, the whole appearance is complemented by the darkness of the pigmentation in the tail and gives the bird an overall pleasing appearance. To date the author has seen the bird only in red, rose and silver examples and has concluded that the paler ground colours best complement the mutation. The eyes are black and the underflue resembles, almost exactly, that of the bronze versions.

The intermediate versions of the four varieties are generally quite different from their pure counterparts. The bronze carries the chocolate-brown colour of the topaz but with a distribution similar to that of a poorly-marked bronze ino. The eye colour is similar to that of the classic brown and also darkens as the bird matures. The underfeather is darker than the bronze ino but paler than the bronze topaz. The brown intermediate resembles, if anything, an even more badly-defined brown ino than the brown topaz, having quite clear striations but also fairly well-defined spangles. It is difficult to differentiate the isabel intermediate from the isabel topaz although it carries a darker underflue. The agate intermediate differs from topaz and ino in that, whilst it carries much clearer striations than the agate ino, it is of a soft grey/beige colour and the characteristic dark feathering of the tail is greatly diluted. The underfeather is a grey brown and the eyes are as the red of a bronze ino.

The mutation, as with the ino, is an autosomal recessive (see Glossary) and the inheritance pattern is therefore predictable:

Pair 1: topaz × topaz will produce all topaz young.
Pair 2: topaz × normal will produce all normal young carrying topaz.
Pair 3: normal carrying topaz × topaz will produce 50% topaz young and 50% normal young carrying topaz.
Pair 4: normal carrying topaz × normal will produce 50% normal young and 50% normal carrying topaz.
Pair 5: normal carrying topaz × normal carrying topaz will produce 25% topaz, 50% normal carrying topaz and 25% normal young.

This second table illustrates the expectations from pairings using the intermediate bird, i.e. a semi-ino and a semi-topaz.

Pair 1: topaz × ino will produce all intermediate young.
Pair 2: topaz × intermediate will produce 50% intermediate and 50% topaz young.
Pair 3: intermediate × ino will produce 50% ino and 50% intermediate young.
Pair 4: intermediate × intermediate will produce 25% topaz, 25% ino and 50% intermediate young.

N.B. In both tables, all pairings can be reversed to give identical results.

History will dictate whether the topaz finds extensive and lasting popularity. What is sure, however, is that arguments will rage for some time on the precise nature of the mutation and the ultimate development of it. This can only be an asset to the coloured-canary Fancy as a whole.

SHOW STANDARDS FOR COLOURED CANARIES

Judging coloured canaries is not easy because of the number of different factors involved but it can be made easier by judging to a points standard. Each factor is then examined independently rather than the bird being considered as a whole, as happens in the comparison system employed in the UK. Although several documents have been prepared by various societies throughout the world, possibly the best descriptive booklet is the one produced by the Commission Nationale des Juges Français on behalf of the Union Ornithologique de France and this is used as the basis of the comments that follow.

With lipochrome varieties, we have two major points to consider: the actual colour purity and the feather type. With melanin varieties, in addition to these two points, we have to take into consideration the presence, or absence, of melanistic pigment according to the mutation under examination.

Lipochrome Varieties – Colour

Lipochrome coloured canaries possess a factor which inhibits the production of melanistic pigment and are judged principally on colour and feather type. In some countries, variegated examples can be exhibited but, in the majority, only examples totally devoid of melanistic pigment are considered to be of show standard. Where variegated birds are accepted, the quality or otherwise of the melanistic pigment is of no consequence and notice should only be taken of the colour and feather type, as with true clear examples.

'Colour' obviously refers to the purity of colour of the subject and normally carries 30 points. The recognised varieties are grouped as follows:

1) Total expression of colour:
   a) yellow (gold)
   b) red
2) Partial inhibition of colour:
   a) dominant white
3) Total inhibition of colour:
   a) recessive white
4) Dilution of lipochrome colouring by mutation:
   a) gold ivory
   b) rose

YELLOW (GOLD) AND RED

When judging these two varieties, one must take into consideration the purity of the colour and its uniform distribution.

For preference, a judge should look for a bird which is of the

291

purest colour uniformly distributed throughout the plumage.

In the gold series, the colour should be of a citron yellow in all birds of the green series (i.e. birds possessing either visible or hidden eumelanin black). In birds of the brown series, again either showing visible brown or not, the colour should be a bright golden-yellow but not an orange-yellow.

All judging standards are based on the assumption that the perfect bird will never exist and thus, even with an exceptional example, points need to be deducted in almost all cases in each of the judging categories, as shown below:

Very Good: Purity and uniformly distributed colour almost perfect. Deduct 3 points.

Good: Good colour evenly distributed. Deduct 4 points.

Average: Impure colour or bad distribution. A tendency to yellow or orange or a violet tinge. Small areas of feather of a different colour (sometimes seen on the wing butts). Deduct 5–6 points.

Bad: Bi-coloured birds or birds of intermediate colour. Deduct 7 or more points.

DOMINANT WHITE AND RECESSIVE WHITE

Three types of white exist: recessive white, dominant white and ivory white (silver ivory).

When judging these birds, it is obviously difficult, if not impossible, to distinguish the different feather types and, for judging purposes, the two factors of colour and feather type are combined to give a possible maximum of 50 points.

The COM rules state that 47 points should automatically be given to every white-ground bird, and heavier penalties should be given to faults in other areas. The French, correctly in the author's opinion, have disagreed with this view and, for shows in their own country, have made the following distinctions between the purities of white presented: luminous white, dull white, or dirty white.

Excellent: Total absence of lipochrome. Luminous colour. Deduct 3 points.

Good: Small traces of lipochrome colouring. Recessive slightly dull.

Deduct 4–6 points.

Average: Lipochrome colouring evident throughout flight and tail feathers. Dull colouring on recessives.

Deduct 7–9 points.

Bad: Lipochrome colouring extending throughout plumage particularly noticeable on wing butts. Dirty birds.

Deduct 10 or more points.

GOLD, IVORY OR ROSE

When judging these varieties one needs to take into consideration not only the degree of purity of colour and the evenness of distribution but also the quality of dilution of the colour. This means not that the colour should appear 'washed out' but that the bird is clearly identifiable as a mutation and not a poorly-coloured normal red-ground or gold-ground bird.

Excellent: Purity, dilution and distribution exceptional.

Deduct 3 points.

Good: Purity, dilution and distribution good.

Deduct 4 points.

Average: Impurity of colour; tendency to yellow or red. Distribution of colour not uniform.

Deduct 5–6 points.

Bad: Birds either bi-coloured or of intermediate colour.

Deduct 7 or more points.

It should be mentioned here that many countries allow only unflighted birds to be exhibited. In first-year colour-fed examples in particular, unless colouring agents are offered to the parent birds when feeding the young, the flight and tail feathers will not carry the same depth of pigment that will become evident after the first full moult. (This occurs in the second year when colouring agents will normally be used.) Some judging standards allow for this, and so judges can disregard the difference in colouration, but others adhere firmly to the uniformity of distribution of colour rule. Where the rules are strict, colour food must be offered to all red-ground stock during the breeding season while a high lutein-based diet should be offered to yellow-ground birds.

Lipochrome Varieties – Feather Type

This refers to the natural structure of the feather. The judge has 20 points at his disposal. There are three categories of feather:

1) Intensive (non-frosted, yellow, etc.).
2) Non-intensive (frosted, buff, etc.).
3) Dimorphic.

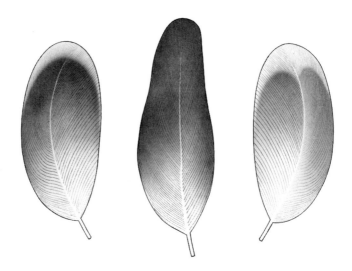

Feather types: non-intensive (left), intensive (centre), dimorphic (right).

INTENSIVE

Here one is looking for birds with no trace whatsoever of frosting on the tip of the feather.

Excellent: No trace whatever of frosting.
Deduct 1 point.
Good: A slight amount of frosting.
Deduct 2 points.
Average: Frosting evident.
Deduct 3–4 points.
Bad: Examples that show as finely-frosted non-intensives.
Deduct 5 or more points.

NON-INTENSIVE

The ideal non-intensive carries a very fine frosting evenly distributed throughout the whole plumage.

Excellent: Frosting fine and evenly distributed, no trace of a concentration of frosting, particularly where the neck joins the back of the bird.
Deduct 1 point.

Good: Frosting less fine with a mild concentration on the back and neck.
Deduct 2 points.

Average: Heavy frosting which is unevenly distributed.
Deduct 3–4 points.

Bad: Defective frosting approaching intensive or dimorphic examples.
Deduct 5 or more points.

DIMORPHIC

In males one is looking for examples which possess a small but distinct mask with lipochrome colour elsewhere being limited to the normal dimorphic 'points', i.e. the eyebrows, wing butts and rump. The colour should be bright and intensive at these points.

Female dimorphics should be basically white with bright red/yellow lipochrome evident only as an extension of the eye, the wing butts and the rump.

N.B. Where melanistic examples are being examined it should be noted that the dimorphic factor influences the striations in three ways:

1) Striations on the head.
2) An absence of lipochrome between striations throughout the bird.
3) Striations wider than with intensive or non-intensive example.

The judging categories for male dimorphics are as follows:

Excellent: Good examples follow the description above. The colour points should be precise and the lipochrome colour intense.
Deduct 1 point.

Good: Colour evident on the chest, slight frosting on the lipochrome of the points.
Deduct 2 points.

Average: Colour evident in the flight feathers throughout the chest/abdomen area, the mask extended to show colour in the cheeks. Frosting very evident on the coloured areas of the dimorphic points.
Deduct 3–4 points.

Bad: Birds which tend to be overfrosted non-intensives rather than true dimorphics.
Deduct 5 or more points.

Female dimorphics are judged according to the categories below:

Excellent: Lipochrome colouring restricted to the wing butts, rump and as a small extension of the eye. A mild colouration of the eye permitted but ideally absent. The remainder of the bird to be snowy white.
Deduct 1 point.

Good: Similar to a bird defined as excellent but with a slight intensity of lipochrome present in the chest area. Slight frosting on the lipochrome colouring of the rump.
Deduct 2 points.

Average: Extension of the colouration of the chest into the flanks, around the eyes and into the flight feathers. Evident frosting of the lipochrome on the rump.
Deduct 3–4 points.

Bad: Birds that can be confused with badly frosted (non-intensive) examples.
Deduct 5 or more points.

N.B. In the lipochrome varieties, subjects exist with red eyes which indicate the presence of ino or satinette factors. The eye colouration should be totally ignored and the bird should judged on its colour and feather type only. Some countries provide separate classes for these birds.

Self (Melanin) Varieties – Classic Colours

As with lipochrome varieties, self (or melanin) varieties of coloured canaries are judged on their lipochrome colour and feather type. In addition, they are judged on the presence or absence of melanin pigment as determined by their mutation.

With their colour and feather type, the criteria for judging is similar but there are fewer points with which to play, i.e. colour – 10 points; feather type – 15 points.

Points for colour are deducted in the following way:

Excellent: Deduct 1 point.
Good: Deduct 1–2 points.
Average: Deduct 2–3 points.
Bad: Deduct 4 or more points.

Deductions for feather type are:

Excellent: Deduct 1 point.
Good: Deduct 2 points.
Average: Deduct 3 points.
Bad: Deduct 4 or more points.

For melanistic pigment, the judge has 25 points at his disposal. The recognised classic varieties are shown in the following table.

Ground colour	Oxidised melanistic pigment	Diluted melanistic pigment
RED	bronze red brown	red agate red isabel
YELLOW	green gold brown	gold agate gold isabel
WHITE	blue silver brown	silver agate silver isabel

GREEN (BRONZE OR BLUE)

These birds should present maximum oxidisation of the melanistic pigment. A typical maximisation of this characteristic occurs in the beak and legs, and in the toes, where it extends to the end of the claws, giving them an ebony-black colour. The feathers of the wings and tail should be black. The striations, of an intense black colour, should be present on the back, head and flanks. Preference should always be given to birds displaying these characteristics to the detriment of phaeomelanin brown.

Excellent: A bird meeting the criteria mentioned above.
Deduct 1 point.
Good: Good black pigment with a minor dilution of pigmentation in the beak and legs. Minor presence of brown.
Deduct 2 points.
Average: Reduction in the intensity of black in the striations, legs, beak and claws. Brown pigmentation very evident. Clear flanks.
Deduct 3–5 points.
Bad: A bird with narrow striations, clear horny areas, difficult to differentiate from an agate.
Deduct 6 or more points.

BROWN

As with the bronze, the melanistic pigment should be heavily oxidised and appear chocolate brown. The horny areas will be clear. The brown, like the bronze, should possess wide, deeply-coloured striations, well defined throughout the back, flanks and head and extending around the chest as far as possible.

Excellent: A bird meeting the criteria listed above.
Deduct 1 point.
Good: A bird almost excellent but perhaps with slight distortion of the striations on the back or flanks.
Deduct 2 points.
Average: A bird well oxidised but not completely meeting the full requirements of a good example. Some dilution in the width of the striations most noticeable in the flanks. Pigmentation of the chest area grey rather than brown.
Deduct 3–5 points.
Bad: A bird showing narrow striations or absence of striations on one or both flanks. Could be confused with a poor isabel.
Deduct 6 or more points.

AGATE

The agate factor is noted by the simultaneous dilution of the two normal melanin pigments (eumelanin black and phaeomelanin brown). The edges of the flight and tail feathers appear grey as, in some instances, do the striations throughout the bird. In the agate mutation, large variations in the density of the colour of the pigmentation appear, from grey through to a fully-oxidised black, although the striations themselves are narrower. Opinions differ on the precise form of the ideal bird, but the majority of fanciers seem to favour the charcoal to the grey/blue colour.

Variations also appear in the extent of dilution most readily seen in the tail and flight feathers. It is preferable for the edges of these feathers to be as broad as possible and for them to carry no trace of brown. The striations of the back and flanks need to be well spaced and symmetrical.

The markings of the head are very important in the agate and are constituted as follows:

1) The top of the head should be black in the case of the intensive and charcoal grey in the non-intensive but should show short compact striations in the dimorphic.
2) The eyebrows should be devoid of pigment and should present the maximum purity and concentrations of lipochrome.
3) The moustache, a necessary and characteristic part of the agate, should be very evident.
4) The horny areas should be skin-coloured.

Between the striations on the back and flanks, no trace of brown should exist thus enabling the lipochrome to stand out. This characteristic does not apply to dimorphics.

Excellent: Maximum dilution of brown. Maximum concentration of black, the edge of each feather evidently clear. Striations of the back and flanks narrow, well pronounced and symmetrical. Moustache well marked.
Deduct 1 point.

Good: Faint presence of brown, striations not extending totally around chest, generally as an excellent bird, but some areas not perfect.
Deduct 2 points.

Average: Evidence of brown pigmentation, evident thickening of striations, moustache not well defined. Colour of the horny areas slightly grey.

Deduct 3–5 points.

Bad: Insufficient dilution of brown, moustache absent. Difficult to differentiate from a poorly-marked green.

Deduct 6 or more points.

ISABEL

An isabel is required to present a chocolate-brown pigmentation reduced in width. This is why the degree of dilution is the most important factor taken into consideration by a judge. All other points are as described in detail for the agate except for the absence of the moustache.

Excellent: Excellent dilution of brown.

Deduct 1 point.

Good: Good dilution.

Deduct 2 points.

Average: Fair but uneven dilution. Some areas very diluted, others less. Striations on the flanks indistinct.

Deduct 3–5 points.

Bad: Insufficient dilution. Difficult to differentiate from a bad classic brown.

Deduct 6 or more points.

Self (Melanin) Varieties – New Colours

INO

The ino factor is evident as one that totally inhibits eumelanin black, but emphasises phaeomelanin brown. Often the factor, when combined with the isabel or agate factors, leaves no trace of melanistic pigment and the bird has the appearance of a clear. There are great differences in the phenotypes of brown and green examples and, in consequence, the birds are judged on the contrast between the areas of feather covered by melanistic pigment and the area exhibiting only lipochrome colouring. The horny areas are skin-coloured and the eyes are ruby red.

BROWN OR GREEN INO

The bird most sought after will carry a chocolate-brown pigmentation presented as a 'spangle', i.e. on the edge of the feather. This will represent itself from the top of the head to the base of the tail. The chest and flanks will carry broad brown stripes. The perfect spangling effect gives a good compromise between a bird totally covered with brown pigmentation and one where there is sufficient space between the spangles to allow lipochrome colouring to show through. This lipochrome should cover the central zone of the feather.

Excellent: The striations are characterised by a deep chocolate-coloured horseshoe-shaped tip to the feather carried in neat lines.
Deduct 1 point.

Good: Indistinct spangle effect. Melanistic pigment not chocolate brown.
Deduct 2 points.

Average: Spangling effect merging into striations.
Deduct 3–5 points.

Bad: Uncharacteristic of the typical ino.
Deduct 6 or more points.

OPAL

The opal factor is characterised by an inhibition of brown pigmentation with black eumelanin concentrated on the underside of the central stem of the feather, thus giving an optical illusion of blue/grey pigmentation.

GREEN (BRONZE OR BLUE) OPAL

The bird will carry the completely-oxidised black eumelanin in its normal format throughout the beak, feet and legs while, at the same time, the striations normal in a classic green will be unaltered except in colour, which should be blue/grey.

Excellent: As the description of the ideal bird with no traces of brown pigmentaton.
Deduct 1 point.

Good: Slight reduction in the intensity of the black colouration of the horny areas. Good manifestation of grey/blue striations.

Deduct 2 points.

Average: Noticeable reduction in the intensity of black in the horny areas. Slight appearance of brown throughout the plumage.

Deduct 3–5 points.

Bad: Horny areas not oxidised. Brown suffusion masking the blue/grey. A bird difficult to differentiate from an over-marked agate opal.

Deduct 6 or more points.

BROWN OPAL

The opal factor should totally repress the appearance of phaeo-melanin brown but leaves the eumelanin brown striations evident but heavily diluted and suffused across the plumage.

Excellent: Birds meeting the ideal.

Deduct 1 point.

Good: A good suffusion of brown striations but over diluted.

Deduct 2 points.

Average: A bird easy to determine as a brown opal, but insufficient-ly typical to be a good example.

Deduct 3–5 points.

Bad: Depth of colouration of brown suffusion insufficient to determine precisely whether bird is a brown opal or isabel opal.

Deduct 6 or more points.

AGATE OPAL

The combination of the agate and opal factors gives a complete disappearance of brown coupled with the fine distinct striations typical of the classic agate but coloured grey.

Excellent: Total disappearance of brown but good distribution of eumelanin black – coloured grey.

Deduct 1 point.

Good: Absence of brown. Grey striations evident but not totally representative of the opal factor.

Deduct 2 points.

Average: Slight presence of brown – most often noticeable on the flanks. Striations broken up.
Deduct 3–5 points.

Bad: Brown pigmentation very evident. Difficult to differentiate from a poorly marked green opal.
Deduct 6 or more points.

ISABEL OPAL

The opal factor should totally prevent the appearance of phaeomelanin brown and confines any trace of eumelanin brown to a slight suffusion on the tail and wing feathers. No trace of striations (the overall phenotype resembles a clear (lipochrome) bird).

Excellent: A bird resembling a non-melanistic variety.
Deduct 1 point.

Good: Slight trace of brown in the flight and tail feathers, otherwise a clear phenotype.
Deduct 2 points.

Average: Traces of brown throughout the plumage.
Deduct 3–5 points.

Bad: A bird difficult to differentiate from a poor brown opal.
Deduct 6 or more points.

PASTEL

GREEN (BRONZE OR BLUE) PASTEL

All mutations have the effect of reducing, to some degree, the intensity that might be considered normal. With the bronze pastel, the effect is to change the colour of the striations from black to a charcoal grey. Within the bronze-pastel mutations, many variations occur. The most sought-after is the one where a symmetrical area of both the flight feathers and tail are of a much paler colour. This phenomenon is called the greywing factor and judging is based on this ideal.

Excellent: Charcoal-grey striations following the pattern expected in the classic bronze. The greywing factor expressed to the

full. Horny areas black.
Deduct 1 point.

Good: Striations excellent but not as distinct as an excellent example. Horny areas dark grey rather than black.
Deduct 2 points.

Average: A noticeable presence of brown pigmentation breaking up the striations. Greywing effect partially expressed. Light-coloured horny areas.
Deduct 3–5 points.

Bad: Indistinct striations black rather than charcoal grey. Obvious presence of brown pigmentation. Greywing factor absent. Horny areas clear.
Deduct 6 or more points.

BROWN PASTEL

The major characteristic of the brown pastel is the overall presence of a beige/brown hue. Striations should be visible but heavily diluted.

Excellent: A brown suffusion covering the entire bird, including wings and tail. Absence of striations on the flanks. Horny areas clear.
Deduct 1 point.

Good: A similar bird to the excellent example but showing a slight presence of striations on the flanks
Deduct 2 points.

Average: A good deep-coloured suffusion present, but not totally sufficient to indicate the mutation. The presence of striations on the flanks and back noticeable.
Deduct 3–5 points.

Bad: A breakdown of the brown suffusion, or an increase in the density of the striations, making it difficult to differentiate between an isabel pastel or, conversely, a classic isabel.
Deduct 6 or more points.

AGATE PASTEL

The pastel factor changes the black of the classic agate to a pearl grey. The extremities of the wing and tail feathers should also display a grey rather than brown colour. As with a classic agate, the striations should be distinct, extending over the head into the back and across the flanks. The characteristic moustache should be present. Horny areas clear.

Excellent: Meeting the description above. Total absence of brown. Moustache very evident.
Deduct 1 point.

Good: As an excellent example but some presence of brown pigmentation evident.
Deduct 2 points.

Average: Grey pigmentation not totally evident some traces of black appearing. Breakdown in distribution of the striations.
Deduct 3–5 points.

Bad: Brown pigmentation very evident. Striations brown rather than grey causing confusion over whether the bird is an agate pastel or a classic isabel.
Deduct 6 or more points.

ISABEL PASTEL

The ideal isabel pastel carries an extremely diluted brown suffusion distributed throughout the whole bird. All striations should totally disappear.

Excellent: No trace of striations. Diluted brown suffusion barely perceptible.
Deduct 1 point.

Good: Good dilution of pigmentation throughout the plumage but some brown apparent in the flight and tail feathers.
Deduct 2 points.

Average: Brown pigmentation noticeable in the flight and tail feathers. Slight trace of striations.
Deduct 3–5 points.

Bad: Flight and tail feathers very brown. Striations apparent on the flanks and/or back. Difficult to differentiate between classic isabel or brown pastel.
Deduct 6 or more points.

SATINETTE

The satinette factor inhibits the production of eumelanin black but leaves neat diluted brown striations. The factor also inhibits the production of phaeomelanin brown. The agate satinette normally carries no pigmentation whereas, in contrast, the isabel satinette is well marked. There exists, therefore, two recognised satinette phenotypes. When an agate satinette showing no trace of melanistic pigment is presented at an exhibition, it is judged similarly to an isabel or agate ino, i.e. a lipochrome bird. However, where pigments are present, an agate satinette can be judged by the same criteria adopted for the isabel satinette. The horny areas are clear and the eyes bright red.

AGATE SATINETTE

With a total reduction of eumelanin black, often the presentation of the bird is typical of a lipochrome. In this instance, whilst it is characteristic, it is not an ideal to seek.

Effectively, the choice for a judge is to choose between two types of birds of the same genotype but totally different phenotypes, i.e.:
a) A bird totally devoid of pigment.
b) An untypical bird well marked and resembling an isabel satinette. Invariably, the latter is considered more interesting and, in consequence, more highly sought-after.

ISABEL SATINETTE

With a total inhibition of eumelanin black and phaeomelanin brown, the diluted eumelanin brown pigmentation remains visible in the form of neat striations similar to a classic isabel but, importantly, with the clear area in between the striations allowing the lipochrome colouring to present itself.

Excellent: An ideal bird. Striations clear and distinct, lipochrome showing clearly in between.
Deduct 1 point.

Good: Less contrast between lipochrome and melanistic pigment.
Deduct 2 points.

Average: Contrast indistinct. Break up in striations.
Deduct 3–5 points.

Bad: Total breakdown of contrast. Birds representing classic isabels or clear varieties.
Deduct 6 or more points.

TOPAZ
There are no written standards for this type.

General Features

OTHER CONSIDERATIONS IN JUDGING
Following the two main areas (colour, which includes feather types and ground colour, and melanin pigment) which, between them, account for half of the available points, the balance of the judgement is split between five further areas.

FEATHER QUALITY
Faults in feather quality for which points may be deducted include:

1) Feathers too long or thin, dry or dull.
2) Incomplete plumage (a moulting bird).
3) Broken feathers.
4) Crossed wings, open tail etc.

Excellent: A bird with a uniform, tight, silky plumage. All tail and flight feathers intact.
Deduct 1 point.
Good: A bird with one small fault.
Deduct 2 points.
Average: A bird with two small faults.
Deduct 3 points.
Bad: A bird with three or more faults.
Deduct 4 or more points.

SIZE
The ideal length from beak to tail tip is 5–5½ inches (130–140 millimetres). Points are not normally deducted for size unless a bird is obviously very small or very large.

SHAPE (TYPE)

A bird considered excellent will have the characteristics listed below.

Head: Round and broad with a short conical beak. Bright, clean eyes above an imaginary line following back from the top of the beak. A thickset neck proportionate in length to the body and blending into the body.

Back: Large and solid, slightly rounded giving a good base on which the wings can rest naturally and symmetrically to the base of the tail.

Chest: Round without being too 'heavy'. Seen from the front the chest should appear broad and strong.

Trunk: Neither too large nor too thin. It should blend in with the chest and back to give the bird a nicely-rounded appearance. Strong but elegant and beautiful.

Tail: Neither too large nor too short, giving a good balance to the overall impression of the bird. The tail should be 'piped' (not open).

Legs and Feet: Robust and solid with well-clipped nails firmly gripping the perch.

Faults in these features are listed below:

Head: Flat, very small, very large or heavy in comparison with the body. Beak thin, long or crooked.

Neck: Thin and long, or too short and thick, giving the impression of being stuck onto rather than blending in with the body.

Back: Convex or hollow.

Chest: Narrow and thin or over-heavy.

Trunk: Too thick or too heavy, upsetting the overall elegance of the bird.

Tail: Swallow- or fish-shaped.

Legs: Too long with thin thighs or too short and hidden under the feathers of the abdomen.

When judging, deduct points as follows:

Excellent: A bird with no faults.
Deduct 1 point.

308

Good: A bird showing one fault.
            Deduct 1 point.
Average: A bird with two to three faults.
            Deduct 2 points.
Bad: A bird with several faults or displaying the overall shape
            associated with another canary breed.
            Deduct 3 points.

PRESENTATION

With presentation, one is looking at the way a bird presents itself in a show cage. A bird needs to 'show' itself properly for the extent of its type to be totally reviewed. One influences the other. A bird presenting itself properly will be alert and active, without being wild, and will hold itself properly in the process at an angle of 45°.

Faults in this area fall into two categories:

1) An over-active untrained bird or conversely an inactive bird squatting on its perch.
2) A bird which, when moving, crosses its wings or drops them down the flanks, the tail spreading, a crouching bird.

Points are deducted as follows:

Excellent: A bird with no faults.
             Deduct 1 point.
Good: A bird with one fault.
             Deduct 1 point.
Average: A bird with two or three faults.
             Deduct 2 points.
Bad: A bird with several faults.
             Deduct 3 points.

OVERALL IMPRESSION

Within this area, one is looking for good health, general condition and appearance, coupled with a pleasing overall impression of the bird and its beauty. Not only should the bird be healthy but, together with its cage, it should be clean. The bird should have no scales on its legs or claws.

AREAS FOR DISQUALIFICATION

Areas for disqualification of birds vary from country to country and it is obviously necessary to study the relevant rules when entering a bird in a foreign show. Listed below are points which vary in importance in different countries and may prevent a bird qualifying for entry.

1) An adult bird.
2) A bird not close ringed.
3) A bird wearing a closed ring oversized for the variety.
4) A cage marked so as to make it identifiable to a judge.
5) A bird with a limb, toe or claw missing.
6) A totally or partially blind bird.
7) Foul (clear) feathers in a melanistic bird.
8) A variegated claw in a melanistic bird.
9) Dark feathers in a clear bird.
10) A bird with a trimmed tail.

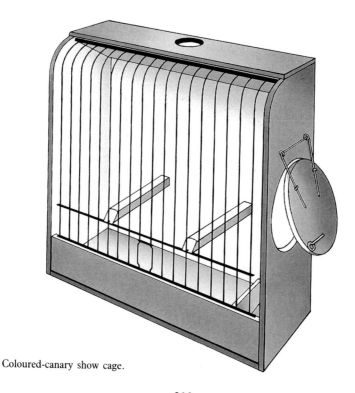

Coloured-canary show cage.

JUDGING TABLES

The following tables are printed to give some indication of how to build up a judging slip. The points given are drawn from the Union Ornithologique de France (UOF) standards but they are similar, if not identical, to most standards viewed. The UOF standard rather than that of the COM has been used deliberately because, in the former, ground colour and feather type is shown separately whereas in the latter they are combined.

Clear Birds – Red or Gold Ground

Categories	Points available	Excellent	Good	Average	Bad
Ground colour	30	28	27	26/25	24–
Feather type (intensive, non-intensive dimorphic)	20	19	18	17/16	15–
Feather quality	15	14	13	12	11–
Type	10	9	9	8	7–
Presentation	10	9	9	8	7–
Size	10	10	10	9	8–
General impression	5	5	4	3	2–

Clear Birds – White Ground

Categories	Points available	Excellent	Good	Average	Bad
Ground colour	50	47	46/44	43/41	40–
Feather quality	15	14	13	12	11–
Type	10	9	9	8	7–
Presentation	10	9	9	8	7–
Size	10	10	10	9	8–
General impression	5	5	4	3	2–

Self Birds – Red or Gold Ground

Categories	Points available	Excellent	Good	Average	Bad
Melanistic pigment	25	24	23	22/20	19–
Ground colour	10	9	9/8	8/7	6–
Feather type	15	14	13	12	11–
Feather quality	15	14	13	12	11–
Type	10	9	9	8	7–
Presentation	10	9	9	8	7–
Size	10	10	10	9	8–
General impression	5	5	4	3	2–

Self Birds – White Ground

Categories	Points available	Excellent	Good	Average	Bad
Melanistic pigment	25	24	23	22/20	19–
Ground colour					
Feather type	25	23	22	21/20	19–
Feather quality	15	14	13	12	11–
Type	10	9	9	8	7–
Presentation	10	9	9	8	7–
Size	10	10	10	9	8–
General impression	5	5	4	3	2–

To give an example, a self bird could be judged as:

Excellent in melanin pigment	24 points
Average in ground colour	8 points
Average in feather type	12 points
Good in feather quality	13 points
Bad in type	7 points
Good in presentation	9 points
Excellent in size	10 points
Average in general impression	3 points
TOTAL	86 points

GENERAL COMMENTS

There will nearly always be variations in the number of points awarded to the same bird at different shows by either the same or a different judge. There can be many reasons for this and listed below are some of the possibilities.

Melanistic Pigment There should rarely be any variation in this category.
Ground Colour In between shows, a bird can accidentally lose feathers which, if replaced in the natural way, without colour food (if applicable), can lead to a bi-coloured bird.
Feather Type There is rarely any variation here.
Feather Quality Feathers can become broken, wet or soiled in transit to the show.
Type A bird may gain weight between shows, spoiling its general outline.
Presentation The reasons given above, plus, for example, fright, may cause the bird to lose its steadiness.
Size There should be no variation.
General Impression There can be variations dependent upon changes within the other categories plus ill health.

Let us not forget that no two show halls share the same lighting conditions and these can give an optical illusion of changes, particularly with regard to ground colour and feather type. Finally, judges are human and, therefore, not infallible. Whilst every judge endeavours to perform to his maximum effiency, inevitably there will be differences in the levels of competence and, whilst it is very disappointing to lose prizes because of bad judging, we must remember that, in the majority of cases, the exhibiting of canaries is a hobby – not a matter of life or death.

· CHAPTER 6 ·
HYBRIDS AND OTHER EXPERIMENTAL PAIRINGS

The fact that most coloured-canary breeders keep a number of birds which are neither clear gold nor green means that they are all, to a certain extent, experimental breeders. This apart, a minority are true experimental breeders because they embark on the pairing together of either different varieties of birds or different coloured mutations. This is often done with a positive aim in mind, such as to determine the phenotype of offspring with a view to deciding whether further experiments should take place in order to isolate a specific point of interest.

RED GROUND
We are indebted to the foresight and perseverance of our forefathers for the fact that we now possess the red-ground colour in canaries. All other variations on the original green canary appear as a result of a spontaneous change in a single gene or a group of genes, i.e. a mutation.

It was our forefathers who first conceived the idea of crossing the South American or black-hooded red siskin (*Spinus cucullatus*) – which, it was hoped, carried genes for the production of red, but not yellow – to the canary, which, it was assessed, carried no genes for the production of red. It was known that South American fanciers had, for a number of years, produced F_1 hybrids when this bird was paired to a canary and, in some instances, they had proved fertile. The term F_1 (or first filial generation) is given to the first cross of two unrelated species. The term F_2 (or second generation), although technically incorrect, is universally used by bird breeders to describe the pairing of an F_1 hybrid to a canary (strictly speaking this term should be applied to the progeny of an $F_1 \times F_1$ pairing). F_3 and F_4 are the terms used to describe subsequent pairings. Once F_4 is reached, the bird produced is accepted as being pure canary.

315

The male siskin is a small bird with a jet-black hood, wings, tail and horny areas and a vermilion-red-coloured body and wing bar. The female is much duller, having no hood and only flushes of red on her breast. The rump is a much deeper red and the rest of the body is coloured grey. This difference in colouring is known as *sexual dimorphism*.

The theory behind the use of this bird was that, as fertility in the F_1 male was known to be limited, pairing with the siskin might ensure continued fertility and make possible the transfer of both red genes to the canary.

In practice, the continued fertility, although present, was extremely haphazard and a disproportionate number of pairings over a number of years had to be embarked upon before the aims of the early pioneers reached fruition. Whether or not their original aim has, to this day, been realised is impossible to say but, with the advent of non-natural colour feeding it can be said that the red canary does now exist.

Although in the UK few examples of the black-hooded red siskin exist today, in mainland Europe, and particularly the southern states of the USA where the climate is more conducive to breeding these birds, comparatively large numbers exist and 'experimental' pairings continue. 'Experimental' is used in parenthesis because rarely are these pairings conducted to achieve anything other than the production of beautiful F_1 hybrids. It is however interesting to note that, in the Benelux countries, where the production of large size has been of secondary importance to the production of colour in coloured canaries, and so the F_1 and F_2 hybrid is more commonly used, the red ground colour is appreciably brighter.

Unlike modern-day breeders who have access to red-canary females for their experiments, early breeders had access only to gold, dominant white and recessive white examples. Thus their progress in transferring the red, in retrospect, is truly amazing. Whilst limited fertility was found in F_1 males, it was not until the third filial generation that females shared fertility and this, according to breeders of the day, was even more limited than in male progeny. Thus a siskin was paired to a yellow or white canary – all three possibilities being used at one time or another – and an F_1 copper hybrid was produced, carrying one gene for red and one for yellow. For reasons still unexplained, when paired to a canary of any ground colour – regardless of whether that canary was clear, ticked, variegated or self, green or brown – copper-coloured self hybrids

316

were invariably produced. There being no other suitable female, the F_1 had then to be paired back to a yellow or white canary female, thus 'diluting' by 50% the existing red genes. Thus F_2 males rarely carried the depth of red colouration of the male parent and this had to be diluted further by outcrossing this male to another yellow or white female canary. Only on the production of fertile F_3 hens – at that time, at best, a pale orange – could the business of rebuilding the red-gene bank progress. By selective breeding over a number of years, the red canary came into being although, as previously mentioned, the earlier pioneers did not realise it.

To dismiss the continued value of using siskins and their hybrids is perhaps short-sighted. We think we are now as close as possible to the ultimate in this area, and have concentrated instead on the production of variations in melanin pigment. Perhaps we are wrong and we await the findings of experimental breeders in this field to inform us accordingly.

BLACK

The desire of breeders to produce free-breeding strains of blue and black canaries has resulted in a certain amount of experimentation over the years. The Bolivian black siskin (*Chrysomitris atrata*) has been used to produce the black canary and the indigo bunting (*Passerina cyanea*) the blue. Records exist of F_1 progeny being produced in both instances but little information has been published on subsequent pairings. We must, therefore, assume that they have either failed totally or have not produced anything resembling the desired effect. Occasionally there are reports of the appearance of black canaries from visually normal offspring but, almost without exception, they revert to normal at the second moult. The one recorded exception is of a bird bred in Brazil in 1980/81 which retained its black colouration through three successive moults. No records seem to have been made of the phenotype of the progeny (if any) of this bird and photographs would seem to suggest that the bird was, in fact, a hybrid rather than a pure canary. It is unlikely that a new mutation will occur giving us the desired phenotype. This is because all known mutations dilute in some form the original green whereas, in the black, we would be seeking the extension of the width of the melanistic striations to give us our aim and, in the case of the blue, a total change in the ground colour. We are, therefore, left with the hope that intelligent experimental breeders

317

will direct themselves to the task and, in the manner of the early pioneers of the red lipochrome, will present us with the formulae for success.

GOLD DIMORPHIC

In more recent times, with the increasing popularity of the gold dimorphic in both the clear and self series, some experiments have taken place using the European serin (*Serinus serinus*).

The original reasons for using the serin (which is a small yellow bird with black streaked plumage, the male being considerably more coloured than the female and less well marked) were:

1) To introduce the luminous yellow ground colour.
2) To profit from the apparent lack of phaeomelanin.
3) Most importantly, to harness the sexual dimorphism and so to improve this characteristic in the self canary.

The first two aims have without doubt been achieved with the production of strains of gold agate, agate opal and agate pastel which display the sought-after improvements. It would appear from limited experimentation, however, that not only has the third and most important aim not been achieved but possibly a deterioration in this quality has been evident. These comments cannot, at this stage, be regarded as conclusive.

For example, a gold dimorphic isabel of good quality as a first-cross female was used with similar quality stock in each generation and no noticeable improvement was apparent. The only two positive advances that appear to have arisen are:

1) Almost total fertility in all males produced in F_1, F_2 and F_3 generations, with some fertility in F_2 females and the majority of the F_3 females also proving fertile.
2) The improvement in ground colour with a corresponding lack of phaeomelanin.

It would appear, therefore, that the advisability of using the serin finch must be questioned. A deterioration in size and shape must be expected, but this may well have been one of the problems faced by the pioneers of the red-hybrid experiments.

MULES

There are a number of breeders in Europe, who hybridise coloured canaries with native species, particularly those having mutations which follow the sex-linked inheritance pattern. The aim is to produce mules for exhibition at shows where classes are provided. The term *mule* is used to describe the offspring from a canary (male or female) paired to an indigenous species. *Hybrid* is used to describe the offspring from one indigenous species paired to a different indigenous species. This is the terminology used in the UK. The term hybrid, outside the UK, is used to describe any pairing of birds to unrelated species, one of which could well be a canary. Invariably, these pairings are made more for the satisfaction of the breeder than with a specific aim in mind and, whilst the resulting offspring are beautiful in their own right, they have no real place in the world of genuine experimental coloured-canary breeding.

LIZARD

Outside true coloured-canary circles, only one variety holds any real interest for the experimental breeder and that is the lizard canary. It seems probable that this variety of canary, uniquely, seems to have come about by mutation rather than by design. Somewhat mysteriously, breeders in general, have failed to fully explore the inheritance patterns involved and to capitalise upon them. The appearance of the lizard canary is, in all probability, due to the result of one or more mutations occurring either simultaneously or over a period of time.

There is, however an interesting hypothesis which, whilst highly improbable, is perhaps worthy of comment. Some investigation by experimental breeders may be rewarding. A bird found throughout Asia Minor is the red-fronted serin (*Serinus pusillus*), a relative of the wild canary (*Serinus canaria*). Apart from displaying striations similar to the rowings of the ideal lizard canary, its other main characteristic is that it possesses a red cap very similar in size and shape to that sought in the lizard. Whilst this could be rejected immediately as coincidence, two further things should be kept in mind. Firstly most members of the genus *Serinus* will readily hybridise with canaries and/or other members of the serin group. When this occurs, some characteristics are passed on from each parent and these can, with patience, be preserved. Secondly, old books describing the lizard are emphatic that the bird carries not a

319

bright luminous ground colour but a rich dark bronzy yellow. Modern-day non-colour-fed lizards are noted for their bright yellow ground colour which is intensified by the almost universal presence of the optical blue (reduction of brown) factor. With this factor present, it is impossible to produce a bronzy yellow. One is therefore left to consider whether the sought-after colour was produced as a result of an outcross to a bird with genes capable of producing red lipochrome at some time in its history. If so, when combined with the normal yellow lipochrome-producing genes of the wild canary (or, in fact, all normal forms of domesticated canaries), a brassy yellow would result.

Whilst this hypothesis is admittedly improbable, it is not impossible and, if the red-fronted serin (*Serinus pusillus*) can be legally acquired in sufficient numbers to make meaningful experiments, it would be interesting to view the results.

In general basic terminology, the lizard canary is regarded as a self but, as will be observed later, this is not by any means a genetically acceptable description.

It is probable that the differences in phenotype when compared with that of the normal green were originally a result of one or more mutations occurring either simultaneously or over a period of time. Throughout its long history, records indicate that, whilst most canary fanciers recognise and appreciate its unique beauty, the lizard canary has never attracted the same numbers of specialist breeders which many other breeds have enjoyed. One reason for this could be the number of specific points which need to be produced to near perfection before the bird can achieve success on the showbench. As a direct consequence of this, the faithful few have been obliged to concentrate solely on attempting to produce show specimens and little time has been spent, or interest shown, in experimenting with the breed. To the author, as a breeder of coloured canaries and, therefore, by definition, an experimental breeder, this is a great pity. Undoubtedly some experimentation has taken place, with outcrossing to other type canaries (self green being high on the list) in order to inject hybrid vigour to a breed that, at times, has been near to extinction. The shame is that such experiments have, almost universally, been carried out in secret, as, in the UK particularly, the stigma attached to such pursuits is great. Because of this, much valuable information on breeding results and inheritance generally has been lost to the Fancy.

It is normally accepted that a variegated lizard is worthless and that not only the bird itself but also its parents should be culled from a strain. Yet it must be admitted that the perfect lizard canary, in true terms, is precisely that, namely, a variegated bird. A true self green canary carries no light feathers whatever, i.e. every feather has normal amounts of eumelanin black and phaeomelanin brown. It also has a black underfeather, dark skin and dark horny area, i.e. beak, legs, toes and claws. A perfect lizard canary exhibits all of these characteristics, except for the cap, which carries no eumelanin either visually, on its underfeather, or on its skin. Why this should occur and why, in particular, it should always occur on the head is quite a mystery. This is in contrast to other breeds where, invariably, the first place for melanistic deposition is the head. Another strange characteristic is that the lizard, invariably, shows no great amounts of phaeomelanin brown. The presence, almost universally, of the optical blue (reduction of brown) factor is a matter of great interest. In other breeds, especially coloured canaries, where this factor is frantically sought, it proves itself to be totally random in its inheritance pattern. Parents, both displaying this characteristic, frequently breed youngsters with no trace of it. A third special characteristic of the lizard is the spangle effect, which will be considered in more detail later, but this can perhaps be more readily attributable to the direct result of a mutated gene.

When mutations occur they normally follow one of the three recognisable patterns, i.e. they are sex-linked, homozygous recessive or heterozygous dominant. In the case of the lizard this is not so. If a lizard is outcrossed to a self non-lizard all normal selfs ensue. Usually regardless of whether the lizard parent has a full cap or no cap at all (non-cap), the youngsters are full selfs displaying no foul feathers. Two of these youngsters paired together will produce, on average, 25% birds showing the characteristic spangling of the lizard and 75% non-lizard, i.e. to the standard Mendelian ratio for a recessive mutation. The problem is that, almost without exception, all of these youngsters, both lizard (showing spangling) and non-lizard will be variegated. Examples varying from three parts dark to ticked prevail. The reason for this has not yet been established but its occurrence suggests that the spangle effect is, in fact, a form of multi-variegation following an abnormal but defined pattern. This variegation problem can continue through several generations. Were this not confusing enough, a quite remarkable feature appears when a lizard is paired to a clear canary. Almost all of the youngsters display some degree of variegation, as would be expected, but what is most unusual is that the areas of variegation are spangled and the head frequently shows a degree of capping. This indicates that, when paired to a self, the mutation is recessive but, when paired to a clear, it is not only dominant in the usual sense but is totally so, and does not follow the 1:1 ratio expected.

Whether as a result of a further mutation or as a result of outcrossing, blue lizards do exist (i.e. lizards where the ground colour has changed from yellow to white). Many are beautiful birds displaying all of the desired characteristics of the breed but with a different background colour. In the UK birds of this type are banned from exhibitions staged under the patronage of the Lizard Canary Association of Great Britain. However, in continental Europe, and even in parts of the UK, they are accepted and can prove delightful additions to a lizard-canary-breeder's birdroom. The blue lizards known at present are dominant white and follow the expected inheritance pattern for that mutation:

Pair 1: blue × normal will produce 50% blues and 50% normal.
Pair 2: blue × blue will produce 50% heterozygote blues, 25% homozygous blues and 25% normals.

Homozygous blues are believed to be non-viable and if so will die.

As we can, on average, expect a 25% death rate in the second pairing, it is not recommended except to establish a defined characteristic and then only in the short term. Blues can appear in both intensive (gold) and non-intensive (silver) forms and the feathers should be fully inspected before deciding on a mate. The normal rules of pairing gold to silver apply.

Lizards have been outcrossed to a variety of coloured canaries with interesting and beautiful results.

Unfortunately, the problems associated with the frustrating variations in the variegation patterns serve to dissuade all but the most dedicated experimental breeder. Over the years, brown lizards have become relatively plentiful and, whilst attempts have been made to introduce other mutations, this has met with little success. A combination of factors which do create prospective visions of outstanding beauty are the rose ground colour combined with the opal and lizard mutations. Such an experiment has been attempted in the UK during recent years, with all the factors being successfully combined, but so large were the areas devoid of pigment that much work still needs to be done to produce full lizard characteristics.

PEARL CANARY

Some 10 or so years ago, experimental breeders were excited by the possibility of combining the new satinette mutation with the brown and the lizard. The new creation was named the pearl. At the time it was not known that the satinette factor could not be produced as a brown, and the theory behind the concept was to produce a bird with brown hyphen-type marks throughout its plumage. Several breeders around the world have attempted to create the pearl, and the closest to the projected ideal was viewed in Los Angeles, USA. This bird, unfortunately, displayed the clear cap of the lizard but its striations were too suffused to really differentiate it from a normally poorly-marked isabel satinette. In consequence, the much-needed full-spangle effect was not evident. The very large number of birds produced which are unsuitable for use in further experiments has acted as a deterrent to many fanciers and, in consequence, relatively few breeders have accepted the challenge. Whether the original concept is truly feasible in a practical sense has yet to be determined. Only time and the pioneer spirit of the few will give us the answer.

· CHAPTER 7 ·
SONG CANARIES

AMERICAN SINGER

Although unknown outside its native country, the American Singer continues to enjoy great popularity in the USA. Unlike most of the singing breeds, however, the American Singer is judged not only for its song but also for its shape and general condition.

The bird originated from a systematic breeding plan whereby the Roller canary was blended with a Border canary. This breeding plan, illustrated opposite, produced, in the fourth year, birds theoretically possessing 69% Roller genes and 31% Border genes. These birds are American Singers.

The aim was to breed birds which did not exceed 5¾ inches (150 millimetres) in length, had tight feathers and met a specific shape. This was defined as a rounded head not showing too much dome, a medium-length beak and a round, well-set eye. A strong neck and full throat to allow for song expansion, with a well-pronounced shoulder leading into the rounded back and similarly rounded features in the breast and lower body completes the overall body shape. The bird, when not singing, should stand at an angle of 35°–45° and should not display the loop shape of the Roller, whether singing or not. The legs, wings and tail should all be of medium length, with the wings folding neatly and the tail held close. Not too much of the thigh should show at any time.

The American Singer was created by a group of ladies in 1934 and the first birds were exhibited in that year at Boston, USA. The name of the breed was adopted by a vote of members following that show. The approved method of breeding true American Singers, and it must be acknowledged that many birds offered for sale bearing the name are not true American Singers, was standardised in 1942, although the described method of production had been practised

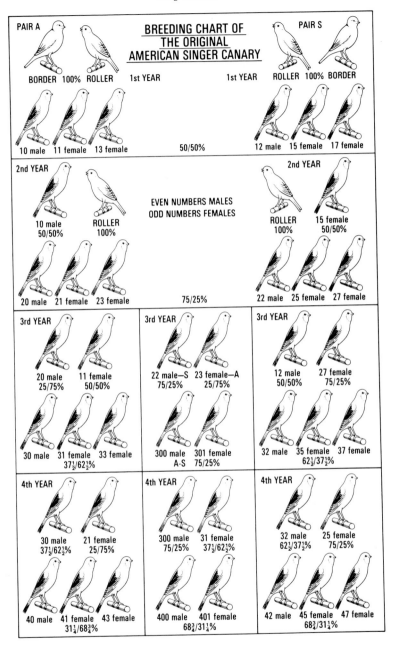

Breeding chart of the original American singer canary.

since 1935. The official judging standard was approved in 1943 and remains unaltered to this day.

It must be remembered that the Border canary of half a century ago does not, to any great degree, resemble the bird of today. In consequence it is now impossible to create a new strain and stock is available only from breeders who possess the strains that date back to the early days.

At an exhibition, 20 points are awarded for the areas already mentioned in the conformation of the bird. A further 10 points are awarded for condition, health, vigour and cleanliness being taken into consideration. The balance of points (70) is awarded for the song. This comprises 10 for the freedom of song (i.e. the willingness of the bird to sing) and 1 further point for each separate song that the bird sings up to a maximum of ten. Fifty points are then left for the rendition of the song. Quality, variety and strength are the attributes sought. A deduction of 2 to 5 points is made for each 'chop' note over the permitted six, with further points being deducted for lack of quality, variety or strength of song.

Unlike the Roller, the songs of the American Singer are not formally predetermined. The great essence of the song is that it should be varied and harmonised. The canary is a great mimic, as has been discussed elsewhere. Unfortunately it mimics unpleasant as well as pleasant songs; thus environment is a major consideration when housing birds. The songs of the Roller and Waterslager breeds are much sought after, as are those of the cardinal (*Richmondena cardinalis*). Less attractive are the songs of, for instance, the budgerigar or the starling and, therefore, the greatest care should be taken to ensure that young cocks in particular are kept out of earshot of such raucous singing birds wherever possible. Unlike other breeds of canaries bred for their song, the American Singer must be trained both for posture and presentation. Thus a combination of the training methods described on p. 59 for posture and a modified form of the training for song, as described on p. 331 for the Roller canary is required. Fortunately, unlike the Roller and Waterslager, where teams of four birds need to be trained and exhibited together, the American Singer is presented for exhibition/contest as a single entry.

The American Singer is an easy variety to breed, although consideration should obviously be given to applying line-breeding techniques so that inherent genetical qualities are retained. A fuller explanation of these systems can be found by studying the origination chart of the American Singer (p. 325) or the passage on

Yorkshire canaries (p. 147). The techniques explained in Chapter 1 on Management and Breeding Techniques are adequate to breed the American Singer successfully.

ROLLER (HARTZ MOUNTAIN)

The Roller canary is the main variety of this section of canary breeds. We have investigated canaries bred and exhibited for shape and posture and also those bred for colour. The third section consists of canaries that are bred and contested for their song, no other considerations normally being made.

All male canaries in good condition sing, regardless of breed. Their song, however, is a spontaneous and natural one evolved from the wild canary from which all breeds originate. The song of the Roller nowadays is a trained song, split into several parts, and the pattern of the song is so inbred that the major training requirement is for tonal quality coupled with the extension of the range of song. Originally the ability of the canary to mimic certain noises was capitalised on to formulate the now accepted repertoire.

The history of the Roller goes back to the mid-nineteeth century when canaries bred by Spaniards were exported to Italy. The Roller, apparently, originated from birds which escaped from the wreck of a ship that sank off the north coast of Morocco in 1842. From there, they made their way, via merchants, to Belgium and Germany. At that time it was forbidden for animals to be kept as pets in Germany and the birds were bought by peasants living in the remote areas of the Hartz Mountains and St Andreasburg. From these areas, two singing strains evolved, the Roller canary from the Hartz mountain area and the Waterslager (p. 336) from St Andreasburg. By the late nineteenth century, so plentiful were the birds that merchants started to bring them to England from where this section of the Fancy came into being.

Such are the complexities of breeding and contesting Roller canaries that many years' practical experience, coupled with help from experienced breeders, will be necessary before anyone can hope to be considered an expert on the subject. The principles of general management, as covered in Chapter 1 apply to the breeding of Rollers but several modifications are needed, particularly when the young are weaned, as their show training is totally different.

To be a successful contestant with Roller canaries, the breeder must be able to differentiate between musical notes and tones – so if tone deaf do not take up breeding Roller canaries.

The song of a canary is caused by a series of beats produced by the throat muscles of the bird. As with human beings, some of whom speak with a deep bass voice and others with a high soprano, the song of a canary can be naturally either high or low. With training, both human beings and canaries can increase the range of noises produced. The song of the Roller canary is divided into a total of thirteen song passages, which have been named according to the sounds recognised by the human ear and graded according to the tempo of delivery. Initially, the songs now recognised and bred for were taught by the continuous playing of various established and home-made wind instruments and water organs; later the repertoire was improved and extended by the continuous tolling of bells with different tones. Five of the song passages are named *rolls* and the other eight are called *tours*. A tour is used to describe the song passages where the beat is discernible by the human ear; a roll is a passage where the speed of delivery is such that the tempo cannot be registered by the human ear. Not only is the Roller canary required to sing as many of the rolls and tours as possible, in scales each ascending in eighth tones, but it is also required to 'pronounce' each song properly, using the correct vowels and consonants. To further determine the quality of the song, each of the passages is divided into three registers: the bottom, where deep tones are required, the middle, and the top where the higher notes are heard. The most sought-after songs and, therefore, those carrying the highest number of points at a contest, are those of the lower register, the songs of the high register being awarded only a small number of points.

The names given to the various songs (which denote the German influence) are as follows:

1) Rolls: bell, glucke, hollow, knorr or bass and water.
2) Tours: bell, hollow bell, deep bubbling water, flute, glucke, water glucke, schockel.

Of these the hollow roll, bass roll, glucke tour, water glucke tour, glucke roll and schockel should be sung in the bottom register but can be sung in the middle register. Water roll and deep bubbling water tour are sung in the middle to bottom register. Flute tours can be rendered in any of the three registers, hollow bell tours in the middle register and the bell roll and bell tour in the top register. The hollow bell tour, when sung in the top register, becomes the bell tour.

The tone in which the bird renders the song, combined with the vowels used, determine the quality of the rendering. The order in which the vowels are used is U-O-A-I-E and these, together with a perfect balance of semi-vowels and consonants added to musical cadences, are required to meet the official song standard for each tour or roll.

Each of the songs should contain a combination of vowels, semi-vowels and consonants. Some of these should be constant throughout a song, others need to change depending upon circumstances (e.g. a change in pitch from bottom to middle register). The actual combinations used need to be heard regularly so they can be readily identified. The detection of the minor faults which are deemed to spoil certain passages totally are also best learned in this manner. Once the basics are fixed in the breeder's mind, the interpretation of the written standards can be more easily understood and, for this reason, in-depth investigation of each song will not be attempted here. Instead, it is recommended that contact be made with experienced breeders, possibly through enrolling as a member of a specialist society catering for the needs of this section of the Fancy, who can explain each aspect in a practical manner.

In the UK the song is the only consideration. In mainland Europe, however, the Roller canary can be judged not only for its song but also as a coloured canary. The bird is first judged for its song and then is transferred to another show cage where it is judged by another judge who considers its phenotype. This practice is thought to have arisen after the discovery of the opal mutation amongst a strain of Roller canaries. This presents a major challenge to a breeder as it is difficult enough to establish the correct degrees of excellence in song *or* phenotype without, at the same time, having to take regard of and improve both. The requirements for establishing standards of excellence in coloured canaries are well covered in Chapter 5 and there is no need to elaborate further.

The acquisition of breeding stock is the first consideration when starting a stud. It is always important to begin with good-quality birds and, when purchasing type or coloured canaries, it is usually the examination of the overall phenotype of various breeders' studs that enables the purchaser to acquire and mix stock to suit his requirements. This, of course, does not guarantee success on the showbench but it does offer the purchaser a fair chance of success. Breeders of Roller canaries, however, carry a separate strain of birds for different ranges of songs, few strains being proficient in the whole range. Keeping in mind the fact that birds, like human beings, have different levels of pitch in their voices, it is difficult to mix birds from different strains and retain the tonal qualities sought. Thus it is considered of prime importance to acquire initial stock from one breeder and to rely on him to sell you birds from the same strain. Whilst the purchaser is totally reliant on the vendor selling him suitable stock with regard to the required singing qualities, he must check for himself that the general health of the birds is satisfactory. To briefly reiterate the points to watch, the bird should be lively and active with feathers held tightly to the body. A bird that has ruffled plumage or one that sits around moping should not be purchased. The eyes should be bright and birds with faecal droppings clinging to the plumage around the area of the vent should also be avoided. To fully maintain one strain, intensive inbreeding and line-breeding is necessary. The methods employed with these systems are explained in the section on Yorkshire canaries (p. 152). Although line-breeding and in-breeding are recommended methods of breeding canaries, inevitably, if pursued for an indefinite period, an ever-increasing number of progeny will be found to be weak and suffering from various diseases, such as epileptic fits. These birds must be culled. No genuine breeder would attempt to pass on such birds to a newcomer and, fortunately, few breeders exist who are unscrupulous. Notwithstanding this, careful observation of stock offered for sale is recommended. The beginner should perhaps take heed of these comments as any problems inherent in a strain will manifest themselves equally in stock purchased and removed to another birdroom. It is far easier to be seemingly kind when viewing weak stock, and to attempt to rectify the problems viewed, than to be realistically hard and to cull immediately any bird showing weaknesses. The latter method is, however, the only one that should be employed. Attempting to breed with weakened stock is a direct route to disaster and is best avoided.

As has been stated, it takes many years to gain sufficient knowledge to be considered an expert on Roller canaries. In consequence, competition winners in a novice's hands can easily be wasted and, rather than attempt to buy such high-quality birds, it is more sensible for a beginner to purchase less highly-bred stock of the same strain and to gradually build up his own strain. Females should always be purchased as soon as possible after the moult has been completed, so as to allow them sufficient time to settle down to their new environment and management. At this time it will be almost impossible to purchase young males as these will still be undergoing training and will not have reached the state where accurate assessment can be made of their quality. If it is possible to purchase males, then those offered will probably be adults. The pairing of adult to young is recommended and thus, providing the bird is not too old (3 years is the recommended upper age limit), and if its health is apparently good, the purchase can safely be made. The bird's age can be ratified from the closed ring all Roller canaries are required to carry. A beginner does not usually know where or from whom stock can be purchased. This information may be obtained by joining a society specialising in promoting the Roller canary and also by studying the list of winners published either at competitions or in the Fancy press.

The method of managing stock and preparing it for the breeding season is the same as for any other breed but modifications need to take place when the youngsters are weaned. As usual, the chicks should be removed either to large flight cages or to indoor and outdoor flights. In the case of the Roller, however, these should never be located in the room used for breeding. As soon as the young males are seen to be attempting to sing, they should be segregated from the females and, if possible, they should be transferred to a third room. At this time, they should still be housed in either flights or flight cages, where they should be left until the moult is completed.

Once the moult has been completed it is time to start training the young birds for contests. Traditionally, a 'schoolmaster', i.e. an adult male possessing a full repertoire of tours and rolls, was used to train the young birds. Nowadays, in some studs, this practice persists but other breeders prefer to allow the inherited song to come through naturally. It is said that some young males become confused if the tutor is not their sire. Attempts have also been made, using the most advanced recording equipment, to produce tapes of the perfect Roller song for use in place of a 'schoolmaster'. These methods have not proved successful, however, and beginners are not recommended to pursue them.

Once the young males have completed the moult, it is time to start encouraging them to use the small training cages and, ultimately, the show cages. Initially they can be transferred to small wire cages or wooden cages, placed on shelves. Partitions of thin wood or cardboard should be introduced to the cages over a period of 3 or 4 days. At first, the partition should be placed to cover about one third of the

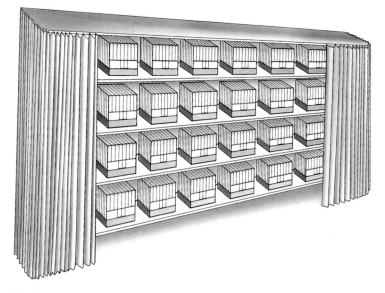

A bank of cages used for training Roller canaries.

cage; it should then be moved a small amount each day until the birds are totally segregated.

For the time being, the birds should be kept in the same position and a small card, marked with the ring number of the bird, affixed to the shelf either above or below the bird. A list of the ring numbers should be kept separately so that the breeder, on hearing, for example, a particular roll can make notes to that effect on his list. The young at this stage need to be watched carefully. It is considered of great merit for a young male to sing very deeply; this is indicated by the bird's throat 'bubbling' whilst, at the same time, the beak is closed. Birds which sing with an open beak are considered 'high' singers. After a week or two, the birds should be grouped into 'deep' singers and 'high' singers. Alternatively, some breeders prefer to keep birds of the same family together.

When the birds have spent 1 or 2 days in the training cages, a lightweight curtain should be hung in front of them. This will reduce the available light but will not place them in total darkness. In an ideal training cabinet, the top shelf should extend 3–4 inches (80–100 millimetres) further than the other shelves. A curtain rail can then be affixed to the edge of this deeper shelf.

The curtains should be opened for a 15–20 minute period two or three times daily, to increase the amount of light, although the birds should not be subjected to direct bright light. Some birds will commence singing immediately this happens but the more reluctant will soon start to mimic their more forward counterparts and thus the preparation for contesting proceeds.

If it is intended to use a 'schoolmaster', it is at this time that he should be properly introduced, either by placing him in the central cage of the training cabinet or in another cage in front of it. In the latter case, this cage should be curtained so that the youngsters cannot see their tutor.

If, at this time, the song of one bird is found to have any major faults he should be taken from the training room immediately. Rollers, being natural mimics, will quickly imitate any noise and the fault can quickly penetrate the 'class'.

Once the young birds start to sing whenever the light source is increased, it is time to extend their training by removing them from the cabinet and placing them in cages next to each other on a table in subdued light. It is advisable to take four birds at a time. After 5 minutes or so, the cages should be stacked on top of each other and a cover should be placed over the top of the cages. After a further 5 minutes or so, the birds will normally start singing.

It is possible to stage either single birds for competition or teams of two to four. If staging teams, the system suggested in the preceding paragraph should be adopted. By ensuring that the birds are stacked in the same order each time, and returned to the training cabinet always in the same order, the chances of achieving the special aims of contesting are enhanced. When the birds are placed on the table, their cages should be numbered from 1 to 4. When stacked '1' becomes the top bird, '2' the second, '3' the third and '4' the base. The birds should be returned to the cabinet, whether they have sung or not, after 15 to 20 minutes. Ideally this procedure needs to be followed two or three times per day.

Once the young birds have become accustomed to singing when the amount of light is suddenly increased, it is time to introduce them to competition cages. These cages are wooden and are fitted with two hinged wooden doors, covering the front. There is a hole $\frac{5}{8}$ inch (15 millimetres) in diameter cut in the top of the cage, about $\frac{3}{4}$ inch (20 millimetres) from the back and centrally placed. A similar hole is cut into the back of the cage near the top to coincide with the hole in the top. This ensures that the birds have sufficient light to find their seed and water at all times. When the birds are first introduced, only one of the doors should be closed; the other door should be closed gradually over a period of a few days. Once this has been done, and the bird is showing no adverse effects from the poor light, care must be taken to ensure that ample circulation of fresh air exists. The cages must be opened and the birds offered fresh seed and water every morning, while the doors are left open for at least 1 hour. This process should be repeated for two further half-hour sessions daily.

At this time it is useful to move the show cages around and open them periodically, particularly if a young bird has been heard singing in the darkened interior of the cage. This allows the birds to sing their full song. After half an hour, regardless of the quality of the singing, the birds should be returned to the training cabinet. When the birds are allowed into full light the breeder is well advised to sit at a table close by and, without being overdramatic, move papers around in a manner such as might be expected by a judge at a contest.

Such is the comradeship found in Roller-canary circles that each breeder will be delighted to assist his fellow fanciers. A most practical approach is for teams of birds to be exchanged for a limited period so that the young birds can become used to singing 'on demand' in different environments. This is strongly recommended.

It will be found that not all young birds will perform the whole Roller-canary repertoire in the first season. Although this is obviously the aim, a bird should not automatically be disqualified as a potential champion in the breeder's mind because the vacant passages may be forthcoming in the second year. If the song is not complete by then, it is improbable that it ever will be. What must be looked for are the faulty passages in the song. If these are apparent, such birds should be withdrawn and housed elsewhere prior to being disposed of as singing pets.

It is hoped that the preceding notes will be a useful guide to the beginner wishing to enter the very specialist world of the Roller-canary contest. Because the Roller is totally different from other types of canary, the author is unwilling, and in many respects unable, to be more specific on specialist features.

In all areas of most countries, clubs exist where experts can be found who will add the detail to the generalisations made in this section. The interested fancier should contact one of these and, it is to be hoped, the complex world of the Roller canary will consequently become much clearer.

334

TIMBRADOS

Attempts to trace the ancestry of the Timbrados have proved difficult and, whilst every attempt has been made to verify the following notes, the author is unable to confirm their absolute authenticity.

Breeders of song canaries, in most instances, are not concerned with the shape or colour of their birds, except where, for example, size of chest is a factor in the final song rendition. We have seen with the Roller and will see with the Waterslager varieties that certain aspects of the song are most highly sought after and what is considered a fault in one race is prized in another. Breeders of the Timbrados sought to produce song birds emphasising metallic notes and this continues to the present day.

Instead of crossing established breeds, the pioneers of the Timbrados chose to hybridise the wild canary (*Serinus canaria*) with the serin (*Serinus serinus*). Hybridising these two closely-related species proved easy and by the F_4 generation a new type of bird, which whilst being accepted as such is not technically a canary, was created. Most of the experimental work was carried out prior to the beginning of the Spanish Civil War and few, if any, records really exist of the experiments carried out, or of how close the breeders came to achieving their aims.

Following the war, experiments again got under way and, in some instances, the original breeding plan was supplemented by various outcrosses to both type and coloured canaries. The main areas of Spain where these experimental breeding exercises took place were the Catalonian villages of Calulla, Vic and Olot. It was in these areas that the wild canary × serin experiments were carried out. In the other main region, Andalucia, crosses were made with the established canary breeds, resulting in the production of bigger birds. These birds, however, did not display the same quality of song as the other type and this form of experimentation seems to have ceased. The breeding of the first true Timbrados is credited to Mr Alexandra Garredo and the first example was exhibited at a World Show staged by Mr Salvadore Marcarnasa. (This was at the Brussels event in 1962.)

Although the spread of the species thoughout other European countries has not been great, breeders in Venuzuela have imported large quantities and the race continues to thrive there as well as in its native country.

The song sought is a metallic one, with deep watery rolls supplementing the main song. Other notes sought are in many instances those associated with Spanish music – the castanet being a good example – and, in consequence, defy translation and explanation. The Timbrados is a small bird and, as such, will readily adapt to normal breeding techniques although, considering its origin, it is probable that it will exhibit nervous tendencies and will need greater training to achieve steadiness and a ready song than other song breeds.

WATERSLAGER

Second in importance to the Roller as a singing breed is the Water-slager. This race is extensively kept in its native Belgium and, whilst breeders exist in other countries, their numbers are limited.

It is rumoured that the Waterslager was, in fact, created prior to the Roller. There are reports of miners in the Imst and St Andreas-burg areas of the Hartz Mountains setting out to breed a canary with the song of the nightingale (*Luscinia megarhynchos*). Such reports go back to the fifteenth century.

We know the canary to be a good mimic and, given ideal circumstances, the miner's task was quite feasible. The problem they encountered, however, was one of the nightingale not singing in the wild, nor in captivity during the period when the young canaries were learning their song, i.e. immediately after the moult. By trapping and raising nightingales in captivity, they were gradually able to alter the normal song cycle so that the birds were in full song at the time when the young canaries were most susceptible to outside influences.

At this time, many breeders in the Hartz area decided to concentrate on breeding canaries with a deeper, softer, more mellow song and their efforts resulted in the production of the Roller. The Belgian fanciers, however, persevered with their original ideal and much experimentation took place to ensure that free, exuberant-singing canaries were bred in great numbers. At this time, the name of Belgische Waterslager was given to the birds which, in part, replaced the previous name given in French – Canari de Chant Belge.

The best results were found in the breeding rooms of fanciers inhabiting the town of Malines and its suburbs – situated some 12 miles (20 kilometres) south of Antwerp and it is as a result of this that the variety is sometimes referred to as the Malinois. Certainly, at the time, any bird acquired and known to be a Malinois automatically carried with it a guarantee of quality.

As was discussed in the section on the Roller canary, the physical aspect of a bird contributes to its singing ability. Also, the actual position it adopts when singing can dramatically alter the tone of the song. Experiments have taken place on outcrossing the Waterslager to other breeds, most notably the Roller and coloured canaries. Because of this, there are fewer pure strains today than is considered desirable. For this reason Dutch officials have published a standard of excellence for the shape etc. of the breed and, whilst it carries no points at a contest – song being the only consideration – by adopting the principle of attempting to produce birds to this standard, the breed should be preserved instead of slipping into obscurity.
The standard is as follows:

Head	Small with a conical shaped beak and black brilliant eyes.
Neck	Thin and long.
Body	Roundish with back well filled in and chest large and round.
Wings	Closed, held tightly to the back, tips not crossing.
Legs	Fine and small.
Tail	Well closed.
Feather quality	Tight, well feathered, no trace of frills.
Colour	Rich, clean, no trace of non-natural colouring.
Song position	Slightly arched back.
Size	6½ inches ± ⅕ inch (165 millimetres ± 10 millimetres)
General condition	In good health, without visible infirmities.

It is not difficult to see why this standard has been written. The bird, at 6½ inches (165 millimetres) is not small and, therefore, can remain active whilst carrying a large body. Equally, with a round chest and a long thin neck, the indications are that the bird is well equipped with the necessary volume and format of the respiratory organs to enable it to produce the desired song. The restriction of the colour to variegated or clear yellow birds goes back to the original Waterslager. This, of course, excludes outcrosses to any other breed, as does the insistence on non-frilled plumage.

Thus, we arrive at the song of the Waterslager. Whereas the Roller is trained to sing tenderly and deeply, the Waterslager is an exuberant, imposing songster with his song composed of ringing sounds, often with a metallic back sound.

Many of the highly prized tours of the Waterslager are often regarded as the weak areas of the Roller, i.e. bell roll and bell tour, water rolls, deep bubbling water rolls, watery bass, high-pitched flutes – very often with aufzug which is a major fault in a Roller presentation.

Thus any breeder who contemplates commencing with a singing variety should visit breeders of all species before deciding which varieties of sound are most pleasing to his ear. Surely nothing can be worse than to breed a large number of birds and then to find that the sheer volume of noise at the stage when the young males are learning their song is irritating to the breeder's ear.

The methods of breeding and training song canaries are well covered in the section on Roller canaries (p. 331) and can be followed with equal success by breeders of the Waterslager.

Show Standards

AMERICAN SINGER

Freedom of song   10 points
(Willingness to sing. Each
song 1 point. Limit 10.)
Rendition   60 points
(Quality, variety, strength
over 6 chop notes per song.
2–5 points deducted per
chop.)
Conformation   20 points
(Well-proportioned body,
good plumage. Maximum
4 points deducted for
each fault.)
Condition   10 points
(Health, vigour, cleanliness.
Maximum 2 points deducted
for each fault.)   ————
TOTAL   100 points

ROLLER CANARY

Hollow roll	27 points
Glucke and glucke roll	27 points
Water tours	27 points
Hollow bell	18 points
Flute	18 points
Schockel	18 points
Bass	18 points
Bell tours and rolls	9 points
General effect and song quality	9 points
TOTAL	**171 points**

FAULTS

Nasal tours	27 points
Defective bass	27 points
Breathing faults	27 points
TOTAL	**81 points**

The points shown are those allocated by a team of three judges i.e. a division of three would occur for each judge's individual score.

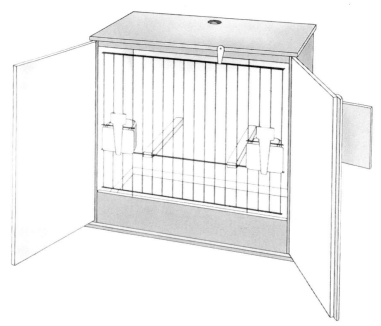

(Roller cage).

WATERSLAGER

		FAULTS	
Glucke	12 points	Shrill rendition	3 points
Bass	9 points	Faulty tours	3 points
Water gluke	6 points	Ausfug	3 points
Gluke roll	6 points	Nasal tours	3 points
Hollow bell	9 points	Faulty flutes	3 points
Flutes	9 points		
Bell tour	6 points	TOTAL	15 points
Bell roll	6 points		
High flute bells	6 points	MAXIMUM TOTAL	69 points
High bell tours	6 points		
Schockel	3 points		
Tour impression	3 points		
General effects of song	3 points		
TOTAL	84 points		

TIMBRADOS

POSITIVE POINTS

Timbre metalico (metallic notes)	9 points
Nota de enlace (joined notes)	6 points
Notas rodadas (rolling notes)	12 points
Nota batida (note of bat hitting ball)	6 points
Cascabel (small bell)	12 points
Cloqueos (clucking noise)	15 points
Castanuela (castanet)	9 points
Floreos basicos (deep flute)	12 points
Floreos adorno (high flute)	15 points
Notas compuestas (compensating notes)	12 points
Campana (large bell)	6 points
Notas de agua (water notes)	9 points
Impresion (general impression)	3 points
TOTAL	126 points

NEGATIVE POINTS

Rascadas (rasping noise)	3 points
Estridencias (faulty song)	3 points
Nasalidad (nasal sound)	3 points
TOTAL	9 points
MAXIMUM TOTAL	100 points

All points standards illustrated are those quoted by the Confederation Ornithologique Mondiale except those listed below. As some associations do not accept these standards, breeders would be well

341

advised to seek advice from specialist societies in their own country to confirm the standards shown.

Giboso Espanol – Club Tecnico Nacional de Canarios de Postura – Spain

Florin – AOB – Belgium

Irish Fancy – Irish Fancy Canary Association – Eire

Columbus Fancy – International Columbus Fancy Association – USA

Timbrados – Federacion Ornitologica Espanola – Spain.

COLOUR PLATES – JUDGES' COMMENTS

Even when faced with a live example in a proper show cage, judging canaries is not easy. To ask, as has been done, two distinguished judges to look at photographs and give critical comment is unfair to both the judge and the bird in question. Most examples in the colour plates were chosen because, at the exhibitions visited, they represented the best of the breed available. Having been transferred to the special box used for photography, not all of the birds were accommodating enough to show themselves to best effect and to adopt the 'show position'. This in some instances emphasises or, in fact, creates faults that would not exist under normal circumstances, which is, of course, more relevant to the type breeds than the coloured canaries. The comments that follow, therefore, are based on what is visible on a projected photographic slide which tends to show the bird in an unnatural and, therefore, unfair light.

I am extremely grateful to Joel Le Banner and Mario Ascheri for attempting the difficult task set and for the constructive criticisms given.

Finally, it is perhaps worth repeating that, throughout continental Europe, a bird scoring between 87 and 89 points is considered to be average to good; a bird with 90 or 91 points is very good and a bird with more points than this is adjudged to be an excellent example with champion status. Rarely is a bird awarded more than 93 points and to achieve this total is uncommon.

G.B.R. WALKER

TYPE CANARIES
Plate 1   BUFF GREEN NORWICH
A good example of a green Norwich. The only noticeable fault which

is minor is that the head does not blend totally into the back, there being a break at the neck. Ideally, the head would blend into the back. The head and body of the bird are excellent, both being superbly rounded.

91 points

Plate 2 CLEAR BUFF NORWICH

In continental Europe, only unflighted birds are accepted on the showbench. This bird is an adult, and, therefore, shows greater length than an unflighted example. Its stance on the perch prevents true examination in a judging sense. This apart, the bird has a fine head and overall roundness; its major fault if judged in Europe would be the long feathers extending from the body around the back covering the flight feathers.

89 points

Plate 3 BUFF CINNAMON NORWICH

A very good bird. Note the differences in the area of the neck from the green example in Plate 1. Here the head blends beautifully into the back. The bird is round throughout and shows good colour, the only fault, which is minor, is that the feathers of the flank are slightly long.

92 points

Plate 4 CLEAR BUFF YORKSHIRE

This bird is unfortunately not in a good 'show' position, i.e. it is resting. In consequence, judging is difficult. The body outline is good but is not emphasised to full extent because of its stance. The thighs should be fully visible and are not in this instance. Also, if fully erect, the wings would fall into their proper position. It is thought that this is an excellent bird showing itself badly.

86 points

Plate 5 VARIEGATED YELLOW YORKSHIRE

This bird is not a particularly good example of the breed. A good Yorkshire will in many respects resemble a 'carrot'. This bird shows a heavy body with the head in consequence appearing too small and unrounded. The bird appears, perhaps because of its heavy body, to be too short.

86 points

Plate 6 CLEAR CAPPED GOLD LIZARD

The back of the cap of this bird, although ending correctly, is not clearly defined, the edges being somewhat ragged. The horny areas are too light in colour, the ideal being an intense black. Although the spangling is good, the melanistic striations both on the back and flanks (rowings) are not completely straight.

87 points

Plate 7   CLEAR CAPPED SILVER LIZARD

The spangle on this bird is excellent. The melanistic striations are good but not totally straight. The position of the bird prevents true evaluation but from what is visible, the bird seems to be a good example. Again, the beak and legs do not display the true black colour sought.

88 points

Plate 8   BROKEN CAPPED GOLD LIZARD

As with all intensive-feathered examples, the melanistic striations are not as well defined as in non-intensive examples. The flank markings (rowings) on this bird, although evident, are not as distinct as would be wished. The position of the bird is not as one would wish which distorts the overall impression. Again the horny areas lack depth of colour.

88 points

Plate 9   BROKEN CAPPED SILVER LIZARD

This bird exhibits almost the ultimate in presence of rowings, these meeting right across the chest. Unfortunately, this is offset by the bird being too fat which distorts the overall profile. This may be a result of the position adopted when photographed. The tail is being held too low which in consequence leads to the wings being incorrectly positioned. A good bird.

90 points

Plate 10   CLEAR YELLOW BORDER

Almost certainly a champion. The body outline is superb with the head and overall shape being exactly to standard. The only faults evident are the feather quality, where the body feathers could be held more tightly to the body, and an absence of sight of the thighs. The break between the head and body is excellent.

90 points

Plate 11   CINNAMON VARIEGATED YELLOW BORDER

Another good bird holding a bad stance when photographed, thus destroying the profile.

90 points

Plate 12   THREE-PARTS DARK CINNAMON BORDER

A near-perfect example of a Border demonstrating all that is sought in an excellent example. The head and body show superb roundness, the break between head and body is excellent with just the correct amount of thigh visible. This bird would certainly prove to be the best in section at a World Show.

93 points

Plate 13   YELLOW GREEN BORDER

Another excellent example which, in the unnatural photographic box, does not present itself perfectly. No major faults are evident.

91 points

Plate 14   VARIEGATED YELLOW FIFE FANCY

The break between head and body is too pronounced. The feather quality, normally excellent in this breed, is not as one would expect; this is emphasised by the flight feathers not laying closely on the tail.

88 points

Plate 15   CLEAR BUFF FIFE FANCY

This bird is not typical of the breed. The overall length is excessive and it does not display the roundness sought.

84 points

Plate 16   CLEAR YELLOW IRISH FANCY

This breed is not included in the official COM list and, therefore, comment is impossible.

Plate 17   VARIEGATED BUFF IRISH FANCY

This breed is not included in the official COM list and, therefore, comment is impossible.

Plate 18   MUNCHENER

This race is not very evident at International shows and in consequence, few excellent examples are seen. The differences between this bird and the written standard are immense, which could be due to the stance shown. The neck of the bird illustrated is not evident whilst the standard calls for a longish thin neck. The head appears too large, a small one being ideal. The body also is insufficiently rounded.

82 points

Plate 19   BERNER

The position of the bird is not sufficiently upright. The head and body are very good, but other areas are difficult to evaluate because of its position. However, sufficient qualities are evident to suggest that this is a good bird.

88 points

Plate 20   SCOTCH FANCY

The bird is standing in a good show position and shows good overall quality. The chest feathers should be held more closely to the body.

92 points

Plate 21   BELGIUM FANCY

A first-class example of the breed standing in a near-perfect show position. Even so the head could be pointed forward and further. The shoulders are magnificent. In many examples of the Belgium Fancy the shoulders are very narrow.

91 points

Plate 22   RAZA ESPANOLA

This breed is the most difficult to photograph as it holds its show position only for a split second when hitting the perch. In this instance, the position is good but the bird should be stretching itself forward. Because this is not happening, other faults are evident; for example the body seems too large both in roundness and in length.

90 points

Plate 23   JAPANESE HOSO

A good example of the breed standing well. If the bird was stretching itself more, giving extended appearance, it would gain a further 2 points.

89 points

Plate 24   GERMAN CREST

This photograph was used to give a proper view of the crest and the bird in consequence is not standing perfectly so as to display its other characteristics well. Notwithstanding this, it is obviously a good-quality bird, the crest being close to the ideal.

90 points

Plate 25   LANCASHIRE COPPY

The head of the bird is excellent with the crest being shown to near perfection. The neck is heavy, showing insufficient outline, with the bottom of the body also failing to taper in sufficiently. The feathering is also a little long showing the probable presence of a Yorkshire canary in its ancestry.

88 points

Plate 26   LANCASHIRE PLAINHEAD

The shape of this bird is better than that of the crested example but it is not standing in a true show position and, therefore, not displaying its virtues to the full.

89 points

Plate 27   VARIEGATED CRESTBRED

A very good bird showing no obvious faults.

91 points

Plate 28 VARIEGATED CREST

The most important features of a crest are the head qualities which this bird displays to perfection. The only criticism that can be levelled is that the bird does not display the 'cock' feathers.

91 points

Plate 29 HEAVILY VARIEGATED BUFF CORONA GLOSTER

An excellent example of the breed showing all that is good. A champion.

93 points

Plate 30 BLUE CORONA GLOSTER

A good example showing no major faults but lacking slightly in the overall quality of the heavily variegated.

92 points

Plate 31 HEAVILY VARIEGATED BUFF CONSORT GLOSTER

This bird is too large to be considered a good example with the head too divorced from the body.

88 points

Plate 32 NORTHERN DUTCH FRILL

A good example presenting itself well.

90 points

Plate 33 PARISIAN FRILL

An excellent example showing all the characteristics of the breed, the voluminous frilling being clearly evident.

92 points

Plate 34 FRENCH FRILL

The main characteristics of the breed are evident in this bird. Although standing well, the bird would, at exhibition, improve the number of points gained by approaching to an even greater degree the continental seven figure. The tail could also be held tighter.

88 points

Plate 35 SWISS FRILL

Unlike many of the birds illustrated, this bird is standing in near-perfect show position, its only fault being that the wings are standing away from the body rather than following the profile, and the legs are bent rather than straight.

90 points

Plate 36 GIBOSO ESPANOL

A good example standing in the proper show position.

92 points

Plate 37   GIBBER ITALICUS

The tail of the Gibber Italicus should be held vertically and in this instance it is not. That apart, the bird resembles the standard well.

90 points

Plate 38   COLOURED FRILL

The rarity of the breed is demonstrated in the lack of quality seen on the showbench. This bird, although one of the better ones seen recently, has many faults when compared with the standard. An almost total lack of frills in the flanks is seen as a major fault.

85 points

Plate 39   PADOVAN FRILL

This bird is not a good example of the breed, showing little that is typical. The frills in all instances are lacking presentation as is the crest which is badly formed. Because of the absence of frills, the thighs are evident with the typical 'shorts' absent. The neck should be frilled and thick.

80 points

Plate 40   JAPANESE CREST

This bird is not included on the official COM list and, therefore, comment is impossible.

Plate 41   CRESTED COLUMBUS FANCY

This bird is not included on the official COM list and, therefore, comment is impossible.

Plate 42   FLORIN

This bird is not included on the official COM list and, therefore, comment is impossible.

OMJ Posture Canary Judge and President of the Union Ornithologique de France and Confederation Ornithologique Mondiale Pour La France.

Joel Le Banner

COLOURED CANARIES

Plate 46   F$_1$ HYBRID

A good example of an F$_1$ Hybrid, in this instance a non-intensive bird. In a good specimen, one looks for a black collar passing round the chest and this is partly absent in this bird. The horny areas are also clear instead of being black. As a breeding bird, this example could be paired with either an intensive red female or alternatively a dimorphic clear or self, depending upon which line the breeder wishes to follow. The lipochrome colouring of the bird is excellent.

89 points

Plate 47   INTENSIVE RED
The colour of the bird is excellent, the tail, however, is too long and too wide.

88 points

Plate 48   NON-INTENSIVE RED
A very good example of the breed. The frosting is excellent being very fine but distinct. The ground colour is also very good.

90 points

Plate 49   INTENSIVE CLEAR GOLD
A good bird in that the lipochrome colouring and lack of frosting is excellent. The breast, however, is too large and follows the shape of a Border canary rather than a coloured canary.

87 points

Plate 50   NON-INTENSIVE ROSE
A finely-frosted non-intensive rose standing well in a good show position. The feather quality and lipochrome colouring are truly excellent.

91 points

Plate 51   INTENSIVE CLEAR GOLD IVORY SATINETTE
The lipochrome colouring is good but could be more luminous. The chest, however, is too heavy for a good show specimen. However, it is an excellent bird for use as a breeding female.

89 points

Plate 52   CLEAR RECESSIVE WHITE SATINETTE
This bird resembles the form of a type canary and is, therefore, too rounded. This is also highlighted by the neck being very pronounced. The feather quality is excellent.

90 points

Plate 53   CLEAR RED DIMORPHIC MALE
The standard for a dimorphic male, whether clear or self, calls for a small distinct mask similar to that of the goldfinch (*Carduelis carduelis*). The dimorphic pattern of this bird is good with a corresponding good-quality lipochrome colouring. The feather quality is less than excellent and the tail is too open.

88 points

Plate 54   CLEAR GOLD DIMORPHIC FEMALE
A beautifully white bird showing the colour points to perfection.
The presentation of the bird and the feather quality are also superb.
91 points

Plate 55   INTENSIVE BRONZE
A well-marked example of the breed which is highlighted by the
striations of the flank and the head. The lipochrome colouring is
also good, as is the absence of frosting. The only major fault is the
lack of real black colouring in the horny areas.
90 points

Plate 56   NON-INTENSIVE BRONZE
This is an adult bird and in consequence it has lost some of the better
characteristics that one would expect in a young bird. This is
emphasised by the lack of colouring in the beak and legs.
87 points

Plate 57   DIMORPHIC BRONZE FEMALE
The distribution of melanistic striations on this bird is excellent
although too much brown pigment is evident. The flanks are clear,
which is a major fault, and the dimorphism is emphasised too much,
thus masking the lipochrome colouring. A useful bird for breeding
but not for the show bench.
86 points

Plate 58   INTENSIVE GREEN
This bird is presenting itself to perfection and is displaying a good
distribution of melanistic pigment. No brown pigment is evident
and the lipochrome is luminous. Again lack of blackness in the
horny areas is considered a fault.
91 points

Plate 59   NON-INTENSIVE BLUE
A dominant white bird with any trace of yellow lipochrome masked.
Little trace of brown pigmentation is evident and it has a good
luminous lipochrome colouring. The horny areas are again lacking
depth of colour.
90 points

Plate 60   INTENSIVE RED BROWN
A good example showing very deep colouring in the melanistic
striations coupled with a good luminous lipochrome. The stance and
feather quality are excellent.
91 points

Plate 61   SILVER BROWN
This bird, a female, shows to perfection the chocolate-coloured

pigment sought, as well as a high presence of phaeomelanin. It is a dominant white version and no trace of yellow lipochrome is evident. A female usually scores more heavily than a male on the show bench owing to the sexual dimorphism accentuating the presence of phaeomelanin brown.

91 points

Plate 62   DIMORPHIC RED BROWN FEMALE

The dimorphism is expressed here to perfection. The feather, however, is rather long. In the dimorphic series of the brown mutation, ironically, the male usually presents itself better than the female because the wider feather combined with sexual dimorphism tends to make the striations indistinct in the female.

88 points

Plate 63   DIMORPHIC RED AGATE MALE

This bird is a carrier of satinette and in consequence the striations are too grey. The dimorphic factor is excellent, as is the lipochrome colouring. This bird is useful as both an exhibition and a stud bird.

90 points

Plate 64 DIMORPHIC RED AGATE FEMALE

A very good example displaying superb distribution of black melanistic pigment and little brown. The dimorphic pattern is also excellent.

93 points

Plate 65   SILVER AGATE

Although the yellow lipochrome sometimes seen in dominant white birds is absent, the lipochrome colouring is dull. This bird is a female and thus presents too much brown between the striations. Its type is spoiled by an overlarge chest.

88 points

Plate 66   INTENSIVE RED AGATE

The lipochrome colouring of this bird is the sought-after bright red. Its melanistic striations resemble that which is sought.

91 points

Plate 67   INTENSIVE GOLD AGATE

A good typical agate exhibiting both a good luminous lipochrome and dilution of striations.

90 points

Plate 68   INTENSIVE ROSE ISABEL

This version of the isabel is rarely seen on the showbench and it is, therefore, pleasing to view such a good example. The dilution of the striations is excellent without any loss of distribution.

91 points

Plate 69   NON-INTENSIVE RED ISABEL

The fiery rich lipochrome coupled with a fine but distinct frosting are the first things one notices with this bird. Coupled to this are the finely-diluted striations. In general, the shape is good with perhaps an excess of breast being emphasised.

92 points

Plate 70   DIMORPHIC RED AGATE OPAL

The dimorphism of this male is excellent and so is the lipochrome colouring. Its stance and feather quality is also good. The striations, however, are not as dark a grey as one would wish.

90 points

Plate 71   NON-INTENSIVE ROSE AGATE OPAL

The frosting on this bird is well presented with good lipochrome colouring also being noted. Again, the striations are not dark enough and lack distribution.

89 points

Plate 72   RECESSIVE WHITE AGATE OPAL

A first-class example displaying good colouration and distribution of striations with no brown pigmentation apparent. The lipochrome is a luminous white.

92 points

Plate 73   NON-INTENSIVE GOLD AGATE OPAL

The lipochrome colouring on this bird is slightly orange which is a fault. Flank markings are indistinct and feather quality is poor.

88 points

Plate 74   INTENSIVE GREEN OPAL

It is unusual to view an intensive opal because of the problems associated with feather quality. This bird has excellent feathering and presents a good lipochrome colouring. The depth of pigmentation is acceptable but could be darker.

89 points

Plate 75   DIMORPHIC ROSE BRONZE OPAL PASTEL

These combination of factors are rarely seen and a judging standard has not been written for a combination of both the pastel and opal factors. The bird would, therefore, be judged as an opal. It is too fat and the feather quality is poor, although the dimorphic pattern is well presented and the lipochrome colour good.

87 points

Plate 76   RECESSIVE WHITE BROWN OPAL
A good bird, the distribution of pigment particularly on the flanks is excellent.

90 points

Plate 77   DIMORPHIC ROSE BROWN OPAL FEMALE
The paleness of the rose lipochrome is lost around the eyes of this bird but, that apart, it is an excellent example of a brown opal.

92 points

Plate 78   INTENSIVE ROSE ISABEL PASTEL
This female exhibits a slight frosting which is not unusual when compared with a male. This is also evident with the lipochrome colouring. The dilution of melanistic pigment is good.

88 points

Plate 79   NON-INTENSIVE GOLD IVORY ISABEL PASTEL
The first impression is of a bird that is too fat. The lipochrome colouring is dull and the bird is overfrosted.

87 points

Plate 80   DIMORPHIC RED AGATE PASTEL MALE
The striations on this bird appear too brown and they should appear grey. The feather is long which leads to 'horns' appearing at the back of the head where the feathers should lay flat against the skull.

89 points

Plate 81   SILVER AGATE PASTEL
A dominant white version made obvious by the excess of yellow in the flights. The bird shows too much phaeomelanin, a common fault in females.

87 points

Plate 82   DIMORPHIC BRONZE GREYWING MALE
Although this is a good bird, it is preferred that the striations are presented in a spangled formation instead of the strongly marked effect illustrated. The dimorphism is not good there being too much lipochrome evident.

88 points

Plate 83   NON-INTENSIVE GOLD IVORY GREEN GREY-WING
Although the greywing effect is evident, there is far too much phaeomelanin present, masking both the striations and the lipochrome colouring. A poor example.

84 points

Plate 84   SILVER BROWN PASTEL
A very good example with both distribution and colour of the melanistic pigment excellent.

92 points

Plate 85   RECESSIVE WHITE BROWN INO MALE
This bird demonstrates the advances made in the quality of male inos over the last few years. Even so, no male will ever compare with a first-class male. Notwithstanding this, it is a first-class example, the only noticeable fault being its shape which emphasises that the bird is a little fat.

92 points

Plate 86   RECESSIVE WHITE BROWN INO FEMALE
This bird emphasises the point raised with the male example, the colour and distribution of the melanistic striations being excellent. The stance of the bird, probably due to the unusual surroundings, would, if repeated on the showbench, cause lost points.

91 points

Plate 87   DIMORPHIC GOLD BROWN INO FEMALE
The introduction of the gold dimorphic to self mutations is fairly recent and in consequence few really good examples exist. The distribution of melanins and spangling effect is excellent.

90 points

Plate 88   DIMORPHIC RED BROWN INO FEMALE
This bird demonstrates the difference in quality between dimorphic examples in red and gold ground colours. The melanin pigment is also excellent.

92 points

Plate 89   NON-INTENSIVE ROSE BROWN INO
The lipochrome colouring is evenly distributed throughout the plumage. The distribution of the melanin pigment is good but lacks depth of colour. The feather is long.

89 points

Plate 90   INTENSIVE GOLD ISABEL SATINETTE
A well-marked example with excellent flank stripes and good luminous lipochrome colouring exhibiting no trace of frosting.

91 points

Plate 91   SILVER ISABEL SATINETTE
The bird shows a slight amount of yellow lipochrome in the flight feathers – a characteristic of the dominant white factor. This apart, it is well marked with distinct striations.

90 points

Plate 92   DIMORPHIC GOLD ISABEL SATINETTE FEMALE
The dimorphic pattern is well presented with the distribution of melanin excellent, particularly throughout the flanks.

91 points

Plate 93   NON-INTENSIVE ROSE ISABEL SATINETTE
The lipochrome is a good shade and is evenly coloured throughout the body. The frosting is well presented. The required striations are not evident, particularly on the flanks.

87 points

Plate 94   SILVER BLUE TOPAZ
No standard has yet to be set by the COM and comment is therefore difficult.

Plate 95   SILVER AGATE TOPAZ
No standard has yet to be set by the COM and comment is therefore difficult.

Plate 96   NON-INTENSIVE RED AGATE TOPAZ
No standard has yet to be set by the COM and comment is therefore difficult.

Mario Ascheri

International Coloured Canary Judge, Centre Technique D'Elevage Du Canari et de Ses Hybrides

GLOSSARY OF TERMS

Allelomorph One of a pair of alternative heritable characters.

Autosome A chromosome other than a sex chromosome.

Body cell The unit of living matter of which animal tissues are composed.

Buff The term used in type-canary circles to describe a feather where the extreme tip is not pigmented.

Cell A unit, consisting of nucleus and protoplasm, which composes the bodies of plants and animals.

Chromosomes Bodies present in the cell upon which are borne the **genes** *q.v.*

Clear A bird totally devoid of melanistic pigment.

Consort A Gloster canary without a crest.

Coppy A Lancashire canary with a crest.

Corona A Gloster canary with a crest.

Craw The frilled feathers of the chest present in all frilled varieties.

Dimorphism The condition of having two different forms.

Dominant character When, on crossing two true breeding individuals that show contrasting characters, all the young exhibit the character of one parent. This character is called the dominant character.

Eumelanin black The black **melanin** *q.v.* centred down the centre of the feather and on the underfeather in green series birds.

Eumelanin brown The brown **melanin** *q.v.* located down the centre of the feather and on the underfeather in brown series birds.

F Symbol for filial generation.

F_1 First filial generation. The young produced from a first cross.

F_2 Second filial generation. The young produced from two F_1 individuals.

Factor See **Gene**.

357

Fertile Able to produce functional germ cells.

Fertilisation Union of a male gamete with a female gamete to form a **zygote** *q.v.*

Fins The frilled feathers of the flanks present in all frilled varieties.

Flighted A bird over 1 year old.

Foul A self bird with feathers in wing or tail that are devoid of dark pigment.

Frosted Old term used to describe feathers which have the extreme tip unpigmented.

Gamete See **Reproductive cell**.

Gene A particle of substance situated on a chromosome in the germ cell which is responsible for the expression of a given hereditary character.

Genotype The genetical constitution of an individual. A group of individuals genetically identical.

Gold The feather of the lizard canary where the **lipochrome** *q.v.* extends to the tip. Also, the term used in coloured canaries to describe a bird with yellow lipochrome.

Heredity The factor in evolution which causes the persistance of characters in successive generations.

Heterozygote A bird which carries both members of an alternative pair of **genes** *q.v.*, hence a bird which cannot breed true to either of the two characters involved.

Homozygote A pure bred. A bird which must breed true to a specific character, as it carries in duplicate only one member of an alternative pair.

Hybrid The offspring of two different species.

Inheritance That which is or may be inherited.

Intensive A feather on which **lipochrome** *q.v.* extends to the tip.

Lipochrome Fat-soluble feather-colouring material.

Mantle The frilled feathers of the back present in all frilled varieties.

Melanins Black and brown pigments on self birds, formed from protein produced by the birds.

Mendelian character A character which is inherited according to Mendel's law.

Mutation A spontaneous change in the constitution of a **gene** *q.v.*

Non-frosted Old term used to describe a feather on which lipochrome extends to the tip.

Non-intensive A feather where the extreme tip is not pigmented.

Ovary The female reproductive gland producing ova.

Phaeomelanin brown The brown melanin located on the edges and tip of the feather in self birds.

Phenotype The sum total of the hereditary characters apparent in an individual. A group of individuals which all look alike.

Recessive character Of a pair of **allelomorphic** *q.v.* characters, the one which will not be manifested in the young if the genes for both characters are present.

Reproduction The process whereby life is continued from generation to generation.

Reproductive cell The gamete or germ cell; the spermatozoon produced by the male and the ova produced by the female.

Roll The term used in song-canary circles to describe a passage where the speed of delivery is such that the tempo cannot be registered by the human ear.

Rowings The term used in Lizard-canary circles to describe the melanistic stripes.

Segregation The separation in a **heterozygote** *q.v.* of the two members of a pair of **allelomorphic** *q.v.* genes.

Self A bird that has pigmentation in all its feathers.

Sex chromosome The **chromosome** *q.v.* in respect of which the male and female differ.

Sex linkage Association of a hereditary character with sex, as its gene is situated on a **sex chromosome** *q.v.*

Spermatozoon or sperm The male germ cell.

Sterile Unable to breed.

Silver In Lizard canaries, the term used to describe a feather where the extreme tip is not pigmented. In coloured canaries, the term used to describe a bird with dominant white **lipochrome** *q.v.*.

Spangle The term used in Lizard-canary circles to describe the **phenotype** *q.v.* where **phaeomelanin** *q.v.* pigment is absent from the tip of the feather.

Ticked A bird with one dark mark that can be covered by a British 1 penny piece.

Tour The term used in song-canary circles to describe song passages where the beat is discernible by the human ear.

Unflighted A current-year-bred bird.

Variegated A bird that has more melanistic pigment than a ticked specimen, but also has some areas of **lipochrome** *q.v.* feathering visible.

X Chromosome The male sex chromosome.

Y Chromosome The female sex chromosome.

Yellow The term used in type-canary circles to describe a feather where the **lipochrome** *q.v.* pigment extends to the tip of the feather.

Zygote The single cell formed by the union of a male and female gamete.

BIBLIOGRAPHY

Andrew, T. (1830) *The Bird-Keepers Guide and Companion* Dean & Son, London.

Blakston, W.A. (1877) *The Book of Canaries and Cage Birds, British and Foreign* Cassel and Co., London

Gill, A.K. (1970) *New Coloured Canaries* Cage Birds, London

Hervieux (1714) *Nouveau Traité des Serins de Canarie*

House, C.A. (1920) *Canaries* Cage Birds, London

Robson, J. (1911) *Canaries, Hybrids and British Birds in Cage and Aviary* Waverley Book Co., London

St John, C. (1911) *Our Canaries* Cage Birds, London

Walker, G. (1976) *Coloured Canaries* Blandford Press, Poole, Dorset.

Wallace, R.L. (1879) *Canary Book* The Country Office, The Strand, London

INDEX

References to line illustrations are in *italic* type.